I0160304

CHRISTIAN PERSPECTIVES ON
GENDER, SEXUALITY, AND COMMUNITY

CHRISTIAN PERSPECTIVES ON
GENDER, SEXUALITY, AND COMMUNITY

Edited by Maxine Hancock

REGENT COLLEGE PUBLISHING
Vancouver, British Columbia

Christian Perspectives on Gender, Sexuality, and Community
Copyright © 2003 Regent College. All rights reserved.

Published 2003 by Regent College Publishing
5800 University Boulevard, Vancouver, BC Canada V6T 2E4
www.regentpublishing.com

Views expressed in works published by Regent College Publishing are those of the authors and do not necessarily represent the official position of Regent College.

All contributions to this volume were first published in *Crux*, a journal of Christian thought and opinion published by Regent College, except for "Theological Foundations for Male-Female Relationships," which first appeared in the *Journal of the Evangelical Theological Society* 41/4 (December 1998): 615-630 and "Homosexuality and the Biblical Sex Ethic," which was first published in *Reflections, Biblical and Otherwise, about Sexuality*, ed. Catherine Clark Kroeger and Tina J. Ostrander (Lenoir, NC: Reformation Press, 2001).

Cover: "In Wrath Remember Mercy" (Habakkuk 3: 2) Copyright © Bruce Herman 1998. Oils on wooden panel, 10'6" x 4'6" middle panel: Adam and Eve are clothed by the Lord as protection before being expelled from Eden. The painting is one of eight in a series of typological murals featuring the connections between O.T. and N.T., and created for the Orthodox Congregational Church of Lanesville, in Gloucester, Massachusetts, USA. Herman's other works may be seen at www.brucehermanonline.com

National Library of Canada Cataloguing in Publication Data

Main entry under title:
Christian perspectives on gender, sexuality, and community
  Papers from a conference held at Regent College, Vancouver, January 4-15, 1999
  Includes bibliographical references and index.

ISBN 1-55361-053-9 (Canada)
ISBN 1-57383-158-1 (United States)

  1. Sex role—Religious aspects—Christianity—Congresses. 2. Sexual ethics—Biblical teaching—Congresses. I. Hancock, Maxine.
BT708.C47 2003   241'.66   C2002-910664-8

Contents

CULTURAL AND HISTORICAL PERSPECTIVES

Contributors

Miriam Adeney is Associate Professor of Global and Urban Ministry at Seattle Pacific University, and Teaching Fellow of Missions and Cross-Cultural Communication at Regent College.

Gordon D. Fee is Professor Emeritus of New Testament Studies at Regent College.

Craig M. Gay is Associate Professor of Interdisciplinary Studies at Regent College.

Stanley J. Grenz, formerly Pioneer McDonald Professor of Baptist Heritage, Theology, and Ethics at Carey Theological College and Professor of Theology and Ethics at Regent College, is now Distinguished Professor of Theology at Baylor University and Truett Seminary.

Maxine Hancock is Professor of Interdisciplinary Studies and Spiritual Theology at Regent College.

Barbara H. Mutch is Assistant Professor of Ministry, Director of Supervised Ministry, Program, and Bentall Professor of Pastoral Studies at Carey Theological College.

Iain W. Provan is Marshall Sheppard Professor of Biblical Studies (Old Testament) at Regent College.

John G. Stackhouse, Jr., is Sangwoo Youtong Chee Professor of Theology at Regent College.

Rikk E. Watts is Associate Professor of New Testament at Regent College.

Loren Wilkinson is Professor of Interdisciplinary Studies and Philosophy at Regent College.

Acknowledgements

"Christian Perspectives on Gender, Sexuality and Community," was the title of a cross-disciplinary symposium held at Regent College, January 4-15, 1999. This colloquy produced a rich and deep discussion of issues with which society at large has been much preoccupied over the past several decades, but which the conservative church has not addressed with sufficient seriousness. Lecturers were drawn from the Regent College and Carey Theological Seminary faculties, with guest lecturers joining us from Trinity Western University, Gordon-Conwell Seminary, and the University of Nairobi. The invitation to participate in this symposium was issued to all professors of the Regent and Carey faculties, with all faculty who accepted the invitation given opportunity to lecture during the symposium. We attempted to ensure that there would be a genuine coming together of independently worked out positions, rather than any attempt to find one voice.

The symposium allowed for lectures to be presented from disciplines as diverse as biblical studies and neuroanatomy. Not all of these disciplines could be represented in this one-volume collection, but the chapters presented here do demonstrate careful thought from a range of disciplinary perspectives on issues of gender and sexuality. The fact that these chapters began as lectures is frequently reflected in an oral-delivery style, with solid scholarship undergirding audience engagement.

The symposium—and this resultant volume of essays—are presented to help "bring the church up to speed" on the issues which we are facing constantly, and to propel us toward more thoughtful discussion on a range of subjects on which we need clarity as believers in and followers of the risen Lord Jesus Christ. To whatever degree there is congruence in the published presentations from these many speakers (along with a few dissenting and warning voices), it represents a new consensus forming among evangelical scholars from a range of disciplines.

The chapters of this book appeared originally in three issues of *Crux*, the journal of Christian thought and opinion published by Regent College, produced under the direction of Editor, Don Lewis and Managing Editor and Designer, Dal Schindell. Loren Wilkinson served as consultant in the planning process and as co-convenor with me of the symposium itself. Thena Ayres gave advance training to a group of teaching assistants who led the small groups throughout the course. My teaching assistant, Sharon Jebb, worked with Academic Secretary, Marilyn Hoeppner, in the many administrative tasks associated with bringing together a total of eighteen lecturers and an additional six seminar presenters or round table participants for the two week symposium. The book presentation of this material is a result of the vision of Bill Reimer, Director of Regent College Publishing, and the work of Rob Clements, Managing Editor, Regent College Publishing.

In both convening the symposium and drawing together the lectures which form this collection, it has been my privilege to work with many gifted and able people. "The gifts of God for the people of God. Thanks be to God."

Maxine Hancock
Regent College, Vancouver

INTRODUCTION

Christian Perspectives on Gender, Sexuality, and Community

Maxine Hancock

At a time when our culture desperately needs models of sexual wholeness and holy relationships, the Christian community is torn by division over issues of gender roles and sexuality. In this collection of essays, a cross-disciplinary and cross-cultural Christian perspective is developed on a solid biblical and theological basis. The essays here began as lectures given by members of the Regent College and Carey Theological Seminary faculty at a symposium held at Regent College, Vancouver, which undertook to consider such issues as: Are there distinct roles appropriate to women and to men within church and home? How do Christians deal with issues of sexuality and identity within their calling to marriage or to singleness? What distinctive attitudes towards gender and sexuality should define the Christian community? How can the Christian community model relationships which truly reflect the Lordship of the Risen Christ?

Participants in the course were challenged—as will be those who read this book—to develop the ability to think Christianly about gender issues, with a fuller understanding of the significance of these issues to our witness to the larger culture; to develop a biblical vision with regard to sexuality and gender within friendships, working relationships, and marriage; and to consider in new and fresh ways the implications of the New Testament concept of the church as a community of brothers and sisters.

Terms and definitions

There are four key terms which anchor the discussion in this book about relationships between men and women within the Christian church. These are: sex, gender, sexuality, and community.

"Sex," of course, has to do with our biological differences, differences built into our humanity. From the beginning, as is clear from the Genesis accounts, God created humankind male and female. Mary Stewart Van Leeuwen, in the book *Gender and Grace* defines "sex" in the following way: "It is common in social-scientific writing to use the term sex when conjecturing about purely biological contributions to male or female behaviour. For example, contributions that seem to be made by genes, hormones, or brain anatomy."[1] In these areas—i.e., differences determined by genes, hormones, and brain anatomy, the scientific community can be helpful in understanding what constitutes "sex." In the simplest possible terms, a person who is male has a penis and testicles; a person who is female, a vagina and ovaries. As Christians, we can talk about sex as creationally determined differences.[2]

"Gender" has to do with those roles and assignations associated with being male and female within culture. Van Leeuwen states: "It is common to use the term gender or gender roles when talking about what seem to be more clearly learned or socialized differences."[3] Gender has to do with roles which are socially set rather than biologically or creationally determined. We can talk about gender differences as those which society has attributed to or which have culturally developed around sex differences. Gender assignment begins with the announcement at the moment of birth: "It's a boy," or, "It's a girl," and progresses through the naming of the child, the ways in which the child is dressed and presented to society, the ways in which the child is spoken to and of, the child's identification with the parent of the same sex, the approved play patterns and ultimately, life role and performance expectations laid on the child.

"Sexuality" is a term which brokers between the two terms, "sex" and "gender." If sex refers to biological differences, and gender to societally assigned or conditioned behaviours, sexuality can be described as the way in which we negotiate our creational and societal differentiations, our societal roles, and our own and others' expectations of us. Sexuality encompasses that part of what it is to be human which is related to our having been created distinctively as male and female. Sexuality is biologically based and socially enacted. For most adults, sexuality encompasses our experience of bodiliness, and hence, a very large part of what it is to be a human person. And so when we talk about sexuality, we are talking about all of that part of us which is grounded in God's original creational intent in making humankind male and female.

By "community," within the context of this series of discussions, we are speaking of a particular community—believers in the Risen Christ. It is a community which Jesus inaugurated with his resurrections and which he announced to Mary in the garden when he made his first post-resurrection appearance. "Go ... to my brothers and tell them, 'I am returning to my Father and your Father, to my God and your God,'" Jesus said, including Mary, and with her, all believers, in a particular relationship with himself as the Eternal Son, and through him, with God the Father, and in a new relationship with each other.[4] In commissioning Mary, to convey this message, Jesus was redefining her relationship to the "brothers" as a "sister." Thus Jesus initiated a new kind of community made up of women and men who, equally sinful and equally redeemed by the blood of Jesus Christ, are equally called back to God's creation mandate and into the mission to bring people to know Jesus Christ as Living Lord and Saviour; a new kind of human community in which we regard each other not as sex objects or as radically "other," but with the mutuality and non-sexualized respect for the person which characterizes brothers and sisters in a family. This is the community which will be the context for all of our discussions about sexuality and gender: the gathered people of a local fellowship, and the body of believers gathered globally and across time as the embodiment of the risen Christ, enacting his will on earth.

Clearly, how we understand our sexuality and interpret gender roles affects how we relate to this community which is called to be different from the surrounding culture, called to enact Jesus' new community within our particular cultural contexts.[5] This collection of discussions is designed to help us articulate who we are, not only individually, but as a community of persons in a highly sexualized and increasingly pagan society. How is the fellowship of believers distinctive in our attitudes and actions as we relate to each other as women and men? What attitudes towards each other should mark it? What graces should this community demonstrate? What holiness ennobles this community? How does it live as a called-out people empowered by the Risen Lord?

What makes discussion of issues around gender and sexuality so difficult?

Talking about matters related as deeply to our fragile sense of self as sexuality and gender is bound to be difficult. We walk between twin dangers when we approach these sensitive issues. On the one hand, there is always the danger that we become conditioned by our culture and so simply accept and endorse the secular status quo—with an appropriate culture lag that is part of being religious and conservative. The danger here is that we continue to let the secular society set the terms of our culture and we merely play catch up. This tends to be most often the problem of liberal Christianity which seems pretty much intent on catching the next wave or trend of popular thought.[6]

There is an opposite and equally serious danger, of course, which is less often recognized by evangelical Christians. And that is that we take the culture of twenty or thirty years ago and we hang on to it as somehow "right" or "biblical," baptising it as Christian because it was the way we were conditioned to think as we grew up. Then we perpetuate—in the name of the church—a culture of nostalgia.

In either response to change—the liberal too-swift embrace of the secular agenda or the conservative clinging to the past with nostalgia—we fail to create a community that is clearly distinctive, because the one approach results in co-option by the secular society and the other creates a conservative sub-culture where people feel safe as long as they know the right language and the right gender role code—but which fails to challenge the culture or bring the reality of the Risen Christ into meaningful connection with it.

With the challenge of what many call "the feminist revolution," the church has reacted in one of the two ways outlined above. We tend to forget that the Christian community must always live in tension with its cultural surround. It did in the first century. It did in the sixteenth century. It does now. If it doesn't live in some kind of tension, it has already been co-opted by the culture. There is no such thing as "a Christian culture," except as it is known within the community of believers. When a culture begins to call itself "Christian," it has already become what is now popularly referred to as "Christendom." That is, it has become an institutionalized form of Christianity, more or less congruent with its cultural surround, and it does not have a cutting edge that challenges power and privilege and works towards the transformation required in order for God's will to be done on earth. The truly vigorous and alive community of the Spirit, seeking to live under the authority of the risen Christ exercised through the Scriptures will always live in a critical tension with cultural norms, and will critique these norms and call for transformation in the direction of holiness, healthfulness and wholeness at every point of human relationship.

Of course, there is another whole level of complexity and anxiety surrounding the discussion of gender and sexuality within the Christian community, and that is grounded in psychological and theological issues. Issues both of sexuality and biblical hermeneutics are involved, and both sets of issues are fraught with anxiety. Almost all adults are somewhat anxious about their sexuality in some way or another, wondering, "Am I okay?" and, in a performance dominated culture, "Am I doing it right?" The natural and irrepressible laughter at the sexual jokes of stand-up comedians is sufficient evidence for a pervasive anxiety about our sexuality. The laughter tells where anxiety is located.

For Christians who care deeply about the Scriptures, there is another anxiety that needs to be addressed: the anxiety about maintaining community standards and living under the authority of Scripture. Here the question seems to be, "Are we getting it right?" It is a proper concern, but sadly it is usually coupled with an invisible hermeneutic—the sense that some one set of readings fully embodies the mind of Christ with no need for any further discussion or interpretation.[7] Everyone, of course, has a hermeneutic. For the great majority of believers, this is a received hermeneutic, learned in the pew through the preaching and teaching of the Word. It is only occasionally examined to discover whether it is consistently applied; whether it fully explores the whole counsel of Scripture; and whether it has become culturally adjusted. As one friend says, "Of course we all read with cultural lenses. It is not the cultural lenses that are the problem, but the cultural blinders, deliberately kept in place, that keep us from seeing more."

The unexamined hermeneutic that approaches difficult texts flatly issues in proclamations like, "the Bible says," without examining the whole range of what the Bible does have to say—not just in a few isolated New Testament phrases, but in the "whole counsel of Scripture" about what it is to be a man, to be a woman in God's creation; to be a woman, to be a man, in Christ. Strangely, whenever a group says, "It's very clear and we don't need to discuss it further"—citing perhaps, "Let your women keep silence in the churches," a selective literalization has already taken place. The same groups tend not to be so literal about say, footwashing, or selling all one's possessions and giving to the poor, as they are about women's roles in the church and wifely submission in marriage. The biblical and theological scholars whose work is included in this volume carefully lay the groundwork so that we can, as a community, set difficult texts in their larger theological, biblical, and historical contexts.

Two more troubling terms

"Feminism" has, for many conservative Christians, been used as a pejorative term for a movement on which most social ills can be confidently blamed, with little real understanding of its history and the range of its meanings.[8] While generally now the academic world uses the term "feminisms" for a range of theories about women as stakeholders in society, the one underlying agreement in a very often fragmented discussion is that throughout the history of humankind, there has been a consistent oppression of women by men. While this culturally-sanctioned oppression of women has been mitigated in some societies by some circumstances, it has been cross-culturally endemic.

The basic cause and result of this systemic oppression of women has been the institutionalization within almost all societies of systems of male privilege, sometime referred to as "patriarchy." Patriarchy has to do with any social or cultural patterns which accord men special privilege on the basis of their maleness—when a person is born male he is born to certain privilege or position or rank which is denied a woman when she is born female. Clearly, the enactment of this privileged position can go all the way from a totalitarian kind of patriarchy where men have absolute rule over the bodies and souls of the women in their households, with women there for their domestic comfort and sexual use, through to a "benevolent" kind of patriarchy in which there is a great deal of kindliness and caring for women, in which the male views his role as protector, provider and carer for women. But even within this more benign form of patriarchy, and rationalized on the basis of the role as protector-provider, the male continues to have particular privilege with regard to vocation or education. Across this whole spectrum—at one end something that most Christians would view as wrong and distasteful, at the other end so familiar that it is hard to critique—one would still be looking at a system of male privilege or patriarchy.

The debate within the church is an intense one, because the question that biblical scholars must address is whether or not patriarchy is rooted in the creation order—or even deeper, within the Godhead itself. The hermeneutic used in reading the Genesis accounts and the Old Testament is fundamental here, as Iain Provan demonstrates in his chapter in this volume, "Why Bother with the Old Testament Regarding Gender and Sexuality?" Equally important is our reading of the New Testament record, discussed in this collection by Rikk E. Watts, "Women in the Gospels and Acts" and Gordon D. Fee, "Gender Issues: Reflections on the Perspective of the Apostle Paul."

Both terms, "feminism" and "patriarchy," have become so highly emotionally-charged that it is hard to have a civil discussion using the terms. And yet they cannot be avoided. In this course, we tried hard not to use the terms pejoratively but as descriptive terms. Because "feminism" is relatively new and "patriarchy" is as old, almost, as human memory, we find it easier to react to feminism than to critique the male privilege to which it is a response.

So—what is the "agenda" of this book?

As with the Regent symposium at which these lectures were given, the agenda of this book is to stir careful thought and respectful discussion within the Christian community, to help us all to think biblically in a way which reflects carefully considered evangelical theology. Two contributions by Stanley J. Grenz, "Theological Approaches for Male-Female Relationships" and "Homosexuality and the Biblical Sex Ethic" model the kind of rigorous theological thought which is necessary to ground further discussion in classical Christian theology. Loren Wilkinson melds philosophical and theological reflection in his chapter, "'Post-Christian Feminism' and the Fatherhood of God." Finally, we attempt to contextualize the discussion of biblical and theological approaches in history and culture. Miriam Adeney contributes an historical perspective on women's contribution to global evangelism in "Women in the World Christian Movement." Craig M. Gay analyzes feminism as a form of thought which is typically post-modern in his essay, "'Gender' and the Social Construction of Reality." Barbara Horkoff Mutch considers the reported experience of women in the church in her chapter, "Women and the Church: A North American Perspective." In the last chapter, John G. Stackhouse, Jr. takes up the question of how history has been invoked in the discussions concerning gender within the Christian community, demonstrating that "The Uses of History in Evangelical Gender Debates" have not always been very honest or very discerning, thereby challenging us to a use of history which has greater integrity.

Throughout this process of discussion, both in the face-to-face context of the symposium and in the lectures presented as chapters here, we endeavour to model discussion about difficult issues in a way which demonstrates courtesy and mutual respect, and thus to show how the community that bears the name of the Risen One can think, grow, stay faithful to the Word, and at the same time both speak into its culture and live in a creative tension with its culture.

What was accomplished by the symposium and will be extended by the publication of this collection is essays is yet to be fully seen: it is our hope that it will have its real outcome in homes in which husbands and wives honour each other in full mutuality and equality as "heirs [together] of the gracious grace of life,"[9] in churches in which traditional barriers to women's full participation are dismantled; in a fresh vigour in evangelism as we confidently invite non-believers into a community where the wholeness of each person, male and female, sisters and brothers together, is acknowledged and called forth.

"Your hands made me and formed me," the psalmist writes, "Give me understanding to learn your commands,"[10] God who has created us male and female, God who has created us as sexual persons, God who has given us the gift of sexuality and gender is the one to whom we turn to ask, "What is your creational intent? What is your redemptive purpose in our lives? How can we engage and live that intent and purpose honestly and earnestly and under your authority?" We invite you as readers to engage with us in hearing and to doing the Word of God.

Endnotes

1. Mary Stewart Van Leeuwen, *Gender and Grace: Love, Work, & Parenting in a Changing World.* Downers Grove: InterVarsity Press, 1990, p. 19.

2. In his lecture during the symposium on "Sexuality and Gender from a Medical Perspective," Dr. Edwin Hui (Regent College) pointed out that there are actually six categories of distinction making up biological sex: chromosomal sex (with the xx chromosome pattern being female and the xy chromosome pattern being male); gonadal sex (ovaries and testicles); hormonal sex; internal anatomical sex; external anatomical sex; and brain sex.

3. Van Leeuwen, *Gender and Grace,* p. 19.

4. John 20:17.

5. "We have ... been reconciled to God and to each other ... we are nothing less than God's new society, the single new humanity which he is creating," says John R. W. Stott in *God's New Society: The Message of Ephesians,* Downers Grove: InterVarsity Press, 1979, p. 25.

6. An historical perspective places late twentieth century secularized "second" and "third" wave" feminism in chronology with "first wave" feminism (1880-1920) which was strongly Christian in its inception, growing out of an application to women's equality of the biblical arguments propounded by the abolition movements in the United States and England. For a comprehensive discussion of what the Bible says regarding women which pre-dates current feminism, see Katharine C. Bushnell, *God's Word to Women,* 1923, rprt. 1988 (no publisher indicated).

7. A book which demonstrates how various hermeneutic approaches have been used in historic debates is by Willard M. Swartley, *Slavery, Sabbath, War & Women: Case Issues in Biblical Interpretation,* Scottsdale: Herald Press, 1983.

8. For full discussion from secular perspectives, see Juliet Mitchell and Ann Oakley, eds., *What is Feminism? A Re-Examination,* New York: Pantheon Books, 1986; from a Christian perspectives, see Elaine Storkey, *What's Right with Feminism,* Grand Rapids: Eerdmans, 1985; Mary Stewart Van Leeuwen, et al., *After Eden: Facing the Challenge of Gender Reconciliation,* Grand Rapids: Eerdmans and Carlisle: Paternoster, 1993.

9. 1 Peter 3: 7.

10. Psalm 119:73.

BIBLICAL STUDIES

CHAPTER 2

Why bother with the Old Testament regarding Gender and Sexuality?

Iain Provan

O Lord, our Lord,
how majestic is your name in all the earth!
You have set your glory
    above the heavens.
From the lips of children and infants
    you have ordained praise
because of your enemies,
    to silence the foe and the avenger.

When I consider your heavens,
    the work of your fingers,
the moon and the stars,
    which you have set in place,
what is man that you are mindful of him,
    the son of man that you care for him?

You made him a little lower than the heavenly beings
    and crowned him with glory and honour.

You made him ruler over the works of your hands;
    you put everything under his feet:
all flocks and herds,
    and the beasts of the field,
the birds of the air,
    and the fish of the sea,
    all that swim the paths of the seas.

O Lord, our Lord,
    how majestic is your name in all the earth!

Psalm 8 is a broad and wonderful statement on what it means to be a human being and, by implication, what kind of person God is who creates us. What does it have to do with the subject that we are here to discuss?

Well, I think it has everything to do with it, and let me explain why by trying to respond to two questions which may be on your minds as we begin. And these questions will help me to engage in some ground-clearing work before we get down to the issue at hand.

First question: Why bother with the Bible?

Bothering about the Bible must seem a very strange thing to do if you are not a Christian, and if you are wishing to ask questions about gender, sexuality and community. It is not where the prevailing culture would go for guidance on such matters. And shaped and molded as we are by the prevailing culture, perhaps even those of us who are Christians feel that beginning with the Bible is a little odd. It seems to me that many Christians inhabit a kind of twilight zone with respect to these issues, hanging on with grim faith to what biblical texts have to say about gender and sexuality, even though every fiber of their beings is shouting out that these texts do not make much sense of modern life and experience. There is, in other words, no deep internal conviction as to the truth of what the Bible says, and so many of us, I think, and more of us than we would like to admit, live as schizophrenics in this area, believing contradictory things at the same time, without any integrated holistic view of Christian faith in relation to these issues. In part, I think this is because we are not thinking in an integrated theological way at all. Our focus is on specific biblical texts and not on the whole thrust of biblical teaching. And of course, generally speaking, things which are out of context often seem strange and alien.

Texts are no different. An individual biblical text, for example, on homosexual practice is always going to look strange and alien when read individually against the background of our present culture, rather than as part of the whole biblical witness. And so I think we need to try to grasp the whole thing and not just the parts. And in particular we need to reject the modern tendency to try to bracket out matters of gender and sexuality as if they had nothing to do with bigger and even more important questions, questions that the culture either does not wish to ask, or to which it has no satisfactory answer. We must insist, I think, that everyone's view of human gender and sexuality—its nature, its purpose and so on—is really only a subset of one's view of human beings more generally, which in turn is a subset of one's overall view of reality, and particularly one's view of God. Conversely there is an implicit theology or worldview in every articulated view of sexuality or sexual activity and in every practical expression of sexuality and sexual activity. There are those whose worldview leads them, for example, to strive to respect and to honour as whole persons everyone of the opposite gender with whom they meet or work or enjoy friendship. There are those, on the other hand, who characteristically only view persons of the opposite gender in terms of their physical attributes and their potential for sexual gratification. In both cases the particular attitude is entirely tied up with whole sets of beliefs and assumptions about the world which may not even be consciously present to the individuals concerned but which cannot be understood outside of that larger context.

There are, in other words, questions prior to questions of gender and sexuality. Who is God?—the first question. What is a human being?— the question of Psalm 8 follows on as the second. And I want to say that I think it is only in the context of these other questions that we can then ask the question, and answer it: "What about gender and sexuality?" It is only within this broadest of all possible contexts that we can approach, with any hope of coherent thought, what the Bible has to say about what it means to be male and female. We cannot speak coherently and helpfully about sexuality until we have set this broader perspective. And I think that the Christian position on particular questions of sexuality and sexual activity is unintelligible to many modern people, including many Christians, when it is not seen as a part of this larger picture. The individual questions are only answerable coherently within this larger framework.

To summarize, we "bother" with the Bible because we believe that here we discover the record of God's revelation to us as to who God is, what it means to be a human being, and then what it means to be gendered and sexual. We do not consult the Bible because it is necessarily obvious in the first instance that individual texts speak truly about gender and sexuality, working up the theological ladder from there, as it were, to questions of human existence and God. And I think it is rather important to get that the right way round. Not getting it the right way around is what causes the phenomenon referred to by Maxine Hancock of plucking texts out of the void and saying, "The Bible says …," which is entirely the inappropriate and unhelpful way to go about biblical exegesis. So that is the first ground-clearing question.

Second, why bother with the Old Testament in particular?

Granted that Christians will want to go and look at the New Testament, granted that we must set this guidance within the whole framework of Christian faith, is not the Old Testament, well, *old*? And does not it present us with perspectives on gender and sexuality which are unhelpful to say the least? Surely the Old Testament is patriarchal to the core, describing abuse after abuse of women at the hands of men, containing legislation that is oppressive of, rather than liberating of, women? Surely this is not the place to go for guidance as to a Christian view of the matter?

Now, this is a very important question particularly if you are aware of the ways in which the Old Testament in particular has been read and used throughout Christian history. The prior question is not "why should we bother with the Old Testament when thinking about gender and sexuality?" but "why should we bother with the Old Testament as Christian Scripture at all?" That is the really important question. And from the early days of the church this question has drawn a decisive answer, which is that the Old Testament must be regarded as Christian Scripture. It was the Scripture of Jesus himself, who often refers to it in terms of the pattern for human conduct: the Old Testament is fundamental to Jesus' ethical teaching. It was the Scripture of the apostolic church. The apostle Paul, for example, constantly refers back to the Old Testament as the Word of God, not least in addressing ethical matters with the churches; when 2 Timothy 3:16 tells us "all Scripture is inspired by God," it is the Old Testament that it is mainly speaking about. The New Testament was never written with the intention of displacing the Old Testament's fundamental position as Scripture within the church. So we do not really in a sense have a choice in this matter, not if we want to stand in the tradition of orthodox Christianity. In fact the first person to question the canonical status of the Old Testament, Marcion, was duly excommunicated for so doing around AD144.

So we are right to begin with the Old Testament, and in particular with Genesis chapters 1-3, the story which the psalmist in Psalm 8 most probably had in mind when composing his psalm. I want to use these chapters on what it means to be human in the context of God's creation as a kind of a base text around which to organize other texts that I am going to draw in to fill out the picture. And so you know where I am going, and can keep track of the argument, I am going to be suggesting the following:

a) that Genesis 1-2 and other texts gives us a vision of what it means to be human in the kingdom of God, and a particular set of perspectives on what that means for gender and sexuality;

b) that Genesis 3, on the other hand, describes the fallen world in which our humanness is distorted leading to fracturing in gender relationships and sexuality, and it is that fallen world which is often reflected in biblical narrative and indeed in biblical law.

Thus I am going to be suggesting that there are two sorts of material in the Old Testament touching on matters of gender and sexuality and that it is crucially important that we understand which is which. And as a subset of that, I shall be suggesting that Christians have often gone wrong on matters of gender and sexuality, as on other matters, by failing to distinguish which sort of text they are dealing with.

First of all, Genesis 1-2. What do these chapters tell us about what it means to be human in the kingdom of God?

We begin with that well-known passage at the end of Genesis 1 about male and female, and dominion (verses 26-30). I think the correct way of interpreting chapters 1 and 2 is neither to think of two sources, telling utterly different stories, nor to collapse the two differing perspectives into one, but rather to take seriously the combination of the two chapters, and particularly to read Genesis 1 as providing the background for Genesis 2. That is normally how we would read a book—taking chapter 1 as coming before chapter 2. It may seem a very obvious point; and if it were not for the recent history of biblical studies I could probably let this pass without further comment. But as those of you who have done Old Testament studies before will know that there has been some dispute about this. It seems to me perfectly obvious, though, that we should read Genesis 2 in the context of Genesis 1, and in particular I want to make this point, which will be important as we go on. Genesis chapters 1-2 do not say what they say with any sense of chronological ordering in mind. If you read both chapters, you will see that the ordering of things is not the same in each chapter. Chapter 1, verses 11-13, tells us already of the creation of plants and trees on the third day, birds and other creatures on the fifth day, the creation of humankind just after the cattle and other animals on the sixth day. Chapter 2, on the other hand, notes the absence of plants and herbs before the creation of Adam from the ground, and only mentions the creation of trees, animals and birds after the creation of Adam. I deduce from this that Genesis 1-2 is not so much interested in chronology, but rather in using two different narrative strategies for emphasizing the importance of Adam in the context of creation. That is the driving force of both chapters. Chapter 1 achieves its goal by mentioning Adam as the pinnacle of creation, coming at the end. Chapter 2 does this by placing Adam at the centre of creation and saying that everything else revolves around him. (Adam is often translated "man" in our English translations, of course, but it is much better rendered "humankind," since chapter 1 verse 27 tells us very clearly that Adam is both male and female.) Both passages share the view that Adam is the focal point of the created order, possessing dominion over it and with everything designed to meet his needs—although it is, of course, not simply Adam's well-being that these chapters are interested in. Taking Genesis 1 as the context of Genesis 2 and noting that chronological ordering is not an interest of the narratives is quite important when we get to male and female issues, as I shall note in a moment.

My second point: we are created, we are told here, "from the dust," with a oneness between human beings and the creation; and yet, we are created by God in the image of God. That is what leads to the wonder of the psalmist in Psalm 8. If we remember the general prohibition of images of God in Israelite religion—one cannot make images, because that is to confuse God with things that are created (e.g., Exod 20:1-4)—then it is clear that "image of God" is a very daring and bold description for Adam. It suggests the very exalted state of the human beings. It also reminds us, however, that human beings have only a delegated authority over the earth. They are not autonomous beings.

Third, we are created by God not only from the dust but as whole people. There is an affirmation biblically of our earthiness "from the dust" as well as of our spirituality, and these things belong together. The human being of Genesis 1 and 2 does not have a soul but rather is a soul (2:7). It is one of the important features of Hebrew anthropology that it does not make compartmentalized distinctions, but prefers to look at the human person simply from different points of view. And so when we see words like "spirit" and "soul" and "heart" and so on in the Old Testament, these are words which are looking at the whole human being from a particular point of view. Human beings are not to be thought of as collections of parts, in the Old Testament way of looking at things. We are to think of one complex entity—body, soul, spirit, emotion—taking each aspect of these things as aspects of our God-createdness. This is, incidentally, why Christians when they are thinking straight believe in the resurrection of the body. The body is not dispensable—

it is an absolutely intrinsic part of who we are. I say that because straight thinking on such matters has not been a mark of the church throughout the ages, which is why Christian tradition has so often come to reject the body, to repress sexuality, thinking that the soul or the spirit is a higher part of who we are; and indeed, it has also sometimes neglected the need for engagement of the whole person (body, soul, mind) in worship, narrowing worship down to something far more limited that has to do with our spirits. A truly biblical theology must emphasize body and soul and spirit together, as it must emphasize createdness and redemption together.

Another fundamental point about this chapter: we are created to enjoy all of God's creation, our totality responding to its totality and through it to the totality of who God is. The Bible, and the Old Testament in particular, has a very great emphasis on beauty and the enjoyment of beauty. Ezekiel 28 celebrates the perfect beauty of the first human being; Song of Songs celebrates the physical beauty of and sexual expression between a man and a woman. In Genesis 1-2 it is above all the trees that are the signs of God's gracious provision, the emphasis falling on abundance and enjoyment with one prohibition; that is the reality that the serpent turns on its head later on. The trees in question in Genesis 1 and 2 are not only good for food—they are good to look at (2:9), a confirmation that the biblical view of human beings is holistic, and that no part of us is more important than any other part. Aesthetics in Genesis 1-2 are as important as pragmatics. Divine provision takes as much account of the human need for beauty as of the human need for food. We have an affirmation of creation here—creation is good. And again, Christian tradition has not always managed to repeat this emphasis, whether we are thinking of the sixth-century Council of Constantinople which outlawed the literal interpretation of the Song of Songs as heretical, or whether we are thinking of the Protestant tradition which has so often opposed aesthetics to other things, assuming that beauty is inevitably corrupting of worship and Christian living. I say this with some feeling as a Scottish Presbyterian! We do not in our tradition have a great deal of place for aesthetics. A biblical theology of humanness has to find a place for sensuality, for beauty, and for this aspect of who we clearly are. And it does us no good if we simply repress that, because it is part of God's givenness to us; it is part of who we are.

We are also created for community. Adam in the Old Testament is always part of a group; there is none of our modern Western, particularly North American, individualism in the Old Testament. There is first of all the community of the man and the woman (Genesis 1 and 2) and as we go on in

Genesis we find still greater complexity of community. The crucial thing here is to remember precisely what I was saying earlier about ordering: that Genesis 1 sets the context in which Genesis 2 must be read. We have already been told in 1:27 that Adam is plural. Adam created in the image of God and given dominion over creation is male and female. Since Genesis 1 provides the context for Genesis 2 we are thus made aware, if we are reading carefully, of the impossibility of reading Genesis 2 as if the order of events in itself was meant to be taken very seriously in this chapter. Whatever the significance may be of the fact that the creation of the woman is mentioned after the creation of the man in chapter 2, no interpretation of this fact can be defended which is not consistent with the basic thrust of Genesis 1:27 and the following verses. I say this because commentators have sometimes been rather over-influenced at this point in their reading of Genesis 2 by a particular interpretation of 1 Timothy 2. Let me underline the point from simply a Genesis point of view, leaving other people to struggle with 1 Timothy 2. It is precisely joint authority over creation which is in view in Genesis 1. Dominion over the world is not to be exercised by one person, or by one gender, but by humankind corporately in sexual differentiation and togetherness. And if that is the general statement, it is very difficult to think that we are meant to draw any theological conclusions simply from the order of events described in chapter 2. All narratives, after all, have to have an order of events. It is what we deduce from them that is the really important thing.

What you will notice if you read chapter 2 carefully is that the chapter itself draws no conclusions at all about the nature of male/female relationships from the fact that the woman apparently comes after the man. Nothing is made of the chronology in terms of hierarchy, subordination, and roles. In fact the emphasis of Genesis 2 is placed quite differently. The emphasis is on kinship and sharing. It is not good for the man to be alone. It is his nature that he is a social being. A search is made, therefore, among the other creatures of God to see if any of them is suitable as the kind of soul-mate that Adam requires. It is thus emphasized, by the way, that Adam is himself a creature, formed out of the dust. There is a commonality between the human and the animal creation which suggests at least the possibility that Adam might have found a creature of another sort to meet his deepest needs and aspirations. There is a kinship there which at least makes the search for some kind of friend a credible one; and yet in the end, Adam's place as God's special creation is underscored. He may well be dust, like the animals, but he is also made in the image of God; and in the end only one who is like him will really supply the need (2:18), a "helper as partner." The word "helper" is most often used in the Hebrew of the

Old Testament of divine assistance; in three places it is used of military aid. The image of the man is of a strength which is inadequate by itself: it requires strength from elsewhere to make it whole. The remainder of the phrase is literally in Hebrew "opposite him," expressing the idea of complementarity, mutual support. In other words, the phrase "helper as partner" means that the woman provides the support and strength for the man without which he is inadequate. The passage celebrates mutuality.

It is only with the disobedience of chapter 3 that other, darker aspects are envisaged as creeping into the male/female relationship. The ideal is framed quite differently. As Phyllis Trible has put it, whether in terms of human relationships or in terms of human creation and the rest of creation, what we find in Genesis 2 is distinction without opposition; dominion without domination; and hierarchy of a kind, but hierarchy without oppression. The community of the man and the woman is a particularly intimate human community involving sexual expression as well as other forms of human relating. They are naked and not ashamed. There is in biblical thinking nothing to be ashamed of. They come together, they become one flesh, or to cite a particularly famous student misquote from a paper submitted while I was teaching in Edinburgh, "the man and the woman became one flash." There is a close intimacy. The Song of Songs offers us a wonderful celebration of the joys of physical love between a man and a woman. Usually, and this is interesting in view of our discussion about subordination, in the Song of Songs the woman is taking the lead in that aspect of the intimacy.

It is important to emphasize all this, for Christian exegesis has not always covered itself in glory when dealing with Genesis or with the subject of sexuality. Of course there is a biblical awareness of the shadow side of sexuality, and the Bible is written in the real world, entirely aware of the way in which sex can be divinized and worshipped, and of the way in which all sorts of brokenness and wickedness can arise from this. The Bible was written in a world like ours in which sex was routinely divinized and worshipped, in which it was widely held that there was an entrance into divinity through the mystery of sexual expression. And that is why fertility cults were a feature of Canaanite religion. So, of course, the Bible opposes that kind of distortion.

The Bible insists that sex, like everything else in creation, has to be placed in the appropriate creation context. And because there is an appropriate creation context, the Bible does of course take its stand against both heterosexual aberration and homosexual practice. But the point about the prohibitions relating to these things is that there is a positive vision being presented in the Bible of what it means to be human and gendered, and we can only understand the negatives in relation to the positive vision. And that, I think, is why so often you get a blank look if you try to explain your Christian view on sexual issues to somebody in the secular culture. They have not the first idea of where Christians are coming from in terms of the larger vision. Things only make sense in terms of the negatives when you understand what the positives are, and we have to be very clear, and in fact be prepared to celebrate much more than we do, the positive biblical vision of humanness and of sexuality, and to say what is good about such things and not simply what is bad. Many of us have grown up in church communities in which the suspicion was rife, no matter what was explicitly said, that mostly everything to do with sex was quite bad, but that one might redeem parts of it if one were particularly lucky. That is not what the Bible is says at all.

Of course there are distortions of creation; and you will find abundant evidence in the Old Testament of those distortions and how they work out. But we must not allow all of these perspectives on the distortedness of the world of experience to swamp all the positive material in the Old Testament on the other side. We must especially not allow these perspectives to distort our exegesis of the early chapters of Genesis, and indeed our understanding of the knowledge of good and evil in these chapters, knowledge that has often been understood in Christian exegesis as sexual knowledge. I am sure that you are aware of this idea that the "apple" represents sexual knowledge and that the eating of it is where everything goes terribly wrong for human beings. It is very bad exegesis.

Genesis 1 presents sexuality as very much part of the created order before we get to Genesis 2, the human pair being told to be fruitful and multiply and indeed the sexual impulse being connected here with being made in the image of God. It is people made in the image of God who are to go and be fruitful and to multiply. It is these positive connotations of sexuality that the Song of Songs takes up. So the idea that the forbidden knowledge of Genesis 2 is sexual knowledge simply does not work exegetically. There is affirmation of both sex and reproduction in Genesis, as one would expect if the creation that God created is indeed good. So to put that whole discussion in a nutshell, sexuality is neither divinized nor despised biblically. It is affirmed in the context of a vision of the kingdom of God which knows of childlike innocence, unselfconsciousness, and a world without shame or guilt. And what the Bible has to say about aberrations from this norm, it does so not arbitrarily (because God simply enjoys making commandments so that he can then punish people for doing wrong), but in the context of what is said positively about what it means to be a human being and to enjoy the good life as ordained by God.

All this is a little of what it means to be human, according to the Bible: what we are created for, the thing towards which we are being redeemed, the vision of the kingdom of God as it is related to our human nature and the way things will be when the kingdom of God breaks in fully and we see in the mirror clearly rather than darkly. It is a rather wonderful vision; a world of joy, intimacy, mutuality, involving (at the level of one-to-one) commitment between a man and a woman and additional sexual intimacy, which is connected with, although not exhausted by, procreation. Here we have the positive vision of what the kingdom of God is about.

What about the reality of our human experience?

Here we have to consider Genesis chapter 3. In our present experience, as in Genesis 3, human reality is fractured and broken because of human disobedience to God. That is why redemption is necessary. Humanness in this world is not commonly nor fully experienced in ways which correspond to the biblical vision of it. Genesis 3 describes this reality and so do many other biblical passages. Now there are many things that might be said about Genesis 3 in terms of exploring the alienation that comes from disobedience to God. One of the great emphases of the chapter is the alienation that comes between human beings and God before we even get to the alienation that comes to the rest of creation. And there is, in addition to that, a tremendous emphasis in the chapter on the alienation between human beings and the environment, the planet; and if we were talking about ecology there would be a lot to be said there.

I want to emphasize in this context what Genesis 3 says about human alienation, one from the other. Genesis 3 knows of a world in which shame has been introduced into these matters, a sense of individuality which takes precedence over any sense of corporateness. So if you are wondering where unhealthy individualism comes from, it comes from this root. People seek freedom from God and with the next step they seek freedom from everyone else as well. This is why C. S. Lewis in his book, *The Great Divorce,* has a vision of hell as a place in which people progressively move away from each other. The people who have been there the longest are distant lights on the horizon, because they are trying to get some peace and quiet. They are on the move into enormous emptiness. That is what is going on in Genesis 3: shame and individualism, symbolized in the relationship between the man and the woman first of all, who were created to be one flesh, naked but not ashamed, and yet are found divided, at odds with each other, concealed from each other with the fig leaves. Something has come between them; nakedness is no longer unproblematic in the midst of unity and innocence, but now has become something shameful, as it is in much of the rest of the Old Testament.

There is not only shame, but also blame. The man blames the woman, the woman blames the serpent and the serpent does not have a leg to stand on! Whereas men and women were created to work in partnership, Genesis 3 insists that they are all too often in practice to be found in unequal relationships. Notice 3:16, where the man "rules over" the woman. The Hebrew verb here is *mashal*: he rules over the woman as if she were simply another part of creation, rather than an equal who has dominion with him over the earth. Psalm 8:6 indeed uses that same Hebrew verb of Adam's dominion over the whole of creation. Something that was once the province of male and female together become something which characterizes male dominance over the female.

The woman's desire for her husband is mentioned here too, although the exegesis is difficult. It may be a reference to a generalized desire for the male/female relationship which leads woman in turn to submit to male domination; or it could refer to an inappropriate desire by the woman, in revenge for this rather forceful domineering spirit in the man, to also have some power to try and meet force with force. Whichever way one interprets it precisely, it illustrates very well the kind of fracturedness that has now come to what used to be commonality. The man now has the power also to define the woman in terms of her role, rather than in terms of her person. In 2:23 the woman is named "woman," whereas in 3:20 she is named "Eve." In the first reference, the word "woman" (Hebrew *'ishah*) is very closely related to the word "man" (*'ish*) in Hebrew, emphasizing commonality, whereas "Eve" is interpreted in the narrative as "mother of the living," emphasizing the woman's role as mother. To my mind that is a narrowing down of her nature to one aspect of her being. The name "Eve" seems to be related to the Hebrew verb "to live," which is a nice ironic touch: the woman's name is "life" and she brings forth the living, but she has been involved with the man in introducing death by listening to the serpent.

So there is a disturbance to the order of things here in Genesis 3. Human relationships are out of order, and the alienation between the man and the woman in due course in Genesis 1-11 becomes alienation of brother from brother, neighbour from neighbour, and the whole of society then breaks down as we get towards Genesis 6. It is this rather uglier vision of gender relations and sexuality that we find widely reflected in biblical narrative elsewhere in the Old Testament, because biblical narrative is the story of the people of God in this fallen, disobedient state living in the world. We should not expect, therefore, to be able to go to biblical narratives and simply read lessons for life out of them without thinking about their nature. We cannot move exegetically from description to prescription without a considerable degree of thought. And so we find in the Old Testament all sorts of very horrendous stories of abuse and violence: the story of Tamar, in Genesis 38, or the story in Judges 11 of Jephthah's daughter, killed as a sacrifice to God because Jephthah makes a vow to sacrifice the one who comes out to meet him after a victory over the Ammonites.

The second is a particularly tragic, terrible story and yet in its horror, it only serves to illustrate the kind of patriarchal society in action which we also see theoretically described in Old Testament law. Jephthah makes a vow which might turn out to apply to any of his possessions, a daughter as well as a goat or an ox. He does not appear to be very concerned to differentiate among these. When the daughter turns out to be the first of his possessions to greet him, Jephthah does not blame himself for the evil he has brought on her, but rather blames the daughter for the evil that she has brought on him (v. 35). The victim is blamed for her own plight. Nor does Jephthah offer himself in her place, or simply refuse to fulfill the vow and suffer the consequences. The daughter simply serves the needs of the father. The only solace that she finds in the story comes from her female friends who weep with her (v. 38), and even then permission for the mourning has to be given by the father. We find here only one act of brutality against an innocent woman, among many biblical examples. There are gentler and nobler stories too. But the Bible does not pull its punches about the nature of fallen reality, especially as it leads to the oppression and exploitation of women.

It is not just the narrative, however, but also the law that reflects the fallen reality. And here I have a few examples because this is a very important issue. I think many people would accept that you cannot move easily from narrative to ethical judgments as to how Christians should live. I think many have more difficulty when it comes to Old Testament law. But let me just illustrate how the law is very far from an expression of God's ideal will for the kingdom of God. In the Ten Commandments for example the wife is clearly the property of the man: "you shall not covet your neighbour's house, you shall not covet your neighbour's wife, or his manservant or maidservant, his ox or donkey, or anything that belongs to your neighbour"(Ex 20:17). The wife is simply one possession among many. Deuteronomy 22:13-21 describes the case of a man acquiring a woman and subsequently coming to hate her (or as the NIV puts it, to "dislike her") and to slander her. The woman does have some protection under Old Testament law, but you will notice as you read through this passage that the implication throughout is that she is not a legal person, that she has no legal role. She is defended in fact, in this case, by her previous owners, her father and mother, the father being the one who gave the woman to her husband in the first place (v.16) and also being the one to whom the fine is paid (v.19). What we essentially have here is a business or a property dispute. Did the father sell damaged goods to the other man? The language throughout is patriarchal: "her father's house," "the men of the city," and so on. The interest is resolutely male, because the background issue here is whether men can assure themselves that their children are really theirs. It has to do with the continuity of the family line. Not only is there no escape for the woman in this situation—she is either put to death, if guilty, or condemned to live with a man who hates her and has publicly humiliated her, if innocent. Clearly, this is not a great choice. It is also the case that the woman's value *vis-à-vis* the man is in question here. For the penalty for the woman if guilty is death, whereas the penalty for the man if guilty is only a monetary fine, even though his false accusation put his wife's life in danger. So we can see that there is a real problem here of equity.

Number 5:11-30 gives us another example of the same kind of thing. If a man suspects his wife of unfaithfulness, while she is under his authority (v. 29), he can compel her to submit to what is called the rite of the bitter waters. There is no provision for the wife to put the husband through this ordeal, since again the basic concerns are those of property and lineage.

In Deuteronomy 22: 22-29 we have a number of further rules about illicit sexual conduct. Certainly in the second and third cases (vv. 23-29) this is clearly rape, and not simply sexual conduct of a less serious kind. Betrothal in Old Testament law is tantamount to marriage, which is partly what explains the Joseph/Mary story in the Gospels; it was taken very seriously. So it is regarded as a case of adultery if the betrothal contract is breached (verses 23-27). The man in both cases here is put to death, but the woman is only put to death if the act took place in the country and thus no one knows if she failed to cry out for help. So again, the choice seems to be death on the one hand, or the risk of violence on the other, for the woman. The third case underlines very clearly that this is not law drawn up with the rights of women particularly in mind. For the rape of an unbetrothed, unmarried woman, the fine for the man is only 50 shekels of silver, half the amount paid in the case of the accusation against the wife (Deut 22:13-21). Yet the woman suffers not only the trauma of rape but the further trauma of having to live with the man who raped her. The fine is again paid to the father to compensate him for the damage to his property. The woman has no say in the matter, because she is not a legal person.

Finally, in this rather alarming array of Old Testament texts, Leviticus 27:1-6 underlines the reality of male-female relations in Old Testament law in terms of the value attached to persons, because you will notice here that females are worth half as much as males in monetary terms.

Now, it is not difficult to see how cultures influenced by the biblical legal tradition should for so long have had statutes on their books which discriminate so thoroughly between men and women in terms of legal status and rights. Jewish law as found in the Mishnah already builds on Old Testament law, e.g., *Tractate Kiddushin*: "by three means is the woman acquired, and by two means she acquires her freedom. She is acquired by money or by writ or by intercourse: she acquires her freedom by a bill of divorce, issued by the husband or course, or by the death of the husband." A modern Christian writer arguing for a fairly traditional Christian view of male-female relations describes the biblical and later the Jewish reality in this way: "The major contribution of Jewish women was in their service in the home. Although their legal rights were practically non-existent, they were accorded a place of honour in carrying out the privileges of motherhood." The last phrase may be thought somewhat romantic in view of some of the legal texts we have just looked at. Indeed the whole question is whether Christians should be at all influenced in a primary sense by texts from the Old Testament legal tradition. And this touches not just on issues of male-female relations, but on issues of homosexual practice and other things like that as well. It has all too often been my experience in Christian debate about gender and sexuality that somebody will pluck a text from Leviticus and whack somebody over the head with it (for example, on homosexual practice), without realizing that they are wrenching a text out of context in so doing. They would not ever take such a negative view of people who, for example, mix seeds in planting out their crops—something that is also prohibited in Leviticus. We need to have a consistent attitude to the Old Testament legal tradition overall.

I want to suggest to you that Old Testament law clearly does not represent the highest vision of the Genesis creation story. And indeed, Jesus himself gives weight to that point of view when in Mark 10, asked about divorce, he makes precisely this distinction between creation and law: "Moses permitted a man to write a certificate of divorce and send her away. It was because your hearts were hard that Moses wrote you this law, but at the beginning of creation, God made them male and female ...." And I take that to be precisely a distinction between the creation order of things and the legal position in a fallen society. The law must always be read in the context of the creation purposes of God, because Old Testament law seems to be aimed at dealing often with ugly reality as it is, rather than enunciating ideal principles of conduct. That is what modern law does too. It does not prescribe virtue; it deals with ugly reality as it actually is. And you can understand many of the laws with which I have just been dealing in a much more friendly way if you do not hear them as ideals, but as attempts to regulate what otherwise would be even worse situations for the woman concerned; for in those ancient cultures, because women had no legal status, a woman with no protector and no provider was in a very perilous and precarious position. So if you understand laws as a barrier to prevent worse things happening, rather than as an ideal, then of course, you will begin to understand what Old Testament law is about. Even the Ten Commandments, which are clearly important principles of behaviour, are not Christian absolutes. Even they are to be interpreted in terms of the command to love God and your neighbour, if they are not to be misunderstood. They do not exist so that people can take refuge behind them as a way of avoiding the command to love. Both law and narrative (which describes only what people did, not what they should do, then or now) must be set in the context of creation.

The church, unfortunately, has often lived out the fallen reality described and legally addressed in the Bible as if it were the vision of the kingdom of God. The church has often read the biblical witness as legitimating fallen reality, rather than as something to be transcended, and has failed to see the trajectory of the kingdom of God from creation through the fall and on through the life and death and resurrection of Christ and into the kingdom of God. And because the church has often taken such a view, it has also done bizarre things, such as opposing the use of anesthetic for women in childbirth, on the grounds that Genesis 3 teaches that women should suffer in childbirth, or supporting slavery. Indeed, in the slavery debate in the United States of the nineteenth century there was a popular conservative Christian argument that ran as follows: we cannot concede on the slavery issue, because the next thing you will be asking for is women's rights. And so we have often found fallen reality lived out as if it were the will of God. The challenge, conversely, is for us is to live the kingdom of God as it has broken into our world, redeeming the creation in the direction of God's purposes for it. And to do that we must always differentiate between those texts which describe for us the way things were in Israel and those texts which hold out before us the vision of God's kingdom as it should be lived out by us now.

That is not an easy exegetical task; it requires effort and thought and struggle and argument. The creation vision of gender and sexuality is of gender equality, of mutual intimacy, of sexual joy and mutual responsibility within a heterosexual marriage. It is a vision of genuine community. And that is the vision that I think we need to grasp, and to run with, and in whose light we need to read the Bible, in its various parts.

CHAPTER 3

Women in the Gospels and Acts

Rikk E. Watts

My allotted inheritance in this series is the place and role of women in the Gospels and Acts, and there are giants more than enough in this land to keep one busy. For example, of what significance is the fact that Jesus did not include women among the twelve, or that the resurrection was announced first to women? Much, if not everything, depends on context, both cultural and literary, and so we will begin with a necessarily brief survey of prevailing contemporary Jewish attitudes toward women.[1]

Survey of background materials

Negative Assessments of Women

In terms of the outrageous, at least to modern ears, few sayings can match Ben Sirach's (ca. 180 BC) "better the wickedness of a man than a woman who does good" (42:14; cf. "any wickedness, but not the wickedness of a woman!" 25:13). Since he claims, "from a woman sin had its beginning, and because of her we all die" (25:24), it is small wonder that his work is peppered with admonitions to avoid the temptations of feminine wiles (9:3-8; 19:2; 25:21).

Philo (ca. 20 BC to AD 50) warns that women are more likely to be deceived because they are gentler, more accepting (*Questions in Genesis* 1.33) and governed by intuition whereas men rely on reason (*On Creation* 165; interestingly, some postmodern feminists might agree with Philo's characterization of men but argue that this is precisely why women and not men ought to be trusted). Women's proper realm is the home (*Special Laws* 3.169-71; *Flaccus* 33)—though not apparently in the case of Cleopatra whom

Philo without hesitation describes as "eminent" (*Embassy* 135)—and so they should not frequent the streets, nor emulate men's violent tendencies (*Flaccus* 89; *Special Laws* 3.172-4).

For Josephus (AD 27-ca. 100), the Law regards woman as inferior in "all things" (*Against Apion* 2.201; in fact, it does not—and maybe neither does Josephus: there are questions regarding the integrity of this text). However, this inferiority provides no grounds for male domination but instead obligates men not to seek material or sexual advantage (2.200). Even so, Josephus can divorce his wife simply because she displeased him (*Life* 426). Reporting a declamation celebrating women's power over men, he speaks of gaping males leaving all their wealth and family for a woman, or working tirelessly crossing land and sea to accrue goods only to lay them at her feet (*Antiquities* 11.49-54). He claims women's testimony is not admitted by the Jews because of the "levity and boldness" of their sex (*Antiquities* 4.219), perhaps alluding to their beguiling power (cf. *Antiquities* 2.49-59).

The Essenes, he tells us, also had a less than positive assessment, regarding women as lascivious and unfaithful (*Jewish Wars* 2.121), and for this reason they practiced celibacy (*J. W.*, 2.120-121; cf. Philo, *Hypothetica*, 11.14-16; Pliny, *Nat. Hist.* 5.17.4). In this he might have in mind 4Q184, "The Wiles of the Wicked Woman." But, based on the similarities to Prov. 7.5-27, this appears more of a warning against the adulteress and prostitute rather than against women in general, especially when there is some evidence of their participation as faithful adherents, if not yet as full initiates, of the Essene community (1QSa 1.4-11; 4Q502; 4Q270).

The *Testament of Reuben*, reflecting on the tradition of Reuben using his father's concubine (Gen 35;22; 49:4) is ambiguous (3:1-6:4). "Reuben" warns that women are evil and scheme treacherously to entice men by their beauty (5:1-2), but freely admits that it was his own sin that led him to take advantage of Bilhah (3:11-14). He obviously lacked self-control even in the face of the wife of Potiphar's persistent attempts at seduction, which is so lauded in the *Testament of Joseph* (3:1-10:2).

Rabbinic material comprises our largest, though most problematic source (see below). Most famous is the Jewish male's thanksgiving that he was not a woman (*t. Ber.* 7.18), though this might be less misogyny than gratefulness for fuller access to the Temple. Still, in a similar thanksgiving, women are likened to illiterate males (neither being educated) though better than slaves (*b. Menah.* 43b). One passage speaks of a "wise" women who asks about Scripture, only to dismiss her concerns as trivial (*b. Yom.* 66b). Not surprisingly, some rabbis disqualified women from giving testimony (*m.*

Yebam. 16.7; cf. *m. Sheb.* 4.1).

Echoing Ben Sirach, men are warned not to speak at length with a woman since this leads ultimately to Gehenna, probably alluding to sexual misconduct (*m. 'Abot* 1.5). A woman could be divorced without financial settlement if she spoke with any man other than her husband (*m. Ketub.* 7.6) though the Talmud specifies "suggestive conversation." Unlike a man, a woman could be divorced without her consent for reasons ranging from infidelity alone (Hillel) to her burning a meal (Shamai) or to the husband's finding a more attractive woman (Akibah; *m. Git.* 9.10).

Women were excluded from the Court of the Men, and during menstrual uncleanness from the entire Temple area (*t. Menaḥ.* 10.13, 17; *m. Kelim* 1.8; *b. Hag.* 16b)—but so were men with bleeding wounds. R. Eliezer declared that it was "better to burn the words of Torah than to give them to a woman" (*y. Soṭa 3.4*) for to do so was like teaching a daughter lechery (m. *Soṭa* 3.4). There was considerable discomfort with the judge Deborah and the prophetess Huldah—the latter being particularly galling since Josiah sent for a word of God through her while Jeremiah was yet living. They are rarely mentioned and only in disparaging terms: "Rabbi Nahman said: Haughtiness does not befit women. There were two haughty women, and their names are hateful, one being called a hornet [literal meaning of Deborah] and the other a weasel [literal meaning of Huldah]. Of the hornet it is written, And she sent and called Barak, instead of going to him. Of the weasel it is written, Say to the man, instead of 'Say to the king [Josiah]'"; *b. Meg.* 14b.[2] Obviously the good rabbi objected mightily to these women exercising authority over men.

The Gospel of Thomas, of later Gnostic provenance, goes further: "Simon Peter said to them: Let Mary go away from us, for women are not worthy of life. Jesus said: Lo, I shall lead her, so that I may make her a male, that she too may become a living spirit, resembling you males. For every woman who makes herself a male will enter the kingdom of heaven" (114). But this should be heard alongside Saying 22 where in speaking about becoming as children, Thomas' "Jesus" speaks of making "the male and the female into a single one so that the male will not be male nor the female be female."

Positive Assessments of Women

All this, however, is only one side of the story. Alongside these negative views are numerous affirmations. Ben Sirach also urges "do not let pass the opportunity to have a wise and a good wife, for her grace is more precious than gold" (7:19). "Children and the building of a city establish a man's name," he says, "but a blameless wife is accounted better than both" (40:19). Indeed, a man without a good woman is like an exile; such a woman is a great gift from God reserved for those who fear him (26:1ff; cf. 36:22ff). Josephus too has no hesitation in recognizing exceptionally able women such as the "wise" Alexandra (*Antiquities* 14.405-32) or the calculating Cleopatra whose machinations rivaled Herod's (*Antiquities* 15.88-107). Philo can even have Leah typify the rational part of the soul (*Preliminary Studies* 26ff). And at Qumran, the *Genesis Apocryphon* (1Q20.20.2-8) recalls the Egyptians' bedazzlement with Sarah's beauty.

Likewise the Rabbis: "he who has no wife lives without joy, blessing or good, ... he lives without a protective wall and without peace" (*b. Yebam.* 62b). While the man was the ultimate authority in the home (*m. Ker.* 6.9), a wife could retain some control over her own property (*m. Ketub.* 8-9) and if necessary precipitate a divorce (*m. Ned.* 11.12; *m. Ketub.* 7.2-10). A husband was to love his wife as himself (*b. Yebam.* 62b) and in contrast to Shamai and Akibah many rabbis regarded divorce as shameful (*m. Ned.* 9.9; *b. Git.* 90b). Strikingly, only women are said to have a right to sexual pleasure (*m. Ketub.* 5.6; *b. Ketub.* 62a; *b. Sanh.* 75a). A mother was to be honoured equally with the father (cf. *m. Ned.* 9.1), even being spoken of as "Shekinah" (*b. Qidd.* 31b), and one rabbi declared his daughters dearer to him than sons (*b. B. Bat.* 141a).

Against Eliezer, others affirm teaching women Torah (*m. Ned.* 4.3; *m. Soṭa* 3.4) with some women actually being consulted on points of oral law (cf. *b. Qidd.* 70a-b).[3] The great feast of Tabernacles took place in the Women's Court (cf. t. Sukk. 4.1; 198.6), women could sacrifice (*m. Nazir* 6.11), slaughter sacrificial animals (*m. Zeb.* 3.1) and maybe even read Torah in Synagogue (*b. Meg.* 73a). While some rabbis prohibited female testimony, others apparently did not (*m. Soṭa 6.4*; 9.8; *m. Ketub.* 1.8; *m. Yebam.* 16.7).

Women not uncommonly appear as role models, leaders, and heroes in Jewish literature (e.g., Aseneth in Jos. Asen, Deborah in Pseudo-Philo, and the mother in 4 Macc 14:11—15:15) and Job's daughters receive the superior blessing of angelic speech, something not extended to his sons (T. Job 46-52). There are several inscriptions, though after AD 70 and from outside Palestine, in which women are described as elders and presidents of Synagogues.[4] Even if merely honourific it is significant that a woman could be so esteemed. In fact, for nearly every negative view a positive counterpart of some kind can be found.[5]

Response

What is one to make of this bird's nest of opinions? First, some small steps. Some of the more negative statements may bear a less offensive reading. In

46

context we might translate, for example, Sirach 42:14: "better the churlishness of a man than the courtesy of a woman," meaning "better to endure the churlish company of men than risk one's heart leading one astray by spending too much time in the company of good but beautiful women" (cf. 42:12f; Sus 1:8-12). Similarly, Sirach's aspersions concerning a garrulous wife (25:20) might be no more than a particular application of the proverbial injunction against foolish speech in general (including men, Prov 29:20; cf. 17:27f).

In the Near East, hyperbole is almost expected in making one's point. Jesus himself admonishes his followers to pluck out the offending eye (Mt 5:29) and to "hate" their parents (Lk 14:26)—neither of which is intended to be taken literally—and likens a Syrophoenician woman to a scavenging dog (Mk 7:27). While not wishing illegitimately to diminish the severity of these remarks, it also seems to be that sensibilities were not as finely tuned back then.[6] Neither is Jesus averse to apparent contradictions: "he who is not with me is against me" (Mt 12:30) and "he is who is not against us is for us" (Mk 9:40). Such apophthegms clearly expect some subtlety on the part of the hearer.

This tension might also reflect a larger principle: that which occasions the greatest good can also cause the greatest harm. In other words, a good, wise and beautiful woman brings joy and delight beyond valuation. But by the same token, a woman can bring a man into devastation. Judging by great romantic literature the world over, this is not an altogether unique notion.

There is also the gap both between theory and practice—for example, it is striking that there are no criticisms of Jesus' teaching women or having them as followers (but see "promiscuous women" below)—and between formal and informal relations—the frequency of complaints about "strong-willed" daughters and "tiresome" wives is prima facie evidence that informally at least male authority was not everywhere meekly accepted. Societies too are rarely homogenous. The wealthy city-dwelling elites might be torn between a desire to closet their women (they could afford to do so) and the influence of the Roman trend of granting matrons more influence. In the country and perhaps among lesser artisans, the need to work fields and run shops rendered strict isolation impractical, as the rabbis realized (*m. Ketub.* 9.4; *m. Ed.* 1.12).[7] Many (or some) may have seen women generically as weak-willed and uninformed. The latter estimation is perhaps not surprising. Women were rarely offered education and apparently often married to men somewhat older and more experienced than themselves. On the other hand, one does not become a heroine, role model, synagogue ruler (assuming we understand the title aright), or, as a widow, successfully manage a large household without having some degree of insight and sophistication.

Now I am not seeking to defend first-century Jewish attitudes to women. Nor am I suggesting that Jewish society was only just a few steps away from achieving modern ideals of gender liberation. It clearly was not. But an unrepentant Wellhausian caricature is unhelpful, whether concerning the Law or women.

Several observations can be made. First, whatever else, this considerable diversity scuttles any notion of there being "a Jewish view" of women or that it was intrinsically misogynist. Second, undoubtedly this was a patriarchal society. There is often little attempt to understand woman in her own right (but see 4 Macc). Woman is mostly discussed in relation to males as wife, daughter or temptress; marriage, for the vast majority, was simply assumed. Is this "chauvinist stereotyping"? Very probably. But a caveat is in order. Stereotyping implies a sophisticated individuation which did not obtain in the first century, either for women or men. Further, women are clearly not merely chattels; there were men who loved their wives and daughters and women who operated with some degree of independence. Third, we actually know very little about the day-to-day situation of women among the common people. Why? Because our Jewish sources derive from elites whether wealthy, religious, educated or some combination thereof and they seem little concerned with recounting the lives of the *hoi polloi*. Finally, although I have tried to use earlier, Mishnaic sources for rabbinic approaches, we still have no way of knowing how representative this second century document is of pre-AD 70 sentiments and whether its various ideas represent a later reactionary conservatism.

Thus, while it is easy to emphasize the inequalities, we should not ignore the complementarian nature of roles in advanced agrarian societies. Likewise, although recognizing the generally androcentric and patriarchal nature of Jewish society, as compared to the modern West, it is important not to overdraw the disparities. They existed to be sure, but at the same time there is also evidence that women could play significant roles and were genuinely valued, almost certainly universally as mothers, and probably in many other spheres.

Women and Jesus in the Gospels

The Birth Narratives

At the outset, Matthew's genealogy contains four women: Tamar, Rahab, Ruth, and Bathsheba. Numerous explanations have been suggested, with the best probably being that their unions were all in some way scandalous. Most likely this is because Matthew records Mary's virginal conception, which almost certainly would have raised many a knowing eyebrow. He reminds his readers that David's line is no stranger to "scandal." Whatever the exact reason it is clear that these women, even if of dubious origin or circumstance, are also part of God's plan.

Unique to Luke, women play an important role in Jesus' birth as agents of prophetic utterance. Elizabeth, on encountering Mary, is filled with the Spirit and praises God. Mary's Magnificat (1:46-55) not only expresses good theology but has been preserved in Scripture to teach us all—unless men are to skip over this section. The prophetess Anna also announces the good news. What is noteworthy, however, is that none of this betrays any sense of provocation or offense against social convention. Whatever the feelings of some Jewish authors, the gospel writers apparently find none of this socially disturbing.

Jesus' Teaching

In terms of the content of Jesus' teaching, women frequently have positive roles and, again, particularly so in Luke. The gentile widow of Zarephath joins Naaman as a recipient of God's blessing (Lk 4:26), the Queen of the south will rise up and condemn this generation (Lk 11:31; Mt 12:42), the persistent widow serves as an example of persevering prayer (Lk 18:1-8), and the woman searching for her missing coin illustrates God's deep concern for the lost (Lk 15:5-8). Concerning divorce, Jesus rejects the notion that women may be discarded whenever fancy strikes (Mt 19:3-9; Mk 10:2-12) and his restriction of grounds for divorcing one's wife to *porneia* surprises even his disciples (Mt 19:10). Intriguingly, in a setting where women were regarded at least by some (if not many) males as lascivious threats to holiness, Jesus in his teaching on lust directs his attention to the problem in men (Mt 5:27-30).

At the same time, his teaching on honouring parents (Mk 7:9-13, but see Lk 9:59-60) and his striking use of children as models of discipleship (Mk 10:13-16) implicitly support traditional notions of family. In his climactic confrontation with the temple hierarchs, Jesus offers a breathtakingly provocative denunciation stating that "the tax collectors and immoral women are entering the kingdom of God before you" (Mt 21:31).

Jesus' Miracles

Although men figure more frequently in the various healing stories (twenty versus six)—probably reflecting the reality that women were less likely to appear in public—Jesus appears just as interested in restoring women. Luke again has a special interest recording five of the six accounts (Mt and Mk four, though Lk 8:1-3 and Mk's longer ending refer to Mary Magdalene's being delivered of seven demons) and he alone includes the story of the crippled woman (and Jesus' condemnation of the hypocritical Synagogue ruler) wherein she is declared a "daughter of Abraham" (Lk 16:10-16).

Responses to Jesus

In terms of responses to Jesus, women have prominent and positive roles. The centurion is commended for the unique character of his trust (Mt 8:10; Lk 7:9) but the hemorrhaging woman and the Canaanite mother are also praised for their faith (Mk 5:34 par and Mt 15:28 par). The women of Jerusalem also weep and mourn for Jesus, probably reflecting a similar tenderness to what they would have toward their own sons (Lk 23:27-31).

Not only so, but on several occasions the insight of marginalized women seems deliberately contrasted with masculine insensibility. The woman who anoints Jesus at Bethany is not only promised world-wide honour (Mt 26:6-13; Mk 14:3-9; cf. Jn 12:1-8), but in Mark is apparently seen by Jesus as grasping what the disciples have not understood: he must die (14:8). The perceptive "immoral woman" who anoints Jesus and washes his feet with her tears, is rewarded with, "Your faith has saved you, go in peace," whereas the contumelious Simon is ironically revealed as the one who does not "know" (Lk 7:36-50; cf. v. 39).

In both cases the women are present at meals, and this raises another issue. Although women were gradually being permitted greater access to public meals, those who attended them risked, at least in some circles, being labeled public or promiscuous.[8] Thus the meal of Mark 2:14-17 has all the connotations of banqueting with "promiscuous" women and pimps and hence the opprobrium—probably more rhetorical than denotative—"he eats with tax-collectors and sinners; a glutton and a wine-bibber" (cf. Mt 11:19; Lk 7:34). It is perhaps also possible that otherwise upright women who joined Jesus and the men in a house to hear his teaching might also have been labelled "sinners." But in the absence of clear evidence we cannot be certain.

In the case of the Samaritan woman (Jn 4:7-26), contrary to the generalizations of some Jewish men, the conversation is every bit as profound as that earlier with Nicodemus (3:1-21). However, her final insight, belief and public affirmation of Jesus stands in sharp contrast to Nicodemus' secrecy, befuddlement and apparent lack of response. She becomes not only a disciple but an evangelist.

But in the one-upmanship stakes, none can match the Canaanite woman who, although an unclean Gentile, is yet rewarded for her persistence, subtlety and wit (Mt 15:22-28; par Mk 7:24ff). It is a matter of sober and striking fact that she alone in all the gospel tradition is able to "best" Jesus in an exchange, no small claim to fame.

That several of these women are of dubious social standing reveals another characteristic of Jesus' regard for women (and men): his willingness to affirm them as recipients of God's compassion and mercy—even if it meant transgressing cultural mores. Rejecting outright Simon's judgmental dismissal, Jesus' tender compassion toward the immoral woman is a wonderful moment of humanizing and dignifying grace toward someone regarded by others and herself as merely an object for male gratification. So, too, Jesus' conversation with the Samaritan, regarded as unseemly by the disciples for both racial and probably sexual reasons. Jesus' concern for the woman as a person overrides any such considerations.

This is nowhere so clear as in the account of the woman caught in adultery (Jn 7:53-8:11). Although most textual critics agree that this is not original to John, there is little question but that the story is genuine. Jesus ignores the wrath of the male establishment and even stands over against their reading of the Law for the sake of this woman—"I don't condemn you, go and sin no more." There is also Jesus' obvious friendship with Mary and Martha (Jn 11). Although of a different nature to the cases above, such a relationship might still have drawn criticism from more conservative circles.

Discipleship

In addition to the aforementioned Samaritan woman, other women appear in discipleship roles. Not only are they included in the crowds who receive his teaching (Mt 14:21; 15:38), but when his family come for him, Jesus points to those around him—men and women (cf. Mk 3:35)—and declares, "Whoever does the will of God is my brother and sister and mother." Although in contrast to some rabbinic material, apparently no one regards this inclusion of women as socially daring.

We have already mentioned Mary and Martha as Jesus' friends, but there is also a clear picture of Mary as a disciple (Lk 10:38-40; the language is similar to the Mishnah's description of a disciple, *m. 'Abot* 1:4). Luke's location of the story is telling. Jesus has just rejoiced that the kingdom is breaking-in in power and says to his disciples, "Blessed are your eyes for they see it." This is immediately followed first by a lawyer who clearly does not "see," asking "Who is my neighbour?" (hence the story of the Good Samaritan) and then the account of Martha. Both stories are about shattered stereotypes concerning who "sees."

Martha behaves in keeping with the stereotype—generally women were just as careful to exclude men from their world as men were to keep women from theirs. She is upset with Mary—apparently because her honour is at stake in providing a good meal and Mary is not helping. Jesus' response, however, seems to say, "Martha, I'm providing the meal that one really ought to worry about." (It is possible that Martha is also offended because she thinks Mary is behaving like a male, not only invading male space but learning Torah.)

Some have argued that Luke's treatment denigrates both women—Martha for her concern for preparations and Mary in being presented merely as a listener—such that both are restricted to a passive role, with the ministry of the table (female role) being subordinated to the ministry of the word (male role).[9] This misses the point. The issue throughout is "hospitality," that is, how one receives Jesus (and his emissaries, the 70 of 10:1-24). However, lest we be too tough on Martha, we ought not forget her confession , "Yes Lord, I believe that you are the Christ, the Son of God, who was to come into the world" (Jn 11:27) which compares well with Peter's confession in 6:68f "To whom else can we go? You have the words of eternal life. We believe and know that you are the Holy One of God." Mary has the right response: discipleship takes precedence over the mores of domestic service (cf. vv.23f). A similar theme emerges in Jesus' comments in Mark 3:31-35 (par Mt 12:46-50; Lk 8:19-21; cf. 11:27-28) where he declares that the claims of discipleship (hearing and obeying the word of God) relativize the traditional and honoured place of motherhood and filial loyalty.

Perhaps the most striking thought of all is Luke's passing reference to a group of women disciples who, with the twelve, followed Jesus while he was in Galilee:

> Soon afterwards he went on through cities and villages, proclaiming and bringing the good news of the kingdom of God. The twelve were with him, as well as some women who had been cured of evil spirits and infirmities: Mary, called Magdalene, from whom seven demons had gone out, and Joanna, the wife of Herod's steward Chuza, and Susanna, and many others, who provided for them out of their resources. (Lk 8:1-3)

These women form part of Jesus' itinerant group, not disciples at a distance but traveling with him (a phrase that in Luke means discipleship, cf. 8:1, 38; 22:56) and are probably represented at Pentecost (Acts 1:14). Not only so but there are some grounds to suggest, based on use of *diakonein* in mission contexts to mean "representative," that they too proclaim the word.[10]

Having followers was not unusual. But what if they included women; surely this would raise questions? Again it is hard to tell. Would the women around Jesus be any more or less noteworthy or "disciples" than those already affiliated with the Hasidim or Qumran? The mere fact that Luke makes so little of this suggests that it is not particularly remarkable. What might be provocative is the suggestion that these traveling women are not staying with relatives, that they are paying the expenses and that Luke—a man—admits as much.[11]

Some of these women are among the many present at Jesus' death (Mt 27:55-56; 27:61; 28:1; Mk 15:40-41; 15:47—16:1; Lk 23:49; 23:55—24:1; Jn 19:25-27; 20:1). The group includes Mary Magdalene, Mary the mother of James and Joseph, Mary the wife of Clophas (maybe one and the same woman), Salome, and according to John, Mary the mother of Jesus, her sister, and the mother of James and John. It is noteworthy that they remain around the cross while the disciples (except John) flee. Again one should not make too much of this since being female they may not have been seen as a threat. It is also a woman—Pilate's wife (mentioned only in Mt 27:19)—who having been warned in a dream unsuccessfully attempts to warn her husband off any involvement. Finally, Jesus, in the midst of an agonizing death, can still show concern for the welfare of his mother (Jn 19:25-27).

Proclaimers of the Message

We have already mentioned the words of the Spirit-filled Elizabeth (incidentally the first person in Luke who is filled with the Spirit), Mary's song which echoes that of Hannah, and Anna the prophetess. These three women stand together with Gabriel, Zechariah, and Simeon, in bearing witness to what God has done. There is also Samaritan woman whose testimony convinces many (Jn 4), and perhaps the women who follow Jesus in Galilee (Lk 8).

Women were, of course, the first witnesses to the resurrection (Mt 28:1-8; Mk 16:1-8; Lk 24:1-12; cf. Jn 20:1-13). Although their gender led Celsus to dismiss the veracity of their witness (cf. Jos, *Antiquities* 4.219), Origen's defense makes it clear that the church stood by that tradition (*Contra Celsum* 2.55-60), and as we noted earlier some rabbis did accept the testimony of women in certain cases.

Is there any particular significance in their being the first to know? It is difficult to tell. The women were not at the tomb because they were expecting the resurrection. They were simply fulfilling a social responsibility. Nor is it clear that they were any more at risk in doing this than they were in standing around the cross.[12] The use of language such as "quasi-apostle" or "commissioning" on the basis of Jesus' simple request that they inform his disciples is several laps ahead of the data. Nor is it likely that a few verses in Mark (15:40f, 47; 16:1-7) are actually the key to the entire gospel such that the women now replace the twelve as the true insiders. Perhaps the simplest explanation is that they hear of the resurrection first simply because they are first at the tomb. But what about Mary (Jn 20:10-18): why does Jesus appear first to her? As John declines to give us any indication, it is wise not to be dogmatic. But given that John of all the evangelists has the most extensive accounts of Jesus' interaction with individuals, it might be that this his meeting Mary reflects as much a relational concern as a gender-oriented theological point.

But it is also interesting to observe how the women's response compares to the various roles of the disciples in the Synoptics. In Mark the women are just as fearful and confused as the disciples and so tell no one (16:8). It is true that in Matthew the women depart in "fear and great joy" to inform the disciples (28:8), but this, too, is more in keeping with his presentation of the twelve as at first misunderstanding but who in the presence of Jesus and his teaching overcome their mistakes. Not surprisingly given his concerns, Luke grants to women an even greater role as witnesses (a major Lukan theme) even to the point of being reminded of the kerygmatic message (24:7: "the Son of Man must be handed over to sinners, and be crucified, and on the third day rise again"). Only in Luke are we told that they "remembered the word spoken" which phraseology recalls Jesus' words to the twelve (18:31-34, cf. 9:22) and provides another indication that Luke sees these women as bona fide disciples.

In the light of the above there is little question that women play a significant and positive role in the gospels.

Negative Examples

But lest we romanticize—and some have wrought wondrous things with, for example, the hemorrhaging woman who becomes a symbol and prototype of women within the worshipping community being at once Authentic Role Determiner, Bulwark of Faith, Legitmizer of Faith Healing, Teacher of the Twelve and Others, Proclaimer of the Truth, Genuine Servant, Voice of God to the Community, and much else besides[13]—there is also another side to the story.

Women can also be examples of faithlessness, notably the foolish virgins

(Mt 25:1-13), and undergo judgment as in the case of one of the women grinding (Mt 24:41; Lk 17:35). While one is not surprised that Herodias and her daughter hardly appear as role-models of piety (Mk 6:14-29, par) the same cannot be said of Jesus' mother, Mary. She fails to appreciate his activity as a youth in the Temple (Lk 2:48-49), and is seemingly rebuffed by Jesus in the wedding at Cana—more perhaps to signal that the mother-son tie has now taken on a different aspect (Jn 2:3-4). Later, she seems to be in charge of a concerted attempt by the family to restrain Jesus (Mk 3:19) and is rebuffed again. These latter two moments are striking in that sons were in some senses still under their mother's authority and were expected to obey them even in adult life. Not to do so was dishonourable.

As already noted, Martha does not feature so well in being more concerned about social proprieties than listening to Jesus (Lk 10:38-42). And then there is the woman who, not unlike Peter, caught up in the wonder of the moment blurts out an ill-considered affirmation which Jesus corrects (Lk 11:27f). The mother of James and John seems to have been interested in maneuvering for her sons' preferment (Mt 20:20-23) and finally, again as noted earlier, the women witnesses to the resurrection are described as being fearful and telling no one (Mk 16:8) and so echo the failure of the twelve in Mark.

Literary Characterization

One final set of observations is in order. It has been pointed out that as far as the mimetic quality of the healing stories go, the gospels reflect the social patterns of their culture. For example, healing stories involving minor male characters outnumber those concerning women by about three or four to one, with the former being on average 15% to 25% longer, and males on average having more to say.[14] Jesus' speech, however, is not so patterned. While in Mark he speaks more often to the men, in Matthew the situation is reversed (an interesting observation in the light of prevailing views on the uselessness of teaching women, given that Matthew is often seen as a teaching document). In Luke the proportion is about equal.

However, when one turns to non-healing stories involving minor characters, although there is approximately an equal number of stories about women as about men, those involving women tend to be longer. Interestingly, when conflict is between men, it involves Jesus' teaching or actions, whereas if the story focuses on women the conflict stems not from Jesus' actions but from the woman's and then men discuss it. So we have men criticizing women, even a woman (Martha) criticizing a woman (Mary), but never a woman criticizing a man. But again one must remember the Canaanite woman who is the only person—male or female—who bests Jesus in public exchange.

What are we to make of this? Some think it demonstrates that the authors of the Synoptic gospels, including Luke who has more stories involving women, are more androcentric than previously realized and as such reflect an increasing redactional trend away from Jesus' original egalitarianism. I find this unconvincing because it confuses the original social reality with redactional intent. Women were not as free to move around publicly as men, and therefore were encountered less often and may have been less accustomed to speak in public or to approach directly a male who was non-family. This would only be heightened in the case of the women who were in positions of public shame (e.g., flow of blood, the immoral woman, or the woman caught in adultery). On the other hand, John's gospel, in keeping with its characteristic style, contains two dialogues involving women: the Samaritan woman and Martha. Both acquit themselves well, especially when compared to male counterparts; the Samaritan woman sees what Nicodemus does not, and Martha gives nothing to Peter in terms of perception of confession. Clearly women are worthy recipients of Jesus' teaching.

Response ... and a last Question

Whatever else, it is important not to romanticize the Gospel accounts of women. There is a range of portrayals, as there is of men. For example, while Luke, as part of his concern to show the gospel is for all, gives greater attention to Jesus' acceptance and affirmation of women, to their faith, to their role as proclaimers both at the beginning and at the end and to Jesus' parables which feature women, he also has more of the less complimentary materials. Women are neither wholly saints nor sinners.

Having said this, Jesus still represents something of a radical change in his response to and perception of women. Contrary to many in his culture, gender distinctions are of no impediment or benefit in relating to Jesus, except insofar that a woman's lower status means the obstacles of pride and potential cost of discipleship are less. Jesus sees women first and foremost as persons, not as gendered beings. Given the present climate of debate, some moderns might take note of this. There is little question that Jesus affirms women, and at nearly every point of discipleship seems to regard them as equal to men.

I say, "at nearly every point," because perceptive readers will be wondering: why does Jesus not include women among the twelve? If he affirmed female leadership, and given his willingness to transgress social norms in other areas (e.g., eating with tax collectors and sinners, apparently challenging elements of Mosaic law), why not do so here and appoint a woman? After all, he chooses a tax collector.

One suggestion is that Jesus, in theological principle, did not regard women as suitable for leadership. While fighting words to many, this position is not so easily dismissed as might be supposed. But the problem is that we have no direct statement one way or the other. Neither does Jesus address homosexuality, although at least in this case the Jewish background material is clearer. In the absence of any unequivocal injunction against women in leadership and in the light of several key examples to the contrary, this position does not seem particularly secure.

Another suggestion concerns ritual impurity. Given both the itinerant and eschatological character of the mission of the twelve, it may not have been appropriate to take a woman on such a ministry tour when for a certain amount of time she would have been ceremonially unclean and presumably unable to be in contact either with the rest of the twelve or the people of Israel. But then, if this did not apparently disqualify Old Testament prophetesses, why should it do so here—unless social mores had changed?

Perhaps the answer lies in a combination of Jesus' conception of the twelve and simple historical realities. Given that the twelve are a reconstituted Israel, he might have chosen twelve men to make the point as clear as possible. There is some force to this. But would a mixed group really have compromised the parallel, provided they numbered twelve? It is difficult to tell from this distance. What is more clear is that, unlike the present time, most women were not as educated or experienced as men and, culturally, would probably have found it hard to get a hearing in more formal settings (tax collectors could on the other hand reform themselves). Jesus had to start in the world in which he found himself and so it was twelve men. If this is so, then we should probably avoid drawing theological conclusions as to gender roles on the basis of the composition of the twelve.

Women in Acts

This question of the composition of the twelve emerges again in Acts where being male is simply assumed ("one of the men," 1:21). The same pattern is evident in choosing the seven qualified men to oversee the Hellenists (6:3). Once again, we need to be careful in deciding whether this is a theologically motivated decision or one that simply reflects prevailing cultural and social realities.

Not surprisingly given Luke's gospel, women are among the 120 and almost certainly include some if not all of the women mentioned in Luke 8:1-3. They are clearly an integral part of the core group of close followers.

Multitudes of both men and women believe (5:14) and both genders are persecuted (8:3, 12; cf. 22:4). Dorcas is an exemplary disciple (*mathetes*), doing good and helping the poor (9:36-42), while Sapphira reminds us that not all were so selfless (5:1-11). We are told that some believers gathered at the house of Mary, the mother of John Mark (12:12). This suggests she is a widow and as such acted legally as a male and the head of her household. Though we cannot be certain, she may have presided over the group that met there.

At Pentecost, the inclusion of daughters and female slaves provides clear evidence that neither gender nor rank have any bearing on whether one receives the eschatological gift of the prophetic Spirit (2:17f). But what does it mean for them to prophesy? Probably not that all have become prophets in the Old Testament sense. Instead it provides an authenticating sign that a new dispensation in God's dealing with his people is at hand (cf. Num 11:24-25; 1 Sam 10:10-11).

Later, in Philippi, Paul goes to the women gathered at the place of prayer by the river (16:13, probably because they could not meet the quorum of ten free adult males, *m. Meg.* 4.3). Lydia, who because she deals in purple is probably of some standing and means, is converted. This signals something of a trend with numbers of leading women joining the movement in Thessalonica and Berea (17:3, 12).

We next encounter Priscilla and Aquila who clearly have a teaching role and are apparently companions of Paul (cf. 18:2, 18; cf. 1 Cor 16:19; 2 Tim 4:19; and Rom 16:3 where they are described as co-workers [*sunergouv*], a word that seems to have some overlap with the term apostle). Initially, Aquilla is mentioned first (18:2)—probably because Luke is recounting their first meeting which appropriately is with the husband (the same order in 1 Cor 16:19 might be due either to the formal nature of the greeting or the presence of "eschatological" women in that church). But after that the order is reversed with Priscilla (Luke uses the informal friendly diminutive, Paul the more formal Prisca) being first. This is striking and suggests that Priscilla is the preeminent of the two, being a teacher of some note.

Finally, there are the four prophetess virgin daughters of Philip the evangelist (21:8-14), with whom Paul stays, one assumes, for mutual building up (cf. Rom 1:12). Allowing that prophecy here follows the general Old Testament pattern, then it probably includes a degree of instruction and giving of direction, suggesting a kind of leadership.

This is a good point to return to the proposal of some noted earlier that Luke restricts women, particularly those who wish to practise prophetic ministry, to appropriately discreet behaviour. On this view, Luke expects that they should listen and not seek to minister; but if they must minister, they should be paired with men, and if not, then at least let them remain "safe" as virgins. But there are problems. With Mary and Martha the issue is not women's silence but the kind of hospitality Jesus seeks, namely, careful, hearing discipleship. In fact, it is this very learning posture that opens the way to the kind of leadership later evident in, for example, Priscilla. She is not only not silent but her reputation as a teacher causes her to be named before her husband. This is less a sign of control through "pairing" than a bell-wether of the expanding role of increasingly learned women, itself a direct result of the new openness to them as persons. Likewise, Philip's four daughters are indeed virgins—but this might be less to render them "safe" as to allow greater freedom to devote themselves to the Lord, to expand their ministry if you will (cf. 1 Cor 7:32-35).

Now, a concluding comment on a particularly Lukan feature (Luke-Acts). At those places where Luke follows Mark he often adds, from his own special source, a second story about a woman resulting in paired stories featuring a male and a female. Several explanations, all of some merit, have been proposed. Given that in Acts women are clearly attracted to the new faith, these inclusive stories provide instruction and edification for them as befits their status as equal members of the people of God. Second, Luke's "formal" preface and style also suggests he has a more public audience in mind, perhaps in order to say something about the relationship between church and society. His use of marital pairs may thus reflect "the increasing prestige and public function of marriage" as the empire sought to increase the population.[15] This pairing of men and women is also found in Josephus who not only writes history (as does Luke) but does so with an eye to Roman reception (as does Luke). But whereas Pliny is concerned that respectable woman be seen and not heard, Luke's women are not always quite so reserved. Already the liberating impact of Jesus' teachings are being felt.

Conclusion: Women in the Gospels and Acts

The gospel accounts seem accurately to reflect the setting in which women found themselves in the first-century Jewish homeland. Their interaction with Jesus bears the marks of an androcentric and patriarchal society. However, where Jesus stands out is in his treatment of women as persons in their own right. The singular feature of Jesus' approach to women is that they are first and foremost human beings, made in the image of God. While he does not deliberately go out of his way to offend, on principle, traditional sensibilities, he is not constrained by them. He does cause offense, but it is because as always for him the person matters more than either the Sabbath or social mores. When the occasion arises where he must choose between personhood and traditional behaviour, he always chooses personhood by affirming the faith, love, understanding and wit of various women, showing compassion, and even on occasion rebuking them just as he would a misunderstanding male. In the meantime, his interest in teaching women cannot help but eventually precipitate change. In Acts, along the same lines and generally in keeping with cultural mores but with an ultimately liberating although not deliberately polemically or confrontational cast, the Spirit uses both men and women to continue the proclamation of the gospel.

In other words, Jesus' agenda is not gender driven. It reflects instead the earliest words of Genesis: "God created humankind in his image, in the image of God he created them; male and female he created them" (Gen 1:27, NIVI). Women are not objects, nor are men the enemy: both are made in God's image and as such the reconstitution of humanity by the Son of Man begins with their mutual restoration and continues with their mutual co-operation in the announcement and extension of that reign.

Endnotes

1. Extensive data (and interpretation) can be found in L. Swidler, *Women in Judaism: The Status of Women in Formative Judaism* (Metuchen: Scarecrow, 1976); Ross S. Kraemer, ed., *Maenads, Martyrs, Matrons, Monastics: A Sourcebook on Women's Religions in the Greco-Roman World* (Philadelphia: Fortress, 1988); cf. J. Jeremias, *Jerusalem in the Time of Jesus* (Philadelphia: Fortress, 1969) 358-76; and Ben Witherington III, *Women in the Ministry of Jesus: A Study of Attitudes to Women and Their Roles As Reflected in His Earthly Life* (SNTSMS 51; Cambridge: Cambridge University Press, 1984), 1-10.

2. Cited in James B. Hurley, *Man and Woman in Biblical Perspective* (Grand Rapids: Zondervan, 1981), 70.

3. Swidler, 97-104.

4. Cf. B. Brooten, *Women Leaders in the Ancient Synagogues* (BJS 36; Chico, Calif.: Scholars, 1982) and Kraemer, 218ff.

5. Amy-J. Levine, "Yeast of Eden," *BibInterp* 2 (1994) 8-33

6. Johnson, Luke T. "The New Testament's Anti-Jewish Slander and the Conventions of Ancient Polemic," *JBL* 108 (1989), especially 428-441.

7. See Witherington, 135n79.

8. Kathleen Corley, *Private Women, Public Meals* (Peabody, MA: Hendrickson, 1993).

9. E.g. Elizabeth Schüssler Fiorenza, "Feminist Criticial Interpretation for Liberation: Martha and Mary: Luke 10:38-42," *Religion and Intellectual Life* 3 (1986) 31 and M.R. D'Angelo, "Women in Luke-Acts: A Redactional View," *JBL* 109 (1990) 442.

10. See R. J. Karris, "Women and Discipleship in Luke," *CBQ* 56 (1994) 8f.

11. K.E. Bailey, "Women," *Anvil* 11 (1994) 8.

12. See Jana Opocenská, "Women at the Cross, at Jesus' Burial, and after the Resurrection," *Reformed World* 47 (1997) 46f.

13. So M. J. Selvidge, *Woman, Cult and Miracle Recital* (Lewisberg: Bucknell University Press; London and Toronto: Associated University Presses, 1990) 94ff.

14. Joanna Dewey, "Women in the Synoptic Gospels: Seen but not Heard?," *BTB* 27 (1997) 53ff.

15. D'Angelo, 448ff.

CHAPTER 4

Gender Issues: Reflections on the Perspective of the Apostle Paul

Gordon D. Fee

The task set out for me in this lecture is not an easy one, because so much of the controversy on gender issues in evangelical circles swirls around the Pauline data. Many of the problems, of course, are of our own making; here in particular examples of poor exegesis and selective hermeneutics are legion.[1] At issue as well is our tendency to throw too many disparate matters (male/female; husband/wives; ministry/structures) into the same container and homogenize them.

But some of the problems clearly stem from Paul himself and the *ad hoc* nature of his letters. Lacking the need to systematize his own thinking, Paul spoke to different situations in different ways. Take for example his advice to widows in 1 Corinthians 7 and 1 Timothy 5, where on the one hand (1 Cor 7:40) he discourages them to remarry, while on the other (1 Tim 5:14) he falls just short of commanding them to do so.[2] So at issue for us hermeneutically is how to handle some of the differences that are actually present in Paul.

Perhaps the worst thing the evangelical tradition has done on gender matters is to isolate them from the bigger picture of biblical theology. Indeed, I think we are destined for continual trouble if we do not start where Paul does: not with isolated statements addressed to contingent situations, but with Paul's theology of the *new creation*, the coming of God's eschatological rule inaugurated by Christ—especially through his death and resurrection—and the gift of the Spirit.

Paul and the New Creation

Two texts in particular serve as the proper starting point here. First, 2 Corinthians 5:14-17, where Paul argues with the Corinthians who are calling into question both his gospel of a crucified Messiah and his cruciform apostleship. He responds that the new creation brought about by Christ's death and resurrection nullifies one's viewing anything any longer from the old age point of view (Gk. *kata sarka*, "according to the flesh"). Christ's death means that the whole human race has come under the sentence of death (v. 14), so that those who do live (in God's new order) now live for the one who died for them and was raised again (v. 15). The result, he goes on, is that from this point on, to view either Christ or anyone/anything else from a perspective that is "according to the flesh" is no longer valid (v. 16). Why? Because being in Christ means that one belongs to the new creation: the old has gone, the new has come (v. 17). It doesn't take much reading of Paul to recognize that this radical, new order point of view—life marked by the cross—lies at the heart of everything he thinks and does.

Which leads to our second text: Galatians 3:26-29. This passage offers the first of two conclusions[3] to the theological-scriptural argument of Galatians 2:16-4:7, in which Paul is adamant that Gentiles do not have to conform to the old covenant boundary markers/identity symbols, in order to belong to the new covenant people of God. The three primary markers were circumcision, food laws, and the keeping of special days. Although each of these is mentioned at some point in Galatians,[4] the major focus is on circumcision, because his opponents regularly appealed to it as the way Gentiles would also be included in the people of God (Gen 17:1-14).

To counter this argument and to recover his Gentile converts from further capitulation to the former covenant, Paul argues first from their experience of the Spirit (3:1-5), and then from Scripture regarding Christ (3:6-22). In his first conclusion Paul's concern is singular: that the old order has given way to the new—promised by God even before the covenant of circumcision. The old order, which helped to distinguish Israel from its Gentile neighbours, was signaled by the law—the legislation of the former covenant that, as Iain Provan pointed out and Paul makes clear, was designed for sinners and assumed human fallenness. Paul's way of putting it in the present argument is that the law served to hem people in until the time for faith to come, with the appearance of God's Messiah (vv. 22-24). All of this because some Gentiles were being persuaded that to please God fully they had to adopt the identity markers of the former covenant as well.

"No," Paul says, as he now appeals to the new creation. Over against former slavery (Jews to the law; Gentiles to idols), he says emphatically: "*All* of you are *children of God* [not slaves] through faith in Christ Jesus" (v. 26), which is further evidenced by their "one baptism" (v.27). All who have been baptized into Christ have thereby been clothed with Christ. Behind this sentence lies the baptismal theology of Romans 6, full of "new creation" eschatological presuppositions. Death and resurrection have taken place in Christ. As believers go through the waters of baptism, we assume our own role in that death and resurrection, thus dying to the old and rising into newness of life—into the new creation.

In verse 28 Paul comes to the conclusion that we have been led to expect, namely, that in the new creation there is neither Jew nor Greek. But right at that point, typically of Paul, he recognizes that the new creation obliterates *all* the old sociological categories that separated people. So he adds, what is true of Jew and Greek is equally true of "slave and free, male and female." His point: In our baptism "into Christ" and through the work of the Spirit we enter the new order, the new creation; and where death and resurrection have taken place, the old distinctions have been obliterated.[5]

Paul, of course, does not mean that the three categories themselves cease to exist in the new creation, at least not in its present "already/not yet" expression. To the contrary, as part of the continuity between the old and the new, all of us are some combination of the three: e.g., Gentile, free, female. What has been obliterated is the *significance* of these distinctions and the (basically divisive) *values*—ethnic-racial (Jew/Gentile), socio-economic (slave/free), and sexual-gender (male/female)—based on them.

Our difficulty with understanding the truly radical nature of Paul's assertion is twofold. First, most contemporary Christians have very little sense of the fundamental eschatological framework which was common to the entire New Testament experience, and which in fact was the *only* way the earliest believers understand their existence. Second, Western culture in particular is quite foreign to that of these early believers at some fundamental points. In the culture into which Paul is speaking, position and status prevailed in every way, so that one's existence was totally identified with and circumscribed by these realities. By the very nature of things, position and status gave advantage to some over others; and in Greco-Roman culture, by and large, there was very little chance of changing status.

Thus Gentiles had all the advantages over Jews, so Jews took refuge in their relationship with God, which they believed advantaged them before God over the Gentiles. The hatreds were deep and mutual. Likewise, masters and slaves were consigned to roles where all the advantages went to masters;[6] and the same was true for men and women, where women were dominated by men and basically consigned to childbearing. In fact, according to Diogenes Laertius, Socrates used to say every day: "There were three blessings for which he was grateful to Fortune: first, that I was born a human being, and not one of the brutes; next that I was born a man and not a woman; thirdly, a Greek and not a barbarian."[7] The Jewish version of this, obviously influenced by the Greco-Roman worldview, is the rabbi who says that "everyday you should say, 'Blessed are you, O God, …, that I'm not a brute creature, nor a Gentile, nor a woman.'"[8]

It is especially difficult for most of us to imagine the effect of Paul's words in a culture where position and status preserved order through basically uncrossable boundaries. Paul asserts that when people come into the fellowship of Christ Jesus, significance is no longer to be found in being Jew or Greek, slave or free, male or female. The all-embracing nature of this affirmation, its counter-cultural significance, the fact that it equally *disadvantages* all by equally *advantaging* all—these stab at the very heart of a culture sustained by people maintaining the right position and status. But in Christ Jesus, the One whose death and resurrection inaugurated the new creation, all things have become new; the new era has dawned.

The new creation, therefore, must be our starting point regarding gender issues, because this is theologically where Paul lived. Everything else he says comes out of this view of what has happened in the coming of Christ in the Spirit.

The Impact

What, then, was the impact of this radical worldview on male/female relationships? We begin by noting that in the new creation both of the essential matters from the first creation—mutuality/complementarity and differentiation—are restored. It is the new *creation*, after all. This can best be seen in two passages in 1 Corinthians—7:1-40 and 11:2-16—where, apparently, some women in the believing community have overdrawn the implications of their new eschatological existence.[9] That is, they appear to have been arguing for, or assuming, a "mutuality" without "complementarity," as well as for the elimination of differentiation. This Paul simply will not allow since these, too, are a part of the creation, both old and new. What most likely lies behind this is their view of speaking in tongues. In 13:1 Paul says, "If I speak in the tongues of men and of angels." You might have heard in passing the text that Rikk Watts cited in the preceding lecture from the Testament of Job, where Job's daughters are given a waistband to put on, by means of which they are transported into heaven by the Spirit, and by the Spirit speak the dialect of the angels. This appears to have been a common understanding, that the one speaking in tongues was speaking the language of heaven.

A kind of ultimate "spirituality" seems thus to have set in at Corinth, which included a disregard for the body. Recall from Iain Provan's lecture that very early on Christians got messed up about the body's being a good thing (given that God created it). Such a view goes back at least to Paul's Corinth. Because they were already speaking the language of the angels, some of the women considered themselves already as the angels (who neither marry nor give in marriage, Luke 20:34-36) and thus were arguing for no sex in marriage (7:1-16) and were also removing a symbol of differentiation (11:2-16).

Paul corrects the former abuse by insisting that each person's body does not belong to oneself, but to the other (7:3-4)—not in an abusive, possessive way, of course, but as gift to the other person. Because of mutuality and complementarity in the marriage relationship, every husband and every wife must be in continuing sexual relations with each other (v. 2) and must stop defrauding one another on this matter (7:5). Thus this passage radically alters the sexual relationship within marriage. Instead of the more common pattern of sex as something the husband does to his wife for his sexual gratification, sexual intimacy is a celebration of belonging to one another, where one's "body" is not one's own private possession; rather, both partners give their bodies for the other in a relationship of mutual love.

In the same way Paul argues in 11:2-16 that wives continue to wear the head-covering because it served as a symbol of differentiation between men and women. Although it is often suggested otherwise,[10] this passage has nothing to do with the subordination of women to men—a view arrived at by making verse 10 say the opposite of what Paul in fact asserts. The Greek text cannot be more clear, that a woman has authority over her own head "because of the angels."[11] If there is still plenty of obscurity about the latter phrase (I think it relates to their being like the angels), there is no question about who has authority over what. The woman in Christ has authority over her own head, even with regard to the traditional head-covering. But Paul wants her to use that authority to maintain differentiation in the new order. That the issue has to do with differentiation between male and female is found in the rhetoric of verses 5 and 6. If she insists on removing the familiar sign of differentiation, Paul argues, why not go the whole way of "shame" (to herself in this case) and have her head shaved or shorn—in that culture evidence of the "male" partner in a lesbian relationship.[12]

The bottom line issue in this text has to do with "shame" (see vv. 4, 5, 6, 13, 14) in a culture much like present-day Asian cultures, where shame counted for everything. With a wonderful word play on "head"—where the issue literally lay—Paul argues that the wife was shaming her husband (her "head" from v. 3) by removing the symbol of differentiation, just as a husband would have shamed Christ by wearing the wife's symbol.

In response Paul does not subordinate the woman, but rather insists that she maintain this symbol of their differences. In a purely *ad hoc* way, Paul argues in verses 7-9, that a wife should not shame the one whose glory she is by creation. To be sure, that is often read as referring to subordination. But nowhere else does "glory" appear in Scripture as having to do with subordination. The woman, rather, is seen as complementary, the glory of the man, as is evidenced in the narrative of Genesis: she was made from man and for man (vv. 8-9), not to be subordinate to him, but as his glory, to complement him. That she has regained her place of mutuality lost in the Fall is made clear in verses 10 to 12. Immediately following verses 8 and 9, he concludes by first stating the reality of the woman's own authority over her (now literal) head: "For this reason, the woman has authority over her own head because of the angels." "Nonetheless," he qualifies in verse 11, with both 8 and 9 and now 10 in view, the wife is not to exercise her "authority" as one who is independent of her husband; nor are they to understand verses 8 and 9 wrongly: because "in the Lord" there is total mutuality. After all, God has ultimately reversed things—man now comes from the woman—so that "in the Lord" neither is independent of the other, because "everything comes from God."

Thus, the thrust of this argument is twofold: that the woman should continue with the cultural symbol of differentiation—because of the issue of shame—but that this should not be understood to mean subordination, but mutual interdependence in the Lord. The new creation has not removed mutuality and differentiation, but has restored it. In the Lord male and female are both one and different. Thus men and women equally pray and prophesy, the two basic forms of worship in the Christian assembly (which took place in homes), but do so as male and female, not as androgynous beings.

The Implications for Social Structures

Given Paul's basic theological stance, and its impact on male/female (especially husband/wife) relationships, the question that remains for us is the problematic one: What are the implications of all this for social structures? To get at this issue we need to return to the three sets of structures singled out in Galatians 3:28, that "there is neither Jew nor Greek, slave nor free, male nor female." It is clear from several passages in Paul that he is not arguing that the new creation eliminates the fallen structures in which some of the differences exist. What Paul does with those structures is to radicalize them by putting them into the context of the cross. Everything is moderated by the fact that the cross rules over all.

Take slavery as an example. On the one hand, in Colossians 3:22–4:1 and Ephesians 6:5-9 Paul calls on both masters and slaves to live as brothers and sisters in Christ, without urging that the structure itself be eliminated. On the other hand, in Philemon he radicalizes the relationship in such a way that it no longer carries significance. Paul does not say, "Philemon, stop having slaves"; what he says is that now "you have Onesimus back for good—no longer as a slave, but better than a slave, as a beloved brother" (vv. 15-16). How, one wonders, can the old structures carry their former significance in this context—where the slave who has stolen and run away, and who in Roman law merited death, is now accepted back as a dearly loved brother in Christ? And remember that both the letter to the Colossians and to Philemon were read publicly in the gathered community, where both Philemon and Onesimus were present together to hear what God had established through the cross. The old distinctions may still exist in a sociological way, to be sure, but they cease to have meaning when both master and slave own the same master, Jesus Christ.[13]

When we turn to male and female relationships (in a culture where this primarily had to do with wife and husband in the home), we find the same thing. The problem for us in reading the texts (especially the "house codes" in Colossians 3:18–4:1 and Ephesians 5:18–6:9) is that we have scarcely an inkling as to how much Paul was in fact radicalizing the Greco-Roman home. Thus before looking at the Ephesians text, one needs to have a sense for the sociology assumed by the passage. And here architecture says a great deal. Although the early believers lived in other kinds of settings—tenements; shopkeepers, who lived above their shops; etc.—this passage assumes a larger household of a kind shown in figure 1,[14] which included wives, children, and slaves.

Figure 1:

A typical *domus*

Key
1. fauces;
2. shop;
3. attrium;
4. impulvium;
5. cubiculum;
6. tablinum;
7. andron;
8. peristyle;
9. triclinium;
10. oecus.

(Drawing by Deborah Wells.)

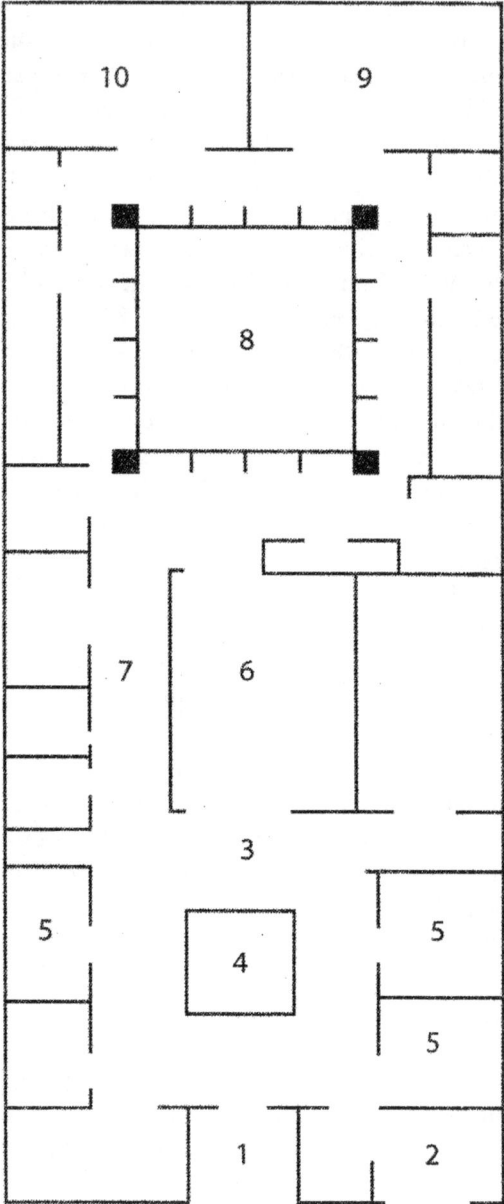

The basic sociological model for this kind of household is that of patronage, meaning a communal relationship between unequals. In this kind of relationship each of the unequals benefits the other. The master of the house benefits the rest of the people in the household by providing for them; they benefit him by doing his bidding (slaves, in particular). The wife would benefit by the fact that she could now exist in a home besides that of her father, and of course the householder benefited because hopefully she would bear him male heirs.[15]

By law, the man was the master of his household (thus the patron). In Maxine Hancock's introduction, she talked about the extreme form of patriarchy known as totalitarian patriarchy. Paul's text, you must realize, is written into a context where such patriarchy was absolute, and sustained by law.[16] Usually, but not always, he required the household to serve his gods. Unlike our understanding of home, such a household was not a place of consumption, but of production; not a private refuge, but often semi-public. His was the only public role, and the atrium often served as a place to do business and was basically open to others. The women, especially daughters, lived in the rear and were not permitted to stray into the public domain of the house—for the reasons Rikk Watts pointed out in his lecture: the fear of her becoming abused or a seductress. Much of this is described in a passage from Philo of Alexandria:

> Market-places and council-halls and law-courts and gatherings and meetings where a large number of people are assembled, and open-air with full scope for discussion and action—all these are suitable to men both in war and peace. The women are best suited to the indoor life which never strays from the house, within which the middle door is taken by the maidens as their boundary, and the outer door by those who have reached full womanhood.[17]

What did it mean for a woman to enter such a household as wife? We know from a large number of census lists from Egypt that the average age of the man when he married was 30, of the woman, less than 18. The reason for marriage was not "love" in our usual sense, but to bear legitimate children, to keep the family line going; indeed, failure to bear children, especially sons, was often cause for divorce. Moreover, almost all men were (from our point of view) promiscuous. As Demosthenes says in an off-handed, matter-of-fact way: "Mistresses we keep for the sake of pleasure, concubines for the daily care of the body, but wives to bear us legitimate children."[18] Wives, therefore, were often promiscuous as well—although they tried to be more discreet, since their infidelity was considered to be a matter of shame.

The idea that men and women might be equal partners in marriage simply did not exist, evidence for which can be seen in meals, which in all cultures serve as the great equalizer. In the Greek world, women scarcely ever joined their husbands and his friends at meals; and if they did, they did not recline at table (only the courtesans did that), but sat on benches at the end. And they were expected to leave after eating, when the conversation took a more public turn. It is especially difficult for most of us even to imagine our way back into such a culture, let alone to have any sense of feeling for it. Which is what makes what Paul actually says so counter-cultural in every way, without eliminating the structures themselves.

Our difficulty in getting back into Paul's text is that we are heirs of a culture in which two major events in the past three hundred years have radically altered Western culture forever, and turned the culture that preceded it completely on its head: the so-called Enlightenment and the Industrial Revolution. The Enlightenment, with its emphasis on the individual, created a culture in which individual rights came to be regarded as the highest good, so much so that by the late twentieth century the concept of individual rights has finally superseded that of the common good.

But the Enlightenment alone did not create the structural changes in our understanding of home and family. Look at the British manor house, with its "enlightened" autocrat, that has got such bad press in a whole series of recent movies. It took the Industrial Revolution to turn things around; and it did so by drawing both men and women out of the home into the marketplace, so that, whereas in 1885 in the United States eighty-eight percent of all goods were produced in the home, by 1915 that was totally reversed.

With these changes, and all the more if we add the onset of the "technological age," also came the wonderful opportunities that women now enjoy: equal opportunities for education, including finally the right to vote and to serve in almost every way in the public domain. But it also resulted in our homes being thought of as havens for rest and, until recently, as the place for the nuclear family to exist—a concept almost foreign to Paul's world.

But the Apostle Paul preceded these events by two thousand years, with the message of a crucified Messiah, which was culturally subversive at its core. Indeed, perhaps the most radical thing was that all people who participated in God's new creation also shared a common meal together and thus celebrated their Lord's death until he was to come again—which, as 1 Corinthians 11·17–34 makes clear, created considerable tension for the traditional household.

When we turn at last to Ephesians 5, we need to begin where Paul's own sentence begins, with verse 18, because "be [keep] filled with the Spirit" is the only imperative in the passage until verse 25 ("Husbands, love your wives"). Thus Paul is urging that believers be filled with the Spirit, and evidence that by singing, giving thanks, and submitting to one another.

In the relationships that follow, three things need to be noted. First, in the ordinary household the husband, father, and master are all the same person, while the wife, children, and slaves were different persons. Second, when Paul tells the wives to submit, and children and slaves to obey, he is not offering some new idea, or countering insubordination, he is merely speaking within the culture. But those who are filled with the Spirit and worship Christ as Lord, do so as those serving their true Lord, not an earthly one.

Third—and here is the truly radical moment—both the structure of the passage and the word count (four words to the husband for every one word to the wife) indicate that the emphasis lies with the householder, the husband/master/father. And the only thing Paul says to him is repeated three times: "Love your wife." Love (*agape*) is what rules, and *agape*, it must be noted emphatically, does not refer either to romance or sex. Rather, it refers to his giving his life in loving service to her for her sake.

One should note especially the regular emphasis on loving his *own wife*. That eliminates the courtesans. Love your wives (v. 25); love your own wives (v. 28); love your own wives (v. 33). She is the one who deserves all of your love and commitment of loving service. The model, as throughout the New Testament, is Christ's love for the church which is expressed in his death on the cross. The imagery Paul uses is that of a man taking a bride, deliberately echoing language from Ezekiel 16, where God betroths the naked and orphaned teenager and washes her and dresses her in the finest of clothes. Paul now images the husband as treating his wife as just such a bride, adorned and glorious to behold.

It is assumed in this text, of course, that the husband will continue to provide leadership in the household. But such leadership will be radically transformed into caring for the people, not having them around to serve his own self-interests. And that is why Paul goes on to speak of the slaves and the children. In each case, the husband, the master, and the father is the person Paul is after. If he can radicalize the home in light of the cross, the life of the child, of the slave, and of the woman is set into new perspective in the new creation.

So where does that put us hermeneutically? I would argue that the structures are ultimately quite immaterial for believers; that is, first-century households can no more serve as models for Christian homes at the turn of the twenty-first century, than the Roman Empire with its self-serving, destructive economic policies and its insistence on emperor worship, should serve for contemporary political structures. All structures, ours as well as theirs, are predicated altogether on cultural givens. There simply is no biblical structure for the household.

Thus in our culture, structures tend to depend largely on the two people involved with regard to their own giftings, personalities, and how they relate to each other. But whatever the structure, at issue is that we live Christ-like in our relationships with one another in our homes. God calls us to *shalom*, to be filled with the Spirit, thus submitting ourselves to one another in reverence to Christ, to love with Christ's love by self-sacrificial giving of ourselves. And I would suggest that if we do that well, the matter of structures will pale into insignificance.

What About Ministry?

The Pauline texts show a rather consistent view with regard to "ministry," meaning serving the church and the world in a variety of ways. Everyone, man and woman alike, minister within the context of their own gifting by the Holy Spirit. At the crucial point of ministering by verbal gifting, Paul consistently says such things as "all may prophesy" (1 Cor 14:23), to which 1 Corinthians 11:2-16 bears corroborating evidence. Despite some voices to the contrary, Paul made no distinction between men and women in the use of any verbal gifting (prophecy, tongues, teaching, revelation, etc.). Gifting by the Holy Spirit was the only criterion, and the Holy Spirit was obviously gender-blind, since he gifted men and women at will.

When we move to the question of "offices" in the church, of course, we move into an arena where Paul supplies us with almost no evidence. The idea that there are some who serve as "priests," and that they should be males (thus keeping alive the strictures of the older covenant), would be about as foreign to Paul as one could get. In any case, it seems clear that "function" preceded the concept of "position." That is, people functioned as prophets or teachers before they were called that; there were not pre-ordained "offices" that they should step into.

Thus the ultimate question before us in the matter of "gender and ministry" is not whether women ministered—of course they did—but whether, given the cultural norm, they also stepped into roles of leadership (which in itself is a nebulous term in light of the Pauline evidence). That they did so in fact would be consistent with the radically counter-cultural sociology that found expression in the believing community, as outlined above.

Thus, one of the more remarkable moments in Paul's letters (but seldom thought so by us, because we tend to read our culture back into the text) is his greeting at the end of Romans to Priscilla and Aquila (16:3-5). That he mentions Priscilla first, that he praises them because "they [plural] risked their lives for me," and that he greets the church that meets in *their*, not Aquila's, house, is sure evidence that something has already been transformed by the gospel.

This is also the significance of such passages as Colossians 4:15 ("Nympha and the church that meets in *her* house") and Acts 16:13-15, 40 (where the first believers in Philippi met at Lydia's house). When a church met in this kind of household, where they would gather in the atrium, the semi-public area where business was regularly carried on, the householder would naturally serve as the leader of the house church. That is, by the very sociology of things, it would never have occurred to them that a person from outside the household would come in and lead what was understood as simply an extension of the household. To put it plainly, the church is not likely to gather in a person's house unless the householder also functioned as its natural leader. Thus Lydia would have held the same role in the church in her house as she did as master of the household.

Other passages reflect the same reality, beginning with the evidence from Philippians 4:2-3. Euodia and Syntyche must have had ministry in the church because of the language Paul uses. They laboured side by side with Paul in the gospel, as did the rest of his fellow workers, meaning the others who ministered in the church besides Euodia and Syntyche. Given this language, had these been men, everyone to a person would grant that they were leaders in the church in Philippi; and even now the only ones who think otherwise, think so simply because Euodia and Syntyche were women. Paul's language is decisive here: they were leaders in the church in Philippi.

The well-known sociology of Macedonia[19] corroborates this as well. Despite what was said above about women in public life, Macedonia was well-known as an exception to the norm; from way back women held significant positions in public life. It is therefore not surprising that evidence of their leadership in the church turns up in Philippi.

Similarly, in Romans 16:1-2, Phoebe is the *diakonos* of the church in Cenchrea, meaning she is the servant of the church. This is the same language Paul uses elsewhere of himself and others, in terms of their giving leadership to the church. In this case he adds that she has also been a *prostatis* to many people, including Paul. There is plenty of good evidence that this word in this case probably means that she has served as the "benefactor" of the church and of others as well.

Finally, in Romans 16:7 Paul singles out Andronicus and Junia, probably husband and wife, who were apostles before Paul himself. Attempts on the part of some to turn Junia into a man (only because she is here called "an apostle"), simply will not do. No such name as Junias is known to exist in the Roman world. She and her husband together served as apostles, pure and simple, although the term in this case, as it almost surely does in 1 Corinthians 12:27 as well, refers to a "function" not an "office."

The only exception to this consistent picture is the *ad hoc*, very case-specific instruction Paul gives in 1 Timothy 2:11-12. And this is clearly the "odd text out," not the norm. In the context of 1 Timothy, the issue is not church order but false teaching. It is equally clear from the evidence of Acts 20 and from the evidence of 1 and 2 Timothy, that the false teachers are local elders who are going astray after false teaching. That is why Paul has such a problem in this letter, and why Timothy is in for such difficulty, because as a younger man he has to stop—even to excommunicate—the elders who are involved in the false teaching. The evidence of 1 and 2 Timothy together makes it further clear, that these straying elders have found fruitful ministry in the households of some younger widows. In 2 Timothy 3:8 in particular, they are said to have wormed their way into the homes of these women, weak-willed and silly women Paul calls them, who are always trying to learn but never able to come to a knowledge of the truth.

In 1 Timothy 5:13 Paul had earlier said of these younger widows, that they go about from house to house being *phluaroi*, which despite our English translations to the contrary, does not—in fact cannot—mean "gossips," but "speakers of foolishness." This word is used in all kinds of philosophical texts of people who "prate foolishness," meaning, of course, who teach a philosophy different from the author. Thus these younger widows were going around from house to house passing on the foolishness of the false teachings. Paul's admonition to them is singular: Because they have already gone astray after Satan (5:15), they are to marry (v. 14; over against his advice in 1 Corinthians 7:39-40), to manage their households well (assume the woman's role in a married household), and "to bear children."

This last piece of advice picks up from the companion passage in 2:11-15,[20] where this is precisely how "they will be saved." Thus in this singular place in the New Testament, these widows, who are in process of repeating Eve's transgression through Satan's deception,[21] are forbidden to teach or domineer. Rather, they are to get married and bear children.

Finally, I would like to remind those who think that this text controls all the others in the New Testament, that if one thinks verse 11 is a verse for all times and all circumstances, then why not verses 9 and 10 that precede it, and verse 15 that follows it, that says that women will be saved by bearing children.

Paul of course surely does not intend that these younger widows will be given eternal salvation by bearing children. This is simply a synechdoche; "bearing children" is one activity (to be elaborated in 5:14) that represents his greater concerns. They are to be "saved" in this case by no longer adhering to, and spreading, the false teaching. This is why he gives his later directive for them to get married, because by getting married they come back into a situation where they will not be spreading false teaching and thus fall prey (as Eve did before them) to Satan's deceptions. What he does later in chapter 5, of course, is to have Timothy excommunicate the elders who are responsible for all this, thus indicating that the two groups in chapter 5 (widows and elders) are the ones causing the trouble for the church.

The point in all of this is that this one text,[22] which has clear case-specific reasons for existing, should not be used to set aside the rest of the evidence. If we do not have more such evidence, we must remember that these texts were written in the first century, into a context like that described above. The wonder is that we have as many such texts as we do. What is significant about them is that the texts that do exist are not trying to "teach" or "correct," they are simply stating what was in place, all of which was the result of the new creation.

Conclusion

The net result of all this seems clear enough: that Paul does not tear down existing structures, but neither does he sanctify them. Everything for him begins with Christ, his death and resurrection, whereby he established the new order, the new creation. In the new creation, two things happen: the relationship between man and woman in the first creation is restored, but that relationship must be lived out under the paradigm of the cross. In Christ Jesus there is neither male nor female, not meaning that differentiation has ceased, but that both alike enter the new creation on the same footing, and thus serve one another and the rest of the church in the same way their Lord did—by giving themselves to the other(s) out of love. Ministry is thus the result of God's gifting and has nothing to do with being male or female, any more than it has to do with being Jew or Gentile, or slave or free.

Endnotes

*The original lecture was not written out, but was given from notes. In this written edition, I have kept much of the flavor of the oral presentation (while removing many of the colloquialisms) and added a few notes for further reference.

1. I do not mean to imply that I am free from such; but just a glance at the literature reveals how much of the exegesis is predicated on what a person was expecting to find before coming to the text.

2. The NIV's "counsel" is much too soft here. The verb Paul uses, "I want" them to, is precisely that used in 2:8 about men and women in prayer; and it is clear in this passage that "want" has all the authority of apostolic command.

3. The second is 4:1-7, which picks up the themes of "sonship"/slavery under the imagery of the pedagogue from 3:24-25 (NIV "guardian," the educated slave to whom the children were entrusted for education) and of the life of the Spirit from 3:1-5, thus tying up the whole of the argument from 3:1.

4. An illustration over Peter's (not to mention Barnabas's) reneging on the Jerusulem agreement over keeping food laws (2:11-14) is what kicks off the rest of the argument of the letter; the matter of "days" is denounced in 4:8-10 as a reversion to slavery. The same three "boundary markers/identity symbols" make up the argument of Romans as well. Circumcision is argued against in ch. 4, while days and food laws come under scrutiny in 14:1–15:4.

5. It has often been argued against this point of view that this is a soteriological text, having to do with people from all of these categories coming to Christ on the equal ground of faith. So it is, but to divorce soteriology from ecclesiology in Paul is theologically disastrous. Salvation in Paul's view has not to do with God's populating heaven with countless individuals, but with creating a people for his name through Christ and the Spirit. It is in the creation of a people for his name that one finds the continuity with the former covenant. Thus, the present text is ecclesiological by the very fact that it is soteriological. The certain evidence for this is the companion passage to this one, 1 Cor 12:13, which is expressed in soteriological categories but is ecclesiological to its core. See G. D. Fee, *God's Empowering Presence* (Peabody: Hendrickson, 1994):178-82.

6. This is one place, it should be pointed out, where change could take place in that culture, because slavery was not based on race as it was in the tragic history of the United States. Rather, it was based primarily on war, captivity and economics, so that people could change status; e.g., in economically hard times people could sell themselves into slavery, and masters often manumitted slaves.

7. 1.33 (Loeb Classical Library).

8. Talmudic tractate *Menahoth* 43b (Epstein translation).

9. This view stems from several realities in the letter, especially the fact that directly following a passage where Paul forbids the men to go to the prostitutes (6:12-20), he takes up the issue of some who are rejecting sex within marriage, on the grounds that "it is good for a man not to touch a woman." When he comes to the issue of divorce (v. 10)—the logical corollary of their position—he does the most non-cultural thing: he argues that a woman should not separate from her husband, and then, almost as an afterthought, says that the same holds true for husbands as well, of course. For the full argument supporting this view, see G. D. Fee, *Commentary on the First Epistle to the Corinthians* (NICNT; Grand Rapids: Eerdmans, 1987):10-13, 267-70.

10. Based primarily on a reading of v. 3 that suggests that "head" equals to be "over the other" in some way. But this sentence is created by Paul as a kind of word play on the word "head," based on the problem lying literally on the wife's head, so that he can establish a point of reference for the issue of shame. The meaning of "head" is much debated, of course, but the so-called "Greek" view, which seems to make the most sense of all the data in the passage is expressed in the interpretation of Cyril of Alexandria (*Arcad.* 5.6): "Thus we say that 'the head

of every man is Christ.' For he was made by him … as God; 'but the head of every woman is the man,' because she was taken out of his flesh…. Likewise 'the head of Christ is God,' because he is of him by nature."

11. For the evidence of this see Fee, *First Corinthians*, 519. There is no known instance in the language where the combination of "subject," the verb "have," the object "authority," and the preposition "over" are passive with regard to the subject, i.e., in which the subject is under someone else's authority, rather than exercising authority over the object of the preposition. There is not a reason in the world to think it is otherwise here, especially so, when Paul immediately qualifies the woman's authority over her own head (with regard to wearing or not wearing the head covering) by insisting that "in the Lord, however, woman is not independent of man, nor man of woman" (v. 11).

12. For the evidence see Fee, *First Corinthians*, 5:10-12. It has often been asserted that the shaved head was a sign of prostitution in Corinth; but there is not a known piece of evidence for such in the literature of antiquity. For Paul same-sex intercourse is a matter of denying the differentiation and mutuality of creation, which is what lies behind Paul's strong denunciation of homosexuality in Romans 1:24-27. Those who have exchanged the truth about God and have believed the lie, Paul says, have expressed their denial of the truth of creation, what God has done, by same-sex intercourse. And God has given them over because they have refused to believe the truth about God. This, of course, sounds like a very harsh word to people who are oriented toward same-sex relationships, but the fact is, "male and female, God created them," and Paul sees very clearly that the obliteration of that created expression is in fact an elimination not only of what God has created but what is also being restored in the new creation. Why else, one wonders, would he single out these two relationships—men with men and women with women? Notice also the language of shame that is persistent in that text.

13. This truth should have brought all the nonsense in North American Protestant arguments in favour of slavery over the past three hundred years to its knees in absolute repentance. What has gone on in my own country (the United States) on this matter is sheer craziness, since Philemon is the clear evidence that "brother in Christ" means that black and white *must* eat together at the same table; the table of the Lord, eaten in the context of a meal, is the great equalizer. Otherwise the gospel of our Lord is betrayed at its core.

14. For this diagram and much of the description that follows I am indebted to Carolyn Osiek and David L. Balch, *Families in the New Testament World, Households and House Churches* (Louisville: Westminster John Knox Press): 8 and throughout.

15. In the Greco-Roman world, girl babies were very often "exposed," put in the dump and left to die. It is the males who count because they carry on the family line. Enough females were obviously kept for the purposes of the male, but a female baby was absolutely chattel and was at the total discretion of the father whether he wanted to keep it or not—and I mean the father, not the parents.

16. We need also to appreciate, of course, that in all such situations where the law allows the most despicable kind of behaviour, there are always people who function as beneficent dictators; and we know of many of these from Greco-Roman culture. My concern is not to paint the picture as utterly bleak, but to point out that a thoroughly totalitarian patriarchy was simply assumed under the law itself.

17. Philo, *The Special Laws* 3.169 (trans. by F. H. Colson in the Loeb Classical Library, 7.581).

18. *Oration* 59.122.

19. For this matter see W. W. Tarn, *Hellenistic Civilization* (Cleveland: World Publishing Co., 1952): 98-99.

20. The only two uses of the word *teknogon* (to bear children) word group in the New Testament occur in these two verses (2:15 and 5:14).

21. Although Paul says that "Adam was created first, then Eve" in v. 13, his point is not that this makes only men qualify as teachers, but that the one who was created second was first in transgression. And it is not her teaching that he takes up, but her "salvation."

22. On the inauthenticity of 1 Corinthians 14:34-35, see Fee, *God's Empowering Presence*, 272-81.

THEOLOGICAL PERSPECTIVES

CHAPTER 5

Theological Approaches to Male-Female Relationships

Stanley J. Grenz

"Dear Dr. Grenz," the letter began. "Please excuse the notebook paper and my handwriting. I would have used my computer and printer to write to you but due to my demise, financially, I've had to sell my printer to put food on the table....Several weeks ago I was browsing the book shelf of a local Christian book store, when your book *Betrayal of Trust* [which deals with clergy sexual misconduct[1]] leaped off the shelf into my soul thirsty hands."

My correspondent then proceeded to pour out a shocking story of abuse and betrayal. She spoke of how one of the ministers of her church and his wife convinced her to divorce her husband and move in with them, how with the blessing of the minister's wife she began to sleep with the clergyman, but then how the wife soon grew tired of the arrangement and turned on her. Publicly parading their rekindled love for each other, the ministerial couple galvanized the support of the senior pastor and the congregation to hound the unsuspecting woman out of the church. No longer able to carry out her job-related responsibilities in the aftermath of this trauma, she soon found herself dismissed from her employment as well.

The woman has since returned to her former husband and found a new church fellowship that is supporting her on the rocky road toward spiritual healing. Nevertheless, the scars linger. "Some days I do well. Some days are more of a struggle," she acknowledged. In fact, the fallout from this experience may never settle. In what for me was the most tragic statement of her letter, the woman stated matter-of-factly, "I don't trust clergy at all."

Our first reaction to this tale of woe might be to excuse it as a bizarre situation or to discount it as the ranting of a jilted lover. In fact, however, the woman's story indicates what can all too readily happen when relationships between women and men go array. Indeed, we all know from first hand experience that our relationships are often not what they could—or should—be. Although not necessarily in as blatant a manner this woman experienced, in a multitude of overt or covert ways we display through our fundamental femaleness or maleness the uncanny human knack to exploit each other for our own ends. In the words of Paul Jersild and Dale Johnson: "As sexual beings we are capable...of reducing another person to an extension of ourselves...It is precisely as sexual beings that we are most vulnerable to the desire to possess another person and to reduce him or her to the object of our desire."[2] Or as Lawrence Kubie noted, "Men and women are infinitely ingenious in their ability to find new ways of being unhappy together."[3]

Is there any hope for this situation? Can we overcome our debilitating tendency? Is it possible to build godly relationships between women and men? As Christians, we boldly declare that the breach between the sexes can be healed. The gospel, we assert with Paul, is the power of God for our salvation. But how does this happen? How can the gospel transform relationships between men and women? Listen to the ancient story once again.

> Then God said, "Let us make human beings in our image, in our likeness..." So God created human beings in his own image, in the image of God he created them; male and female he created them....God saw all that he had made, and it was very good. (Gen 1:26, 27, 31)

> The Lord God said, "It is not good for the man to be alone. I will make a helper suitable for him." Now the Lord God had formed out of the ground all the beasts of the field and all the birds of the air....But for Adam no suitable helper was found. So the Lord God caused the man to fall into a deep sleep; and while he was sleeping, he took one of the man's ribs and closed up the place with flesh. Then the Lord God made a woman from the rib he had taken out of the man, and he brought her to the man. Then the man said, "This is now bone of my bones and flesh of my flesh; she shall be called ['female'] for she was taken out of ['male']." (Gen 2:18-23)

Then I saw a new heaven and a new earth...I saw the Holy City, the new Jerusalem, coming down out of heaven from God, prepared as a bride beautifully adorned for her husband. (Rev 21:1-2)

In the biblical narrative, we find three insights that assist us in our quest to build godly relationships between women and men.

The Foundation for Godly Relationships: The Mutuality within the Trinitarian God

First, the biblical narrative indicates the foundation for godly relationships between men and women. The first creation narrative begins with God: "And God said, 'Let us make...'" In this manner, the story points to what the Bible everywhere assumes: God is the foundation for human existence, including existence as male and female. Even more significantly, our human relationality as sexual creatures finds its source in the divine reality. But what about God provides the foundation for godly relationships between women and men?

For much of its history, Christian theology has been dominated by an emphasis on the oneness of the transcendent God. This view pictures God as the powerful, solitary sovereign over the world. God is characterized by the supposedly "male" traits surrounding designations such as "Lord" and "King." This characterization has tended to lead to a conception of human relationships that gives prominence to the male and fosters a hierarchy of male over female. According to this model, men represent God, whereas women symbolize creation.

The twentieth century, however, has witnessed a renewal of interest in the doctrine of the Trinity and its implications for the Christian understanding of human relations. Simply stated, the doctrine declares that the eternal God is not an undifferentiated reality. Although one, God is nevertheless a unity-in-diversity. The one God is the social Trinity, the fellowship of Father, Son and Holy Spirit. Consequently, God is fundamentally relational. Hence it comes as no surprise that when God fashions the pinnacle of creation, a unity-in-diversity—humankind as male and female—emerges.

Contemporary trinitarian theologians find this idea latent within the enigmatic words of the first creation account: "Then God said, 'Let us make human beings in our image...'" Of course, we would be overstepping exegetical propriety were we to claim that the plural divine reference means that the biblical writer was somehow a crypto-trinitarian. Nevertheless, reading the narrative in the light of the entire canon does indeed suggest that the One who stands at the genesis of the plurality of humankind as male and female is internally a plurality. And consequently, we can look to the dynamic among the trinitarian persons for the clue to understanding what characterizes godly human relationships.

But what is this fundamental dynamic within the triune God? In a word: "mutuality." This mutuality is evidenced in what provides the best window into the divine dynamic, namely, Jesus' relationship to the one he called "Abba" (or "Father").

Some theologians, in contrast, argue that the life of our Lord demonstrates anything but mutuality. Didn't Jesus declare, "The Father is greater than I"? And didn't he live in total obedience to, even dependence upon the Father? Advocates of a "top-down" ordering of human relationships find in our Lord's demeanor the confirmation for a hierarchy of male over female they believe is likewise operative in God's relationship to creation. These thinkers argue that women ought to reflect the same kind of subordination to men that characterized Jesus' relationship to his heavenly Father.

This interpretation, however, goes beyond what the biblical texts in fact assert. Nowhere does the New Testament declare that the Son's obedience to the Father is a model of how one gender (women) should relate to the other (men). We would do better to see in Jesus' obedience to the One he called "Abba" the model as to how all human beings—whether male or female—should live in obedience to God. And we ought to find in Jesus' example a grand illustration of the proper attitude that all Christians, female and male, should demonstrate toward one another. Rather than encouraging the establishment of lines of authority and submission, Jesus' life calls us to mutual submission to one another. Indeed, Paul instructed the Ephesian believers to "submit to one another out of reverence for Christ" (Eph 5:21).

The life of our Lord offers a model of the mutuality that ought to exist between women and men. But we have not yet arrived at the goal of our journey to the divine foundation for godly human relationships. We must take our considerations of the relationship of the earthly Jesus' to his heavenly Father one step farther. We must probe the divine dynamic lying behind it and then tease out more clearly the implications for us of the Christian understanding of God as triune.

At the heart of the doctrine of the Trinity is the declaration that God is an eternal dynamic. According to the theologians of the ancient church, the primary movement within the Godhead is the eternal generation of the Son. As the church father Origen declared, from all eternity the Father begets the Son in one eternal act.

On the basis of this ancient Christian assertion, some theologians construct

86

a linear or asymmetrical model of the Trinity, in which authority flows from the Father to the Son (and finally to the Spirit). This linear conception, in turn, provides the transcendent foundation for an asymmetrical model of human relationships. These thinkers claim that just as authority flows from the Father to the Son, so also men have authority over women, and whatever authority women have derives from men.

Such a conclusion, however, fails to see that the dynamic Origen referred to as "the eternal generation of the Son" moves in two directions. As the church father Athanasius realized, not only does this dynamic generate the Son, it also constitutes the Father. In that the Son is none other than the eternal Son of the eternal Father, the Son is not the Son without the Father. But in the same way, the Father—being the eternal Father of the eternal Son—is not the Father without the Son.[4]

Allow me to illustrate this seemingly opaque idea. The generation of my firstborn (Joel) not only marked him as the son of his father, it also constituted me as father, or more specifically, as the father of my son. Indeed to call me "father" is a shorthand way of designating me as "the father of Joel" (and subsequently, "the father of Corina" as well). My situation reminds us that there is a reciprocal relationship inherent in human generation.

Of course, this illustration has an obvious short-coming and therefore ought not to be pushed too far. Human generation is temporal; it always happens at a point in time. As a result, I know of a time before I was Joel's father, and I can speak of myself as a person apart from my role as the progenitor of my son. Not so with God, the ancient theologians declared. The generation of the Son—the act which constitutes the Father as Father—is an eternal dynamic, so that the Father never was apart from the Son.

Despite the limitations of the analogy, the point ought to be clear. The idea of generation within the triune God means that we must balance the subordination of the Son to the Father with the dependence of the Father on the Son. In short, the eternal generation of the Son indicates that the First and Second Persons of the Trinity enjoy a mutuality of relationship. In a certain sense, each is dependent on the other for his own identity.

What is true within the eternal divine dynamic (or what the theologians call the "immanent Trinity") is in turn visible within salvation history (that is, the "economic Trinity"). At the heart of the biblical narrative is the recounting of how Jesus willingly submitted himself to the One he called "Abba." At the same time, however, the story also suggests that in the sending of Jesus the Father made himself dependent on the Son.

Our Lord himself declared, "All things have been committed to me by my

Father" (Lk 10:22; cf. Mt 11:27). Of course, in its context within the synoptic Gospels, Jesus' statement refers primarily to his role as the one who reveals the Father. But reading our Lord's bold assertion in the context of the entire Gospel narrative suggests that the principle he announced here is applicable to his ministry as a whole. With these words, Jesus offered a profound truth about the nature of his vocation. In sending the Son into the world, the Father entrusted to the Son the entire divine program, which focuses on the establishment of God's reign and hence sets forth the Father's own deity.[5] The patristic theologian Athanasius rightly perceived the significance of Jesus' mission for the one who sent him: "Since the Father has given all things to the Son, he possesses all things afresh in the Son."[6]

Considerations such as these suggest that we cannot appeal to the example of Christ's subordination to the Father alone and hence an asymmetrical model of God as definitive for male-female relationships. Rather, the foundation for godly human relationships lies in the subordination of the Son to the Father together with the dependency of the Father on the Son. The application of this transcendent mutuality within the divine dynamic to the human sphere leads quite naturally to an emphasis on the interdependency of, and mutuality between male and female.

Hence Paul's words to the Corinthian believers: "Now I want you to realize that the head of every man is Christ, and the head of the woman is man, and the head of Christ is God....In the Lord, however, woman is not independent of man, nor is man independent of woman. For as woman came from man, so also man is born of woman. But everything comes from God" (1 Cor 11:3,11-12).

This brings us to our first conclusion: Godly relationships between men and women find their foundation in, and therefore are to be patterned after the relationship between the First and Second Persons of the Trinity. Whatever else ought to characterize our life together, we must take seriously the fundamental mutuality exhibited between Jesus the Son and his heavenly Father.

The Goal of Male-Female Relationships: Reflecting the Very Character of God

Three years after breaking up with Irving, the comic strip character Cathy finds that her former boyfriend has been hired by her firm to engineer its down-sizing program. After her encounter with Irving, Cathy complains to the receptionist: "Even when there's no way to get to you, men get to you, Charlene.... They're some deranged, mutated species all their own!" Cathy then offers a theological conclusion: "God created women. Men invented themselves."

In addition to providing the foundation, the biblical narrative indicates the goal of godly relationships between women and men. As the curtain on the biblical narrative rises, the spotlight focuses appropriately on God. But the flow of the plot quickly moves to humankind, as the divine speaker declares, "Let us make human beings in our image." This phrase, "in our image," indicates the goal of the creation of humankind. God intends that humans be the *imago dei*. But how are we the image of God? And are men and women equally the bearers of the divine image?

Our initial inclination upon hearing this second query may be to wonder whether such a question even warrants mention. How could anyone assert that one or the other sex is not created in the image of God? While some might agree with Cathy that "men created themselves," more common in the Christian tradition is the assumption that women reflect the divine image only in a derivative sense. Many theologians have in fact concluded that in the final analysis men more completely reflect the divine image than do women. Such treatments often attempt to construct an understanding of the image of God from a prior view of God's lordship, defined by concepts such as "control" and "authority." This line of reasoning then concludes that men are more completely God's image-bearers[7] and thus are a more appropriate expression of the divine sovereignty.

In the words of one proponent, "As a vassal lord, Adam is to extend God's control over the world....He has the right to name the animals, an exercise of authority in ancient thinking....And he is to 'fill' the earth with his presence."[8] What comes through here in a somewhat subtle manner is stated more directly by another apologist for the primacy of the male: "The image of God is in man directly, but in woman indirectly."[9]

In contrast to statements such as these, egalitarian thinkers affirm unequivocally that both male and female are fully the image of God. They see clear indication of this in the first creation story, in that God gave to both sexes the responsibility of multiplying and subduing the earth. Or stating this in Reformed theological terms, the Creator charged humankind—male and female—with the "cultural mandate."

Although it offers a better interpretation of the creation story, the egalitarian position often shares a debilitating liability with the viewpoint it seeks to refute. Both readily assume that the divine image is something we possess as individuals. In contrast to this view, I would argue that the image of God is primarily a relational concept. Ultimately we do not reflect God's image on our own, but in relationship. Thus, the *imago dei* is not primarily what we are as individuals. Rather, it is present among humans-in-relationship. In a word, the image of God is found in human "community."

The creation narratives themselves point to the communal nature of the divine image. Implicit in the first but more explicit in the second creation narrative is the idea that God makes the first human pair so that humans may enjoy community with each other. More specifically, the creation of the woman is designed to deliver the man from his isolation. The narrative indicates that Adam's solitude arose from a void that could not be filled by his companionship with the animals nor, interestingly enough, even by the presence of the solitary Adam before God. The appropriate antidote for this situation was the creation not merely of a human counterpart, but more specifically of a female counterpart.

This indicates the sexual nature both of Adam's solitude and of his awareness of his solitude. The void in his existence was sexually based, for he was fundamentally incomplete. And his sense of incompleteness gave birth to the cry of joy, when he was introduced to his sexual counterpart: She is "bone of my bones and flesh of my flesh" (v. 23).

In this manner, the Genesis story reminds us that as humans we can only exist as male or female—as sexual beings. To be sexual creatures entails being incomplete in ourselves. Our sexuality not only participates in our incompleteness, it allows us to sense this incompleteness. Indeed, as we are confronted with the other who is sexually different from us we are reminded of our own incompleteness. Our sexuality, then, is a sign that rather than isolated entities existing solely unto ourselves, we are fundamentally social beings. And rather than finding fulfillment within, human completeness arises from outside the individual self. Hence, our fundamental sexuality gives rise to the desire to come out of our isolation and enter into relationship with others.[10]

In Mary Stewart Van Leeuwen's poignant words, "...we are so unshakably created for community that we cannot even develop as full persons unless we grow up in nurturing contact with others. Moreover, the fulfillment of our sociability depends on fellowship with the opposite sex."[11] Similarly, on the basis of his work with mentally challenged persons, Jean Vanier, the founder of the worldwide l'Arche communities, drew a similar conclusion: "Each human being is incomplete; our bodies are incomplete: man has need of the woman, woman has need of the man....each is made for the other."[12] In what sense? "Man and woman are as mirrors to each other; their differences reveal to each other who he is or she is. These permit each one to be himself or herself in his masculinity or her femininity."[13]

Our fundamental incompleteness as isolated individuals means that in ourselves we simply cannot live according to God's design for our existence, namely, that we reflect the divine image. To live out fully God's purposes for humankind requires that we be in relationship with each other, for the fullness of the *imago dei* is present only in community. This is reflected not only in the creation narrative, but also in the vision that concludes the book of Revelation. According to John the seer, God's will is the establishment of a human society in which God's children enjoy perfect fellowship with each other, all creation and the Creator:

> Then I saw a new heaven and a new earth ... I saw the Holy City, the new Jerusalem, coming down out of heaven from God, prepared as a bride beautifully adorned for her husband. And I heard a loud voice from the throne saying, "Now the dwelling of God is with human beings, and he will live with them...." (Rev 21:1-3)

From beginning to end, therefore, the biblical narrative draws from a relational understanding of the image of God. But this observation doesn't tell us why the *imago dei* is relational. For the ultimate answer we must return again to the eternal divine reality. The doctrine of the Trinity makes clear that throughout eternity God is the fellowship of the three Persons. No wonder, then, that God's image bearers best reflect the divine nature in their relationality. The first creation narrative asserts that when God made humankind, God built into human existence as male and female the unity-in-diversity that characterizes the eternal divine reality. For this reason, neither the male as such nor the isolated human is the image of God, but humans-in-relationship ultimately are the *imago dei*. Such human community illustrates what is present in a prior manner within the divine reality.

But we must take this a step farther. In our task of showing what God is like, we are designed above all to reflect the divine character so essential to God's own nature. What is this character? John speaks for the entire biblical tradition when he offers the seemingly simple, yet profound answer: "God is love" (1 Jn 4:16). Just prior to this statement, the biblical writer asserts that "if we love one another, God lives in us and his love is made complete in us" (v.12) and then explains how this can be: "We know that we live in him and he in us, because he has given us of his Spirit" (v.13). In this manner, our quest to determine what it means to be the image of God leads to the Holy Spirit.

The connection between the divine character (love) and the Spirit arises out of the observation that the divine character is concretized in the Third Person of the Trinity. This conclusion, in turn, is the extension of the interesting manner in which the Bible speaks of God's essence as "Spirit" (Jn

91

4:24) and then uses this word to delineate the third trinitarian person. To understand how the Spirit is the concretization of the divine love, we must unpack the second movement within God, what the patristic thinkers called the "procession" of the Holy Spirit.

The great theologian Augustine perceived that the Spirit is the love binding the Father and the Son.[14] As a consequence, he—and the Western tradition after him—spoke of the Spirit as proceeding from the Father and from the Son. Throughout all eternity, the great theologian explained, the Father loves the Son and the Son reciprocates the Father's love. This unique bond is the personal Holy Spirit.

As a consequence, the pouring out of the Spirit in our lives facilitates our sharing in this eternal love. Hence, it is this particular love—the divine love concretized in the indwelling Spirit—that God intends to be in evidence in our relationships. As we love one another, we show forth the divine essence and thus are the *imago dei*. Hence, with good theological reason Paul exclaims, "And now these three remain: faith, hope and love. But the greatest of these is love" (1 Cor 13:13).

According to the Genesis narratives, the social nature of our creation in the divine image emerges in the relationship between women and men: "So God created human beings in his own image, in the image of God he created them; male and female he created them." In what sense is this the case? The obvious answer is: through marriage, as man and woman become husband and wife. Indeed, the second narrative concludes with this very point: "For this reason a man will leave his father and mother and be united to his wife, and they will become one flesh" (Gen 2:24). Subsequent biblical texts utilize marriage as a fitting earthly picture of the divine love. Marriage is a reminder of God as the One who loves. More specifically, it presents the exclusive nature of the divine love.

The second creation narrative hints as to the sense in which marriage can be a metaphor of the divine love. The narrator presents marriage as the joining of two persons who share a fundamental sameness as "flesh of one flesh" and yet differ from each other as male and female. This human dynamic reminds us of the dynamic within the triune God. As we noted earlier, the divine life entails the relationship between First and Second Persons who share the same divine essence but are nevertheless differentiated from each other. The bond uniting them is the divine love, the third trinitarian person, the Holy Spirit. As marriage incorporates its divinely-given design to be the intimate, permanent bond arising out of the interplay of sameness and difference, this human relationship reflects the exclusive relationship of love found within the Trinity, the unique relationship between the Father and the Son concretized in the Holy Spirit.

Not only does marriage represent the relationality within the eternal divine life, it also reflects God's great love for creation. Here again, marriage speaks of the holiness or exclusivity of the divine love. As is indicated by the Old Testament prophets and reiterated in Ephesians 5, marriage is a fitting picture of the kind of relationship God desires to share with God's people. The marriage bond—i.e., shared love—binds together a specific man and a specific woman in an exclusive relationship that each of them is to honor. In a similar manner, God's love for us creates a bond that is exclusive and holy. God desires that we honor no other gods and that our relationship to God be threatened by no rival loyalties.

Understanding the metaphorical significance of their marriage ought to motivate each couple to live out in the various dimensions of their life together God's desire that their relationship be an ongoing witness to the character of the eternal God and an appropriate picture of the glorious connection that binds Christ and the church. As this occurs, their marriage can become a godly relationship between this man and this woman, which brings honor and glory to God.

Marriage, however, is not the only relationship through which men and women can reflect the divine love. Most of the bonds we form are non-marital. Perhaps the most obvious type of non-marital bond is the relationship formed among single people, which unlike marriage is neither necessarily permanent nor exclusive. The non-exclusive nature of all non-marital bonds provides a powerful image of another dimension of the divine love. Whereas marriage is by its nature intended to be exclusive, the non-marital bond is expansive, unbounded, always open to the inclusion of others. As a result, it is an appropriate representation of the openness of God's love. Non-marital relationships remind us that the loving God continually seeks to include within the circle those yet outside the boundaries of God's covenantal people. As the popular hymn reminds us,

> The love of God is greater far
> Than tongue or pen can ever tell.
> It goes beyond the highest star
> And reaches to the lowest hell.
> (Frederick M Lehman, "The Love of God")

Although the Old Testament elevates marriage as the primal bond uniting man and woman, in the New Testament we discover an even more theologically important relationship. Drawing from the words of Jesus himself, the New Testament writers present as the primary relationship into which humans can enter the covenant with God in Christ which in turn leads to membership in the covenant community, the fellowship of Christ's disciples. Consequently, within this relationship we become most completely the *imago dei*. And hence within this context, godly relationships between men and women ought to emerge in the most pronounced manner.

To summarize our second conclusion: Godly relationships between men and women emerge as we direct our life together toward the highest human task, namely, reflecting the divine character and thereby being the image of God. God's goal for us arises out of the procession of the third trinitarian person, the Holy Spirit who as the concretization of the divine love is the one who creates that character in us. God's loving character becomes visible as we love one another, whether as partners who share the exclusive love relationship of marriage or as participants in the more inclusive non-marital bonds that bring persons—both male and female—together within the context of Christ's fellowship. Within this fellowship, our task is to help others, in the words of Jean Vanier, to "grow toward wholeness and to discover their place, and eventually exercise their gifts, in a network of friendship." This requires, he adds, "the integration of one's sexuality in a vision of fellowship and friendship. It implies that each one, man or woman, in his or her sexual being, must learn to love others, entering into relationships of communion … tenderness and service, using their genital sexuality only in that particular covenant which is blessed by God."[15]

The Means to Godly Relationships: Empowering the Other

The movie *When Harry Met Sally* raise a question we continually face: Can men and women enjoy being companions and friends or are they condemned to think of each other solely as potential "lovers"? The male lead (played by Billy Crystal) concludes that non-genital relationships are impossible. "Men and women cannot be friends," he says matter-of-factly to his female co-star. "The sex thing always gets in the way."

We have noted that the primal biblical narrative moves from the chief acting agent (God) to the product of God's creative action (humankind). The narrator then adds one additional crucial detail, the purpose of the differentiation of the sexes: "The Lord God said, 'It is not good for the man to be alone. I will make a helper suitable for him.'...Then the Lord God made a woman from the rib he had taken out of the man..." (Gen 2:18,22).

In response to the perceived loneliness of Adam, God created another human being who would deliver Adam from his solitude, not only by being a sexual partner, but in all dimensions of their existence.[16] The creation of the woman with which came the differentiation of the sexes, therefore, arose as the Creator's desire to make a suitable helper for the man. In this third observation, we find the means to nurturing godly relationships between men and women. Our task now is to determine what this entails. More specifically, we seek to understand what the creation of the woman as a suitable helper suggests for godly relationships between men and women.

Many theologians conclude from this aspect of the Genesis text that God outfitted men and women to fulfill different functions. In the words of the Danvers Statement of the Council on Biblical Manhood and Womanhood, "distinctions in masculine and feminine roles are ordained by God as part of the created order, and should find an echo in every human heart."[17] And what are these distinctions? One widely-held suggestion asserts that man is equipped to lead, whereas woman is created to support; man is to initiate, woman to enable; man is to take responsibility for the well-being of woman, woman to take responsibility for helping man. In short, godly relationships emerge as woman serves as man's assistant.

Despite its long pedigree in Christian tradition, the assertion that strict gender roles are rooted in creation actually runs counter to the point of the narrative. Alvira Mickelson has pointed out that of the twenty other Old Testament appearances of the Hebrew term translated "helper" in this text, seventeen refer to God as our helper.[18] To speak of God in this manner is to acknowledge God as our strength or power. On the basis of an examination of all the Old Testament uses of these words, Semitic language specialist David Freedman concluded, "When God creates Eve from Adam's rib, His intent is that she will be—unlike the animals—'a power (or strength) equal to him.'"[19] Rather than requiring that we view the woman as man's assistant, therefore, the narrator intends that we see her as the one who rescues the man from his solitude. Far from being cast in a subservient role, she is thereby elevated in the narrative as the crowning achievement of God's saving intent for life in the Garden.

The Genesis narrative does speak about a hierarchical arrangement of male-female relationships traditionalists find in the text. But rather than being part of God's creative intent, in the narrative such a hierarchy arises as a consequence of the first sin. God's statement, "Your desire will be for your husband, and he will rule over you" (Gen 3:16), is not a prescription of what is morally necessary for godly relationships, but a description of life after the fall.

A clue as to why the fall led to male, rather than female, dominance is found in God's words to sinful Adam: "Cursed is the ground because of you; through painful toil you will eat of it all the days of your life. It will produce thorns and thistles for you, and you will eat the plants of the fields. By the sweat of your brow you will eat your food" (Gen 3:17-19). The research of anthropologist Peggy Reeves Sanday indicates that in addition to biological sexual distinctions, the nature of the environment in which a society emerges determines the type of relationships between the sexes that develop. A hostile environment readily leads to male domination, whereas relative equality between the sexes is most frequently found when the environment is beneficent.[20]

The most widely-held theory today explains that male/female roles developed in the pre-historic hunting and gathering societies in response to women's need to be protected during pregnancy or nursing children.[21] Obviously, these conditions are no longer operative in western culture. As tasks related to procreation and rearing offspring lost their determinative influence over gender roles, the door was opened to the assumption of new social functions especially for females.

These considerations led some theorists in recent decades to throw out completely the traditional view. At the foundation of this revisionist position is an idea known as "androgyny," which declares that apart from obvious differences in reproduction, no fundamental sexual differences exist between male and female. In the words of the Roman Catholic scholar George Tavard, "Men and women are complementary in sexual activity, yet identically human in everything else."[22]

In contrast to the traditional model of fixed sex roles, proponents of the androgynous understanding call for the eradication of all such roles. To this end, they draw a sharp distinction between sex and gender, arguing that gender is a social construct. In the words of Robert Stoller, "Gender is a term that has psychological and cultural rather than biological connotations: if the proper terms for sex are 'male' and 'female', the corresponding terms for gender are 'masculine' and 'feminine', these latter may be quite independent of (biological) sex. Gender is the amount of masculinity and femininity found in a person, and obviously, while there are mixtures of both in many humans, the normal male has a preponderance of masculinity and the normal female a preponderance of femininity."[23]

Although this proposal may have provided a needed corrective to the traditional view with its focus on inherent gender roles, it overlooks the important distinctions that do exist between the sexes. Lisa Sowle Cahill offered this helpful summary of one recently proposed, albeit controversial[24] trajectory of anthropological research: "It appears that different physical characteristics, deriving at least in part from their reproductive roles, may create in men and women a tendency toward certain emotional (nurturing, aggressive) or cognitive (verbal, visual) capacities, which may in turn influence the ways they fulfill various social relationships."[25]

Others point to a more psychological foundation for role distinctions, namely, in the emergence of gender awareness in early childhood in contexts in which the mother is the primary care giver. In such a situation, to develop a sense of gender identity, young girls need only to continue to stay close to, and model the behaviour of their primary care giver. Little boys, in contrast, become aware that they are "not like" this seemingly powerful person and that to build their gender identity they must detach themselves from her so as to identify with their less involved male parent.[26]

Whatever the reason, men and women do seem to view the world differently, and they bring differing skills to the task of living. Awareness of this has led to a mediating position between the static roles advocated by traditionalists and the total fluidity of roles arising out of the idea of androgyny. The mediating position calls for what proponents call "role flexibility."[27] Based on biological findings, Milton Diamond, for example, offered this advice: "A goal for our culture might be to recognize and accept that generalities can exist simultaneously with allowable deviation from the typical."[28]

Diamond's advice has found echo among evangelical thinkers as well. Kaye Cook and Lance Lee have advocated what they call an "identity-flexible" model of gender roles, which "finds a breadth of appropriate roles and functions for the biblical woman or man." This position "is less interested in asking 'What is the appropriate behavior for a man or woman?' as it is in asking 'How can both genders most creatively fulfill their potentials in the effort to glorify God?'"[29]

The newer theory of gender roles offers helpful direction for our search for the means to nurturing godly relationships. It suggests that such relationships come neither through static sex roles which view women as subservient to men nor through the denial of any sex-based distinctions between men and women. Instead, godly relationships emerge as men and women offer their unique perspectives as gifts to each other, so that together they might become the community of persons God intends humans to be.

And what are the unique gifts of each gender? Drawing from the psychoanalytical view of gender distinctions, Celia Allison Hahn has offered one model. She concluded that by working together the sexes present a "life-giving tension between connection and separation, commitment and personal boundaries."[30] In this tension, masculinity contributes the emphasis on separation from others, whereas femininity offers the complementary focus on connectedness with others.[31]

Whatever the distinctive contributions of women and men may in fact be, one conclusion runs throughout the various proposals: Men and women exist to empower each other, and hence need to discover expressions of their fundamental interdependence which empower both sexes.[32]

Indeed, this is the final lesson found in the biblical narrative. As we noted above, sexual distinctions remind us of our fundamental incompleteness. Whether male or female, we need each other and are dependent on one another. This is the point of the narrative of God's creation of the female to be the counterpart of the male, which finds echo in Paul's declaration, "In the Lord, however, woman is not independent of man, nor is man independent of woman" (1 Cor 11:11). If we do indeed need each other, then we dare not view our fundamental masculinity or femininity as the means to gain power over the other or as a vehicle through which to enhance oneself by using the other. Instead, God has entrusted our fundamental masculinity and femininity to us for the sake of serving each other.

For this to occur requires that we come to grips with what power is meant to be. We must eschew the widely-followed assumption that we live in a context of competition and therefore that power primarily entails the ability to dominate the other. Instead, we must embrace an understanding that focuses on effectiveness in assisting the other. We must see power as power for, rather than power over others. And rather than believing that it is a scarce commodity which must be hoarded for ourselves, we must come to realize that such power-for-others actually increases as it is given away.

For a consistent example of this understanding of power as empowerment we need look no further than to Jesus of Nazareth. The gospels are replete with stories in which Jesus not only relates to men, but also interacts as a man with women. In each case, he consistently refused to view women as occupying a lower place on the social order and hence as those over whom he needed to exercise dominance. Instead, our Lord used his power to empower each woman he encountered. In each situation, he modeled his own countercultural teaching:

> You know that those who are regarded as rulers of the Gentiles lord it over them, and their high officials exercise authority over them. Not so with you. Instead, whoever wants to become great among you must be your servant, and whoever wants to be first must be slave of all. (Mk 10:42-43)

But the greatest illustration of this principle came at the end, as our Lord fulfilled his own prediction: "For even the Son of Man did not come to be served, but to serve, and to give his life as a ransom for many" (v. 45). His death on our behalf opened the way for him to pour out the Holy Spirit, God's personal presence empowering Christ's community for their divinely-given task.

Our Lord's example takes us back once again to our starting point in the eternal dynamic within the divine life. In his own life and above all in his death, Jesus of Nazareth revealed the divine way of life. For in the end the mutuality and love shared among Father, Son and Holy Spirit entail an eternal empowerment by each of the others, an empowerment that binds them together as the one God. Hence, Jesus' life indicates that in the Father's love for the Son, he empowers the Son to be the Son of the Father. By reciprocating the Father's love, the Son, in turn, empowers the Father to be who he is, namely, the Father of the Son. And as the divine love shared between Father and Son, the Holy Spirit empowers them to be who they are and is thereby empowered to be who he is, namely, the personal concretization of the divine character, which is love.

I admit that the path I have invited you to follow in this address may appear to be so much heavy theological reflection. Yet its practical implication is profoundly simple. Larry Crabb put it this way: "Beginning with the data of divine relationships rather than our experiences with each other, we can come close to defining a good relationship. A good relationship is one in which each member willingly and actively devotes whatever he or she has to give to the well-being of the other. In such a relationship, the highest criterion for deciding what to do at any moment is a person's understanding before God of what would be the greatest service he or she can offer to the other."[33]

This is the key to nurturing truly godly relationships between women and men, regardless of the context of those relationship. Let us therefore pledge ourselves anew to reflect in our life together the kind of godly mutuality, love and empowerment that reflects the eternal dynamic within the triune God, as we journey toward the glorious New Jerusalem that awaits us in God's eternal community.

Endnotes

1. Stanley J. Grenz and Roy D. Bell, *Betrayal of Trust: Sexual Misconduct in the Pastorate* (Downers Grove, IL: InterVarsity, 1995).

2. Paul T. Jersild and Dale A. Johnson, *Moral Issues and Christian Response*, fourth edition, (New York: Holt, Rinehart and Winston, 1988), 50.

3. Lawrence Kubie, "Psychoanalysis and Marriage, Practical and Theoretical Issues," in *Neurotic Interaction in Marriage*, ed. Victor W. Eisenstein (London: Tavistock Publications, 1956), 15.

4. Athanasius, *Contra Arian* 3.6.

5. Wolfhart Pannenberg is an important contemporary proponent of this idea. For a summary statement of his position, see Stanley J. Grenz, *Reason for Hope: The Systematic Theology of Wolfhart Pannenberg* (New York: Oxford, 1990), 50.

6. Athanasius, *Apologia Contra Arian* 3.36.

7. On this issue, see Ruth Tucker, *Women in the Maze: Questions and Answers on Biblical Equality* (Downers Grove, IL: InterVarsity, 1992), 36.

8. John M. Frame, "Men and Women in the Image of God," in *Recovering Biblical Manhood and Womanhood: A Response to Evangelical Feminism*, ed. John Piper and Wayne Grudem (Wheaton, IL: Crossway, 1991), 231.

9. Roger Beckwith, "The Bearing of Holy Scripture," in *Man, Woman and Priesthood*, ed. Peter Moore (London: SPCK, 1978), 57.

10. A corresponding relationship between loneliness and community is presented by Dwight Hervey Small, *Design For Christian Marriage* (Westwood, NJ: Revell, 1959), 30.

11. May Stewart Van Leeuwen, *Gender and Grace: Love, Work and Parenting in a Changing World* (Downers Grove, IL: InterVarsity, 1990), 41.

12. Jean Vanier, *Man and Woman He Made Them* (New York: Paulist, 1984), 8.

13. Vanier, *Man and Woman He Made Them*, 57.

14. Augustine, *The Trinity* 6.5.7; see also 15.17.27; 5.11.12; 15.19.37. For the connection of this Augustinian idea to the Greek tradition, see Yves Congar, *I Believe in the Holy Spirit*, trans. David Smith, three volumes (New York: Seabury, 1983), 3:88-89, 147-48. For a contemporary delineation of this position, see David Coffey, "The Holy Spirit as the Mutual Love of the Father and the Son," *Theological Studies* 51 (1990): 193-229.

15. Vanier, *Man and Woman He Made Them*, 97-98.

16. The broader interpretation of helper is offered by many exegetes of Genesis 2:20. See for example, Samuel L. Terrien, *Till the Heart Sings* (Philadelphia: Fortress, 1985), 10-11.

17 Advertisement in *Christianity Today*, 33/1 (Jan. 13, 1989). See also Gene A. Getz, *The Measure of a Family* (Glendale, CA: Gospel Light, Regal Books, 1976), 41-43. Getz attempts to chart a middle position by concluding, "Woman's submissive role to man, then, antedates the fall, but was complicated by the fall" (p. 43).

18. Alvira Mickelson, "An Egalitarian View: There Is Neither Male nor Female in Christ," in *Women in Ministry: Four Views*, ed. Bonnidell Clouse and Robert G. Clouse (Downers Grove, IL: InterVarsity, 1989), 183.

19. David Freedman, "Woman, a Power Equal to Man," *Biblical Archaeology Review* 9/1 (Jan-Feb 1983): 58.

20. Peggy Reeves Sanday, *Female Power and Male Dominance* (New York: Cambridge University Press, 1981), 172. Sanday's study in noted by Lisa Sowle Cahill, *Between the Sexes* (Philadelphia: Fortress, 1985), 95.

21. This theory is based on part on the studies of the anthropologist George Murdock. For a helpful presentation of the theory, see Peter DeJong and Donald R. Wilson, *Husband and Wife* (Grand Rapids: Zondervan, 1979), 68-75.

22. George H. Tavard, "Theology and Sexuality," in *Women in the World's Religions, Past and*

Present, ed. Ursula King (New York: Paragon, 1987), 78-79. See also Tavard, *Woman in Christian Tradition* (South Bend, IN: University of Notre Dame Press, 1973).

23. Robert Stoller, *Sex and Gender* (New York: Science House, 1968), 9-10.

24. For a critique of the attempt to reaffirm gender differences on the basis of scientific findings, see Beryl Lieff Benderly, *The Myth of Two Minds: What Gender Means and Doesn't Mean* (New York: Doubleday, 1987).

25. Lisa Sowle Cahill, *Between the Sexes* (Philadelphia: Fortress, 1985), 91.

26. See, for example, Mary Stewart Van Leeuwen, et. al., *After Eden: Facing the Challenge of Gender Reconciliation* (Grand Rapids, MI: Eerdmans, 1993), 397.

27. A call to move in this direction was issued already in 1968. See Vance Packard, *The Sexual Wilderness* (New York: David McKay Co., 1968), 360, 361-379, 392.

28. Milton Diamond, "Human Sexual Development: Biological Foundations for Social Development," in Frank A. Beach, ed. *Human Sexuality in Four Perspectives* (Baltimore: Johns Hopkins University Press, 1977), 58. His understanding is developed further in Milton Diamond and Arno Karlen, *Sexual Decisions* (Boston: Little, Brown and Co., 1980), 441-61.

29. Kaye Cook and Lance Lee, *Man and Woman: Alone and Together* (Wheaton, IL: Victor/BridgePoint, 1992), 49.

30. Celia Allison Hahn, *Sexual Paradox: Creative Tensions in Our Lives and in Our Congregations* (New York: Pilgrim, 1991), 26.

31. Hahn, *Sexual Paradox*, 15-16.

32. See, for example, Stephen B. Boyd, *The Men We Long to Be: Beyond Domination to a New Christian Understanding of Manhood* (San Francisco: Harper, 1995), 203.

33. Larry Crabb, *Men and Women: Enjoying the Difference* (Grand Rapids, MI: Zondervan, 1991), 109.

CHAPTER 6

"Post-Christian" Feminism and the Fatherhood of God

Loren Wilkinson

People who still speak dismissively of feminism are likely to do so on the assumption that feminism is primarily about power. For the movement did have its origins in the recognition that women have regularly been excluded from positions of power. It is easy to forget that in most areas of North America women were not permitted to vote till less than a hundred years ago.[1]

But from the beginning feminism has been much more than a protest against closed doors to such activities as voting, medicine, law, and the ordained Christian ministry. Underlying all these specific exclusions have been assumptions about the nature of women which have said in effect, "women *in their very nature* have (or lack) characteristics necessary for these activities. So the deepest feminist cry has always been not "I want to have power" but "I want to be human."

It is no surprise then that feminism has become increasingly concerned with those explorations and expansions of human potential which have, in the last part of the twentieth century, flourished in reaction to the dehumanizing aspects of modernity. Many feminists argue that a "postmodern"[2] critique of the modern era must be feminist and reasons are not hard to find for this conviction. Feminists argue that all the main aspects of the modern way of knowing—fragmentation, detachment, mechanism—are the result of masculine (and ultimately patriarchal) attitudes. Men are more inclined to distance themselves from their bodies; hence from the earth, and to promote a "spirituality" of dominion. Men are thus more likely to describe the world and themselves in terms of a detached analysis, not "holistically;" men are more likely to image the world as a machine; women, as an organism, a growing thing, a womb.

In every case, "modern" traits which are understood as contributing to the de-spiritualizing, desacralizing movement of modernity are linked to the masculine; the spiritual is seen as a feminine force, countering sterile modernity with life and nurturing. The appeal of feminism, therefore, to both women and men is that it embodies attitudes which are equally needed by both in the desert of modernity, for it holds out the promise of healing some of the major alienations of our time: alienations from *ourselves*, from *other persons*, from the *earth*, and from *God*. Let us consider in order some of the feminist responses to these alienations.

1) For a variety of obvious reasons (most of them having to do with childbirth and nursing) women are less likely to pretend that they are, in their essence, merely a mind thinking about dead matter. Thus the women's movement has nourished a greater comfort with a person's *being* a body. Perhaps it is easier for women to be at home with their bodies than men, which may be one of the reasons why sexuality means different things to men and women. So it is not surprising that a part of the women's movement has been its opposition to any attitude which would treat the body as a mere thing: pornography, rape, and loveless intercourse—all of which are primarily male ways of trying to come to terms with alienated masculine existence. (Walker Percy, in his superb study of modern spiritual homelessness called *Lost in the Cosmos*, suggests that the average modern man is "a ghost with an erection."[3] Caricaturing the male attitude, Percy writes "not *cogito ergo sum* [I think, therefore I am] . . . but rather: If I enter you, I am alive, even human.") By challenging those sadly inadequate ways of being masculine, feminism has thus been indirectly responsible for "the men's movement" in which men explore ways of being men which acknowledge their weakness, their feelings, and much which has been traditionally dismissed as "womanly."

2) Likewise, feminism holds out the prospect of a genuine community which is not marred by the patriarchy—or by hierarchy of any kind—which, it is said, has done such damage to modern civilization (indeed, a spiritless modernity is sometimes seen as patriarchy's chief monument). The symbol of such a community is the circle: decision by consensus rather than decision from above or without. Radical feminism speaks of a mythic, non-hierarchical, goddess-worshiping past of genuine community, in which there

was no war, men and women lived at peace with each other, their bodies, and with nature. This reconstructed history is largely wishful thinking (goddesses and matriarchies seem to have been no less bloodthirsty than their masculine equivalents) but it represents an age-old longing for a lost golden age—a glimpse, perhaps, of Eden.[4]

3) More fundamentally, feminism argues that much of our alienation from the earth is the result of the dominance of masculine ideas of exploitation. (Common phrases like "rape of the land" and "virgin forest" support the claim.) Much of this argument turns, again, on a woman's biological—and psychological—preparation for giving birth and nurturing. The introduction to *Reweaving the World,* an important collection of ecofeminist writings, makes the point by its dedication to one of the pioneers of the environmental movement, Rachel Carson:

> Men of science have believed for hundreds of years that naming preceded owning, that owning preceded using, and that using naturally preceded using up. Some even believed that scientific understanding of the world would, if shrewdly managed, become something human beings could with considerable profit do to one another. . . . We have so many hard jobs ahead of us, so much education, so much organizing, so much action. But we do have that other way of understanding, a revolutionary understanding that we call feminist and ecological, in which we share the world with all creatures and living things and know that their stories are our own.[5]

The very existence of "ecofeminism" is thus a recognition that women may have unique insights into the healing of our alienation from the earth.

4) Finally, some feminist critiques suggest that most of the problems of modernity can be understood as the consequences of worshipping a God who is imaged in masculine terms—thus placing as the source and meaning of all things a detached, distant being. It is no surprise, goes this line of argument, that the worship of such a deity produced the self-alienating, spirit-destroying aberrations of thought which characterize the modern era.

Thus feminism asks, and seeks to answer, deep questions about what we are, and what our place is in relationship to each other, to creation and our Creator. Many of the answers given to those questions are inadequate, reflecting both a misunderstanding of human nature and a misunderstanding of Christianity. But Christian men and women dare not ignore either the questions or the answers, however flawed. Not only do they come from deep and genuine need, but they may enable us to recover truths about the triune

God (and hence about ourselves and other creatures) which have been all-too-easily overlooked in our reading of the books of Scripture and Creation.

So feminism is both a kind of spiritual quest and (like the environmental and neo-pagan movements with which it is almost inseparably intertwined) a kind of "post-modern" critique of modernity. Feminists too are looking for a way out from the spiritually airless and arid world which the modern vision has increasingly produced. At the same time, sadly, many women are looking for a way out of Christianity. Many women perceive the Christian understanding of God to be the main source of the attitudes which have kept them from full personhood.

In particular, the exclusion of women from many types of Christian ministry (and generally, the more orthodox the theology, the greater the exclusion) has been a particularly bitter fact for many women. More painful than the exclusion have been the reasons given for it. Apart from appeal to occasional texts, the most frequent argument has been that in some sense— perhaps because Jesus was a man, perhaps because of a more fundamental masculinity in God—males are more suited to represent humanity to God than are females. So for many women it is hard to resist the implication that though all of humanity is made in God's image, men are a somewhat less-clouded picture of God than women.

I must make clear at this point that I believe these complaints are answered fully in Jesus' treatment of women, and in the unequivocal biblical declaration that male and female are in the image of God, and that in persons united to Christ, the "fully human one," there is neither male nor female, slave nor free. There is a rich, deep stream of Christian feminism—indeed it can be convincingly argued that feminism is, in its origins, a Christian movement. That fact is largely ignored, however, by the ideological feminism which dominates most "women's studies" departments in the contemporary university, and which is a pervasive influence in the culture at large. This article is concerned to hear, and speak to, that radical, ideological and "post-Christian" feminism.

To write with critical sympathy about radical feminism, as a male Christian committed to biblical orthodoxy, is to enter an area swept by crossfire from two sides. Feminist theologians (an increasing number of whom identify themselves as "post-Christian") tend to see the Bible, Christianity, and Judaism as the last bastions of a patriarchal attitude which for centuries has denied women their full humanity. The idea that the Christian Gospel which (they believe) has so many times become bad news for women might in fact be the water for which their souls thirst is received by many with incredulity.

They hope to persuade women and men alike to leave Christianity behind. At the same time many thoughtful Christians rightly perceive that this sort of ideological feminism is inimical to orthodox Christianity, and thus, in reaction, want nothing to do with feminism of any sort.

Daphne Hampson is a former Anglican whose work *Theology and Feminism* is perhaps the most thorough and consistent of these attempts to construct a "post-Christian theology." She puts the matter very clearly:

> . . . for a feminist to be a Christian and also to be true to herself and to her feminist beliefs is, I am suggesting, not possible. . . . In practice I note that the women I most admire, while they may be profoundly spiritual people, have discarded Christian belief.[6]

Hampson shares with many other women the conviction and hope that feminist criticism of Christianity is likely to be fatal. In the introduction to *Theology and Feminism* she argues for the idea "that feminism represents the death-knell of Christianity as a viable religious option." Hampson has little regard for many women who try to redefine Christianity in such a way as to avoid its offensiveness to feminism.

The only other people, she observes, who recognize the seriousness of the feminist challenge are orthodox Christians. As she puts it: "It is conservative Christians who, together with more radical feminists, perceive that feminism represents not just one crisis among many. For the feminist challenge strikes at the heart of Christianity." Recent works by those Hampson would call "conservative Christians" bear out this alarm. For example, in *Speaking the Christian God: The Holy Trinity* and the *Challenge of Feminism* (an anthology which one Christian feminist dismissed as a "backlash volume against feminist theology"[7]), all of the essays make clear that arguments about the language with which we speak of God are not trivial. To call God "mother" and "Goddess" is no longer to worship the Christian God. Stephen Smith in his essay in this volume ("Worldview, language, and Radical Feminism: An Evangelical Appraisal") says of feminist attempts to change the language with which we speak of God that here "the church faces a crisis of identity possibly unmatched since the second century. An alternative worldview, not just a theological variation, contends with classical orthodoxy for the mind and heart of the church."[8]

I agree with these and other "conservative Christian" judgments about the seriousness of the feminist challenge. At the same time, I must agree with the radical feminists that for the most part Christians have been quite comfortable with the close connection between Christianity and the modernity which the feminists reject. We need to view the world differently. The various versions of monism proposed by feminism misrepresent the Christian God. But so also does the modern world, and feminists have done a great service in protesting it, and the God (however secularized and humanized) it assumes. Such a God—and such a world—is a construct much more of deism than of trinitarian Christianity. So Christians need to share the feminist quest for "an alternative worldview."

Most of the criticisms which feminists make of the world which we have built, often in the name of Christ, are valid. Only rarely, and then always imperfectly, have Christians tried to shape their cultures in the light of the triune God. Yet we have no choice but to engage in such a worldmaking, and for that task it is important to understand the feminist critique of the modern world—a world in which Christians have often felt all too much at home.

The Feminist Critique of Theism

The major feminist critique is against patriarchy—the belief that authority is properly vested in the male—and the reinforcement of that belief by the assumption that God, the ultimate source and ruler of all, is masculine. This patriarchal understanding is, it is argued, particularly embodied in the "Abrahamic" religions: Judaism, Christianity and Islam. The belief in the cruel and distant patriarch whom feminists conceive such a God to be is seen as underlying millennia of cruelty to women. Carter Heyward puts this attitude clearly in a book whose title—*The Redemption of God*—makes her thesis clear. She describes the God of theism in terms which, at many points, evoke the worst aspects of modernity. Such a God, she says, is in fact "an idol":

It is in the nature of our idol to be intolerant of ambiguity. His first and only love is Himself. He is an impassive unflappable character who represents the headship of a universal family in which men are best and women least. He is the keeper of an ethical scorecard on which "reason" gets good marks and "relation" fails. He is a master plan-maker who maps out, and by remote-control, directs our journeys before we have learned to walk. His narcissism is unquenchable. He demands that he be loved. This cold deity is the legitimating construct of the patriarchal desire to dominate and control the world. He is the eternal King, the Chairman of the board, the President of the institution, the Guru of the youth, the Husband of the wife, the General of the army, the Judge of the court, the Master of the universe, the Father of the church. He resides above us all. He is our superior, never our friend. He is a rapist, never a lover, of women and of anyone else beneath Him. He is the first and final *icon of evil in history.*[9]

This is a harsh picture, an unrecognizable caricature of the God of biblical faith. But harsh as it is, it nevertheless forms part of the mental landscape of a great many of our contemporaries. Here, for example, is novelist Ursula LeGuin's picture of the patriarchal worshipers of one God (called "One") in her Utopian novel, *Always Coming Home*:

> One made everything out of nothing. One is a person, immortal. He is all-powerful. Human men are imitations of him. One is not the universe; he made it and gives it orders. Things are not part of him nor is he part of them, so you must not praise things, but only One. . . . They say that as there was a time when One made everything, there will be a time when everything will stop being, when One will unmake everything. Then will begin the Time Outside of Time. He will throw away everything except [those] who obeyed him in every way and were his slaves. They will become part of One then, and be forever. I am sure that there is some sense to be made of this, but I cannot make it.[10]

The passage reflects a deep repugnance at what is perceived to be a belief in a God who is uninvolved with what he has made, who cares only for some humans, and who will "throw away" the non-human. The same sort of horror at God's alleged unearthliness is evident in a remark of Susan Griffin in an anthology of "ecofeminist" literature. She calls the idea of

> the divine as immanent . . . a concept foreign to those raised in Judaeo-Christianity. The view that we've grown up with is that the divine and matter are separate and that matter is really dangerous. The material world belongs to the devil. What's under your feet is closer to hell. . . .[11]

Christians rightly will answer: this is not the God whom we meet in Jesus, and worship through the Spirit. The fact remains, however, that this is the God whom many feminists are (quite understandably) rejecting, for it is the God whom they have seen embodied both in the actions and words of Christians, and in the whole modern attitude toward the earth as a resource and receptacle.

Most feminists do not, however, wish simply to replace such a "patriarchy" with a corresponding "matriarchy" (as one woman put it, the worship of "Jehovah with a skirt"). For the problem with patriarchy and patriarchal religions is not, they say, so much their elevation of masculinity as it is their deep *dualism*. The patriarchal God of Christianity, say feminists, is always and necessarily transcendent: lofty, aloof and utterly beyond creation. In this radical separation of God and creation there is a necessary devaluation of the rest of creation, or "nature." Since—for reasons of their mysterious ability to give birth and to nurture, an ability like that of the earth itself—women have often been associated more with "nature" than with men, they have suffered from that same patriarchal dualistic devaluation.

Carol Christ and Judith Plaskow, in an influential early (1979) anthology of essays on women's spirituality called *Womanspirit Rising*, put this central feminist premise very clearly in their introduction: "God in 'his' heaven is both a model of divine existence and a model for women's subordination to men."[12] Mary Daly put the point even more succinctly in her work *Beyond God the Father*: "If God is male, then the male is God."[13] But again, the problem is not so much intrinsic maleness, as it is the *dualism* which accompanies it. As Christ and Plaskow explain, drawing on Rosemary Reuther:

> . . . the sexism of Christian tradition is related to the dualistic and hierarchical mentality that Christianity inherited from the classical world. This dualistic mentality opposes soul, spirit, rationality and transcendence to body, flesh, matter, nature and immanence. God is identified with the positive sides of the dualism, and "the world" with the negative sides. In this view, a human being stands between God and the world, spirit and nature, and must learn to subdue the desires of the flesh. This is a model for domination, because reality is divided into two levels, one superior, one inferior. . . . Scholars have noted that the dualistic world view contains the seeds of the ecological crisis; for if the world and nature are seen as mere matter, then they are subject to human control and exploitation. Classical dualism also became the model for the oppression of women when the culture-creating males identified the positive side of the dualism with themselves and identified the negative sides with the women over whom they claimed the right to rule.[14]

Despite this rejection of the Christian God on the grounds of dualism and patriarchy, ideological feminism is by no means without a religion.[15] The worship of "the goddess" who is immanent in the earth and in the self, is common. In support of such goddess spirituality some posit a pre-history in which the immanent goddess was worshipped in all things, and men and women lived in harmony with each other and the earth. Such a golden age stands as a shining myth to contrast with the "satanic mills" of masculine modernity, and from such a myth many contemporary women seek to draw strength.

As we noted earlier, there is a great deal of wishful thinking in such historical reconstructions: we can find little evidence that the neolithic, hypothetically monist, past was noticeably less bloodthirsty than more recent "dualist" times. At this point, however, the historicity of the feminist past is not the issue. Whether or not an original pre-dualist age of peace ever existed, it still stands as an important symbol for many feminists in their attempt to provide an "alternate worldview"—that is, a worldview characterized not by a set of dualisms, but by a great underlying unity of God, nature and humanity. We turn now to a consideration of that essential monism of the vision of ideological feminism.

Feminism and Monism

One prominent neo-pagan feminist is Starhawk, a practitioner of Wicca. She declares that she still feels very close to her Jewish roots, but:

> For me the goddess is immanent, she is the world, she is us, she is nature, she is the changing of the seasons, she is the earth herself. It is as if the whole universe were one living being that we are a part of.[16]

Here the monism of much feminist spirituality is explicit. And it is set over against a dualistic theism which distances God from creation. "God [that is the deity spoken of as masculine] is found outside the world."

Many feminists propose that instead of a patriarchal male deity transcendent over creation, we ought to recognize a kind of total immanence of God and nature, an immanence in which we play a part. Sometimes this is expressed philosophically, sometimes mythically (as in "Starhawk's" words, cited above).

The connectedness of autonomous selves

We consider first the more philosophical description. It is laid out carefully in the work of one of the most ruthlessly consistent of feminist theologians, Daphne Hampson.

Hampson is particularly helpful, for she clarifies a central conviction of feminism which is often concealed beneath the appeals to a mythical monist past: that the fundamental wholeness sought by feminists is that of the self. Consider these words from *Swallowing a Fishbone*, a dialogue with other feminist theologians, all the rest of whom would call themselves Christian. In attempting to persuade them of the error of their Christian theism, Hampson begins by pointing out the inseparability of truth from the world:

> Truth, whatever truth may be, is present in and with the world. It is either waiting to be discovered (as in a scientific subject) , or it is something (such as in arts subjects) in which each age expresses itself as it will. In the same way, one may see God as a dimension of all that is, present to every age in so far as that age is able to discover that truth.[17]

"Truth" in other words, is inseparable from the world in precisely the same way that God is inseparable from the world. There is no God apart from the world. Just as it would be meaningless to speak of a transcendent God, so it is useless to speak of a transcendent truth. God must be found in the world says Hampson, or not at all: God is not transcendent, but " a dimension of all that is."

How then does one find such a God in the world? Hampson does not at this point appeal to a mythical goddess. Rather—placing herself firmly in a modern line that goes back at least to Kant, if not to Descartes, she argues that the locus of truth—and hence of "god"—must be in the autonomous self. "In these circumstances human beings take control. It is they who are at the centre of the picture. It need not follow that one believes that 'God' is no more than the individual. . . . But there is no heteronomy involved. God is one with all that is."[18]

Though God may be "one with all that is," it is clear that God has no standing apart from the free, conscious human self. (Hampson does not elaborate on what it can mean, in her view, to say, "it need not follow that . . . God is no more than the individual.") The central need for women—as for men—is not worship, which implies subservience and "heteronomy" (rule by another). It is rather the need for autonomy—the need, as Hampson puts it, "to take control." This self-rule by the human (male or female) stands at the opposite extreme from the Christian ideal. In her words: "To be a Christian is to be placed in a heteronomous position. Feminists believe in autonomy." There is indeed an inclusive circle at the centre of feminist consciousness, a circle which admits of no dualisms. But it is the circle of the independent self. As she puts it:

> . . . Autonomy is what feminism has been about. To be "autonomous" is to let one's own law rule . . . to be autonomous is to overcome heteronomy. Heteronomy is the law of another ruling one, is the situation of the child. To be an adult is to come into one's own.

"Enlightenment," said Kant, with reference to the movement of the late eighteenth century, is the "exit of humanity from its self-incurred minority". . . . Feminism might well be understood as the natural working out of the Enlightenment. Women are those, last but not least, who are able to claim their maturity and think for themselves.[19]

In search of a basis from which to attack modernity Hampson thus goes back to the very foundation of modernity—the Enlightenment idea (first clearly stated in Descartes) that the self is sovereign. Her words are a lucid exposition of a fact often concealed in postmodernist reactions: the absolute centrality of the modern idea of the autonomy of the self. Individual freedom or "autonomy" is the feminist bedrock, as it is for modern individualism. This is a monism of sorts—but it is remarkably like the individual atomism of patriarchy which feminism rightly protests.

Hampson does indeed seek to resist such an interpretation of the autonomy she advocates:

[Autonomy] need not imply conceiving of oneself as an isolated atom in competition with others. Indeed, that it has come to hold such connotations may tell us much about the male psyche within patriarchy; as though the only way to be oneself, to take responsibility for oneself, were to set oneself up over against others.[20]

Hampson, committed to the autonomy of the self and to the idea that feminism is the last triumph of the Enlightenment, is aware of how easily her arguments for autonomy could be subverted by an atomist dualism of self-against-other. She makes her ultimate stand against dualism, therefore, by appealing to the ideal of *connectedness*:

In what then in a word does the feminist vision consist? . . . if I were to choose one word I should say that it is a vision of connectedness. Of feminism Eleanor Haney writes that it offers us individually and collectively the possibility of making connections with ourselves, one another, the earth, and all that is and can be. . . . Women may well, on a political level, see sin as a break in connectedness, and salvation as a reweaving of the web of life. Creation, or the relationship to nature, is a theme in feminist writing because feminist women want to elevate the profound connectedness between humankind and the rest of nature. It may be because women live, to a greater extent than do many men, in a web of relations with others that Angst may not be such a dominant theme in their lives. . . . In their drawing of the vision as to what humanity might become, women create a relationship between people, and between people and earth. Haney adds: "Indeed, humanity literally yearns for what feminism intends."[21]

Hampson's vision of salvation as a restoration of broken relationships in many ways resembles the biblical one—but it is a vision which can only be developed from within the trinitarian framework which, sadly, she rejects. Thus she, like many other protestors against the excesses of modern individualism, finds herself in a tension between the need to fully affirm the self, and the need to not be alienated from all of the "others" outside the circle of selfhood. The tension is basic to the human condition—and resolved only in the Cross. We will return to a consideration of the centrality of the Cross to the resolution of that tension.

God(dess) As Mother

The other, more mythical, way which feminists have taken to avoid dualism is simply to affirm a more ancient monism in some form of goddess spirituality. "Starhawk"'s words are representative:

> There is no dichotomy between spirit and flesh, no split between God-head and the world. The Goddess is manifest in the world; she brings life into being, is Nature, is flesh. Union is not sought outside the world in some heavenly sphere or through dissolution of the self into the void beyond the senses. Spiritual union is found in life, within nature, passion, sensuality—through being fully human, fully one's self. . . .
>
> The Goddess is also earth—Mother Earth, who sustains all growing things, who is the body, our bone and cells. She is air . . . fire . . . water . . . mare, cow, cat, owl, crane, flower, tree, apple, seed, lion, sow, stone, woman. She is found in the world around us, in the cycles and seasons of nature, and in mind, body, spirit, and the emotions within each of us. Thou art Goddess. I am Goddess. All that lives (and all that is, lives), all that serves life, is Goddess.[22]

It is no surprise that the scientific "Gaia hypothesis" has been so enthusiastically adopted by those environmentally-sensitive women who also find oppressive the idea of a transcendent patriarchal deity. In a society longing for connectedness, connection with the whole planet—and even, perhaps, with the cosmos itself—is tremendously appealing.

Whatever the motivation for speaking of the divine as Goddess, many women, including many who still call themselves "Christians" have embraced

114

such an idea. Perhaps the most notorious instance of such an attempt to bring Christianity and goddess worship together was in the "Re-Imagining the Divine" conference in 1994. Here women from many of the American Protestant denominations gathered in Minneapolis with the purpose of expunging all hints of patriarchy from Christian worship and expression. An often-cited liturgy from that conference, in worship of Sophia (widely asserted to be a feminine face of God) underlines how total such a "re-imagining" can be— and how cut off it is from any control in Scripture:

> Our maker Sophia, we are women in your image: With the hot blood of our wombs we give form to new life. With the courage of our convictions we pour out lifeblood for justice. Sophia, creator God, let your milk and honey flow. . . . Our sweet Sophia, we are women in your image: with nectar between our thighs we invite a lover, we birth a child; with our warm body fluids we remind the world of its pleasures and sensations. . . . Our guide, Sophia, we are women in your image: with our moist mouths we kiss away a tear, we smile encouragement. With the honey of wisdom in our mouths, we prophesy a full humanity to all the peoples.[23]

Most feminists who approve of such worship would not deny that it is quite different from orthodox Christianity. Rosemary Radford Ruether, for example, remarks, acknowledging approvingly the similarity to Canaanite religion, that such a feminist faith

> combin[es] the values of the world-transcending Yahweh with those of the world-renewing Ba'al. In a post-technological religion of reconciliation with the body, the woman, and the world, its salvation myth will not be one of divinization and flight from the body but of humanization and reconciliation with the earth.[24]

But once again, it is not enough for Christians simply to denounce these attempts to shift Christianity into worship of a goddess; we need to understand why they are being made, why we have so misrepresented the Gospel of Jesus as to drive women to such a position.

First, however, we must agree with the feminist charge that the Judaeo-Christian religion is unequivocal in calling God "Father." Its determination not to see God as "Mother" is one of the most striking differences from the surrounding Canaanite religions. All are agreed on this point. As Elizabeth Achtemeier puts it:

More pressing for the feminists, however, is the question of why God reveals himself only in masculine terms. Elaine Pagels is quite correct when she states that "the absence of feminine symbolism of God marks Judaism, Christianity and Islam in striking contrast to the world's other religious traditions, whether in Egypt, Babylonia, Greece and Rome, or Africa, Polynesia, India and North America."[25]

Achtemeier goes on to ask the obvious question:

But why could a personal God not have revealed himself in feminine metaphors instead? God is never called "Mother" in the Bible and is never addressed or thought of as a female deity. That was unique in the ancient Near Eastern world; Israel was surrounded by peoples who worshipped female deities—Asherat and Anat, Nut and Isis, Tiamat and the Queen of Heaven, Demeter and Artemis. And such a masculinizing of the deity is still unique in our world.[26]

The answer is not far to seek. It is that the monism or pantheism so clearly expressed by Starhawk and by many others (as though it were a new discovery) is indeed the basic human religion—what Huxley called approvingly "the perennial philosophy." It is entirely "natural" for human beings to worship "nature" as divine. As Achtemeier (again) puts it:

In most of the cultures of the world, deity and world are not differentiated. Rather, the divine is bound up with and revealed through the natural world. . . . [T]he expanse of the sky, the heat of the sun, the growth and death of vegetation, the fury of the storm—these were to those ancient peoples not impersonal happenings and objects but cosmic Thou's which affected human life and demanded adjustment to them. Nature was alive for primitive peoples as it still is for many today. . . . In the worship of the biblical Canaanites, any natural object could be a medium of revelation—a stone pillar, a sacred grove, a stream. . . .

It is precisely the introduction of female language for God that opens the door to such identification of God with the world, however.[27]

Natural as it is, however, such worship is a kind of trap for it deflects our attention away from the otherness of God, and encourages us in our attempts to make God a kind of projection of ourselves. Above all, it is a religion which implicitly denies or ignores the possibility of revelation. The longing for a closeness to God cannot be overlooked. But it is a closeness sought by *God*, and to see God as a kind of "mother-nature" bountifully, and in a sense "naturally" producing all, is to miss the real personality of the God who chooses to create. Feminists like Hampson rightly long for autonomy; but in denying that autonomy to the living God, they cut themselves off from the possibility of genuine autonomy for themselves. The curious fact (biologically speaking) that the Creator God is spoken of as "he" makes it easier to avoid the mistake of seeing God as a kind of cosmic principle of fecundity. Rudy Wiebe makes this point very well in his novel, *My Lovely Enemy* (a very strange novel: the words are spoken by Jesus to a literature professor in the stacks of the University of Edmonton library):

> All words are image, speaking is the only way human beings can handle large reality. But the difference between the image and the reality has to be clear, and when man speaks of "God as Mother" her acts usually become so closely identified with nature—the physical world everywhere—that he forgets the image-ness and begins to think the words as physical actuality. For a person to say "All is brought forth from the womb of God" is so close to what actually happens every minute in animal nature that he starts acting out copulation and birthing and begins to think he's God while he's doing it. . . . But God subsumes and is far beyond both Nature and Image. So it is better to contemplate the concept of GOD THE FATHER because no natural father ever brings forth any life by himself. You are then forced to contemplate the creation of the world not as an act of physical birth out of God's womb, but rather as the act of being spoken into existence by Words coming out of God's mouth. This is an image so strange, so profoundly human, that no one can ever mistake it for what happens in nature.[28]

Almost everyone, whether feminist or patriarchalist, agrees that our language for God is, at best, analogical: God is neither male nor female, "father" nor "mother" in any literal biological sense. Even when this is granted, however, the fact remains that metaphors and analogies profoundly affect our thought. So the feminist question remains: how can the Gospel be good news for women when God is always pictured in masculine terms? Wiebe's observation, made by many others as well, suggests an answer. The most common human tendency in worship is to confuse creation with Creator, and it is vastly easier to make that mistake when God is imaged as mother. Much must be rediscovered, in Christianity, about God's intimacy with creation. But it must be recovered first of all on the basis of the infinite difference between God and creatures.

Paradoxically, the feminist case against patriarchy (well expressed in

Hampson's impassioned argument for "autonomy") is relevant here. We live in a universe of freedom and distinctness—even, it seems, right down to the sub-nuclear, quantum level of things. Freedom and integrity—on the human level, *selfhood*—requires otherness, separation, "space." It is a commonly recognized paradox that such individual integrity is a necessity if there is to be genuine relationship; otherwise the relationship is not "I-thou" but "I-I," or at best "I-It." The various versions of monism proposed as alternatives to patriarchal dualism miss this point. To make God simply part of all that is, is to speak of a God unavailable for relationship, for he/she/it is simply a part of ourselves. To make ourselves nothing more than a part of nature is to render such ideas as stewardship of nature unintelligible. One of the deepest of psychological problems is the desire to "return to the womb." Such a state necessarily precludes action and relationship, qualities which depend utterly on separateness. To speak of God the creator as "father" rather than "mother" is in the long run a way of honouring the creature, not enslaving it. No bondage is greater than that of foetus to mother in the womb. Separation is necessary for relationship, and to speak of God as mother is to lessen that separation. It is a curious theology which argues (rightly) for human autonomy, yet denies that autonomy to God. All monisms, however—particularly the monism of "goddess spirituality" attempt to do this.

Yet this imagery of being in the womb of God is inevitable when we begin to speak of God as mother. (Recall the "re-imagining God" liturgy, cited above, full of imagery of the womb.) David Scott points out how the imagery of being in the womb of God is entering Christian worship these days under considerable feminist pressure. He cites these lines from *Supplemental Liturgical Texts* of the Episcopal church: "O God, from before time you made ready the creation. Through your Wisdom, your Spirit moved over the deep and brought to birth the heavens . . . earth . . . plants and animals; and finally, humankind," and goes on to observe that:

This metaphor . . . implies that the creation is of God's nature, since a child is of the same (human) nature as its mother. It was precisely for this reason that classical Christian theology insisted on the eternal generation of the Son from the Father and differentiated this act from God's creation of the world. That which is generated of God is God.[29]

To be a *creature*, on the other hand, is a far different relationship than to be a biological child, and it is precisely this creaturely state which is evoked by the paradoxical language of being created by the word of God the Father. Our relationship to the Creator is not one of birth, or emanation, or descent, or any kind of physical continuity: it is a gift from the Other, who does us the great and dangerous honour of allowing us "autonomy" however we misuse it. Scott elaborates on the uniqueness of this creaturely relationship:

> Classical Christianity teaches that God made the world; God did not generate or beget the world. That is, the created world is not of God's own nature. Rather, the creation has its own unique constitution and nature, marked by real existence, dependent on God's creative and sustaining will yet real in its own right. Thus . . . the early theologians intentionally and consciously made a fundamental distinction between the eternal Word's relation to God and the creation's relation to God. This was the distinction between the generation of the Son and the creation of the world. The begotten Son, the second person of the Trinity, issues forth from the being of the Father. He shares the divine substance and nature. He is of the Godhead. The creation, on the other hand, is made out of nothing by the will and pleasure of the Creator. It is not of the divine nature; it does not participate in the eternity and being of God, but enjoys its own kind of reality—dependent, contingent, and real in its specific creaturely way.[30]

Elizabeth Achtemeier makes the same point about the strange fact of male language for the creator. Like Scott, she makes it in response to the recent, unprecedented appearance in Christian worship of feminine language for God:

> The United Church of Christ's *Book of Worship* prays, "You have brought us forth from the womb of your being." A feminine goddess has given birth to the world. But if the creation has issued forth from the body of the deity, it shares in the deity's substance. Deity is in, through, and under all things, and therefore everything is divine. . . . If God is identified with his creation, we finally make ourselves gods and goddesses—the ultimate and primeval sin. . . . But we can never rightly understand ourselves and our place in the universe, the Bible tells us, until we realize that we are not gods and goddesses. Rather, we are creatures, wondrously and lovingly made by a sovereign Creator: "It is he that made us and not we ourselves" (Ps 100:3). The Bible will use no language that undermines that confession. It therefore eschews all feminine language for God that might open the door to such error, and it is rigorous in its opposition to every other religion and cultic practice that identifies creation with creator.[31]

Perhaps it is clear, therefore, why feminine language and imagery for God is not appropriate, even analogically, for it opens the door to the inveterate human tendency to make ourselves divine, part of God.

Yet the powerful feminist criticism remains. The merging of self, God and universe may be a danger in feminine language for God. But is the danger any greater than the implications of a *masculine* language for God? The bitter legacy of Jewish and Christian patriarchs "lording it over" women because they are not as fully in God's image is undeniable. Mary Daly's bitter aphorism—"if God is male, then the male is God"—is mistaken in both its premise and its conclusion. But it is nevertheless a mistake which generations of Christian men have been all too likely to make. For those who are willing to set aside the language and imagery of Scripture, it seems reasonable to risk erring on the other side of the question and speak of the motherhood of God. In what sense then can we speak of "God the Father"?

God our Father through Jesus

There is a profound and biblical answer to that question, one which ultimately is inseparable from the event and the meanings of the Incarnation and the Cross. Put briefly it is this: The "Fatherhood of God" is ours not through the patriarchy of Old Testament religion—which, if it is understood simply as a kind of apotheosis of patriarchy, comes under the same judgment as "matriarchal" religions, and all human idolatries. It is only through Jesus that we call God "father." God is our father only in as he was the father of Jesus. Surprisingly (especially in view of all that has been written, by feminists and others, about the patriarchal father-figure of the Old Testament Jehovah) this is the witness of Scripture as well. The biblical witness is steadfastly against the kind of patriarchy which feminists rightly oppose.

Janet Soskice makes this case clearly in an essay in *Speaking the Christian God* entitled "Can a Feminist call God Father?" Her argument is extraordinarily important for Christians, feminists and (as the title indicates) for all those who make the difficult attempt in these late-modern times at being *both*.

After restating the feminist case against patriarchy—adding a few more horrendous details gleaned from church history, Soskice observes:

> It should be clear from this by no means exhaustive discussion that what disturbs feminist theologians is not simply that God has been styled as male in the tradition, but that God is styled as male in particular ways and especially has been styled as powerful, dominant, and implacable.

This is the feminists' real objection to the rhetoric of patriarchy: not just that it subordinates women, but that it also gives divine justification to a hierarchical reading of the world invariably conceived in terms of powerful/powerless, superior/inferior, active/passive, male/female.[32]

If this is indeed the reading of the human condition that one receives from Scripture, then it is no surprise that many feminists abandon Christianity entirely. Here Soskice is inclined to agree with those "post-Christian" feminists who (like Hampson) feel that language of God as "father" cannot be disentangled from the Christian tradition so as to leave much behind. In her words:

> Moreover, it could be argued that any of these strategies, if employed not to complement but to actually replace the Christian language of "God as Father," would result in the institution of a new religion, that the language of "fatherhood" is too deeply rooted in the Christian texts and the religion itself too intimately tied to those texts. Accordingly, the best course for the feminist who could not accept the language of "divine fatherhood" would be not to tinker with models of God but to abandon Christianity, a step from which post-Christian feminists have not shrunk.[33]

It is clear, however, that Soskice herself does not make this move, and her next question is one which all Christians must ask (though the "post-Christian" extreme of feminism has made it a daunting one for most Christians, male or female, to contemplate):

> And as for feminists who find they cannot abandon Christianity? Must we accept all the apparatus of patriarchal religion if we accept the language of God's fatherhood? Is there not another way, a way by which the language of divine fatherhood may be detached from the male idol of patriarchal religion? This is what I would like now to explore.[34]

Many orthodox Christians, committed to the God of Scripture, will cringe at Soskice's use—following what has come to be ideologically-laden rhetoric—of phrases like "the male idol of patriarchal religion." But her question is crucial: does prayer to God as "our Father" imply worship of the God who (for example) spoke no word disapproving Lot's suggestion that the people at the gate violate his daughters instead of his male guests? We cannot easily overlook such "texts of terror" as Phyllis Trible calls them. Yet our commitment to Scripture does not allow us (like some postmodern Marcion) to reject the God of the Old Testament for a kinder and gentler "our Father."

Soskice, drawing heavily on a seminal article by Paul Ricouer, points out first of all that God is described as "father" over 170 times by Jesus in the New Testament, and is never invoked in prayer by any other title.[35] But in the Old Testament, God is spoken of as "father" only eleven times—and is never addressed as father in prayer. He is often described as "God of our fathers," but *never* addressed as "Father." In fact, the central revelation of God in the Old Testament—to Moses at the burning bush—makes clear that he must be recognized as beyond all such analogical descriptions as "father." God's relationship to his people is one of covenant—adoption, not descent or kinship:

> God is not described as "father"; the people of Israel are not true "sons." The prime name of God in Exodus is that given to Moses from the burning bush, I AM THAT I AM. . . . it is a "name" that casts itself in the face of all names of God.[36]

Soskice here quotes Ricouer: "the revelation of the name is the dissolution of all anthropomorphisms, of all figures and figurations, including that of father. The name against the idol."[37]

In the context of the paganism of the religions of the Near East, the question of whether God is to be called "father" or "mother" pales into insignificance before the revelation of God's otherness in the name by which he reveals himself: "I AM THAT I AM." As Soskice says: "The God of Israel is defined, then, over and against father gods, gods who beget the world. . . ."[38] And also, obviously, against all "mother gods" who bear the world in the womb. In the Old Testament, the full intimacy of God with his creatures is yet to be revealed: but it will not be revealed so long as people continue to confuse the created with the Creator.

Soskice continues, to her main point:

> paradoxically, it is this abolition of the biological father God that makes non-idolatrous , metaphorical "father language" about God possible. By means of a number of other designations (liberator, lawgiver, the bearer of name without image) space is created where God may be called father. Movement may then take place to the designation of God as father, which occurs in the prophets, to declaration of the father, and finally the invocation to God as father, complete only with the prayer which Jesus asks us to pray, with him, to the Father.[39]

It is only through Jesus that we can call God father. The "fatherhood of

God" is ours not through our participation in a real or imagined hierarchical past; rather it is a possibility which calls us from the future, a future opened by Jesus' death on the cross, and by his resurrection from the dead.

In the Christian understanding, the death of Jesus shows us the most important part about God: not that "He" is a distant and domineering father—nor that "She" is the nurturing breasts and womb of the Universe; rather, that God, the totally other, has, from the beginning of time, poured himself out for us, allowed us to be a person, by graciously inviting us into relationship with the One who is, from all eternity self-giving relationship. "Abba" is above all a term of intimacy and relationship—a term which comes from within the family. Soskice quotes Ricouer's words again: the "Fatherhood" of God for us "does not look backwards towards a great ancestor, but forward, in the direction of a new intimacy on the model of the knowledge of the son . . . there is a father because there is a family and not the reverse."[40]

The feminist cry is not "I want power," but "I want to be human." But that is the cry of every human, out of the deep spiritual poverty of our times. We can speak of "the fatherhood of God" not because he commands us with patriarchal strength and wealth, but rather because he woos us, in a self-giving that overturns all our human notions of power, into the communion and love which is the very nature of God: "For you know the grace of our Lord Jesus Christ, that though he was rich, yet for your sakes he became poor, so that you through his poverty might become rich." Thus, through Jesus, can we prodigal sons and daughters say "Abba, Father."

Endnotes

1. "Feminism" is an inadequate term, not only because it can mean such a wide range of things, but because it is often used (especially by Christians) as a term of reproach. I use it in what follows as a kind of shorthand for "any way of thinking or action which encourage reflection and action on the full humanity of women," but I am speaking mainly of *ideological* feminism: that is, feminism when it is considered as one's central, guiding philosophy of life.

2. "Postmodernity" (like feminism) is not a very satisfactory term, but I use it nevertheless in this paper to describe the many critiques of the depersonalizing consequences of the modern era which surfaced in the last quarter of the twentieth century. The term is unsatisfactory because all "postmodernities" are themselves thoroughly compromised by the modernity they critique. Nevertheless the term retains some usefulness as a way of describing a critical awareness of the "iron cage" of the modern.

3. Walker Percy, *Lost in the Cosmos: The Last Self-Help Book* (New York: Washington Square Press, 1983), p. 47.

4. The ideological feminist attitude to the body on the matter of abortion, however, reflects the deep inconsistency which runs all through postmodern "spiritualities." On the one hand, feminism stresses the importance of connectedness: a concern reflected in the frequent appearance of circles and cycles in feminist literature. However, when it comes to the connection of the foetus to the mother and to the actions of the mother and the father, the circle of personal freedom quickly becomes more important than the circle of connectedness. The right of a woman to be absolute mistress of her body transcends and cancels those other connections. This elevation of personal fulfilment and autonomy above all other concerns underlies the considerable change in sexual ethics which marks the postmodern period.

5. Dedication to *Reweaving the World: The Emergence of Ecofeminism,* ed. Irene Diamond and Gloria Orenstein (San Francisco: Sierra Club Books, 1990), p. iii.

6. Margaret Daphne Hampson, *Theology and Feminism* (Oxford: Basil Blackwell, 1990), p. 2.

7. Sarah Coakley in *Swallowing a Fishbone? Feminist Theologians Debate Christianity,* ed. Daphne Hampson (London, SPCK, 1996), p. 185, n. 6.

8. Stephen Smith, "Worldview, language, and Radical Feminism: An Evangelical Appraisal," in *Speaking the Christian God: The Holy Trinity and the Challenge of Feminism,* ed. Alvin F. Kimel, Jr. (Grand Rapids, MI: Eerdmans, 1992), p. 274.

9. Carter Heyward, *The Redemption of God: A Theology of Mutual Relation* (Washington, DC: University Press of America, 1982), p. 156.

10. Ursula K. Leguin, *Always Coming Home* (New York: Harper and Row, 1985), p. 200.

11. Susan Griffin, "Curves Along the Road," in *Reweaving the World,* p. 87.

12. Introduction to *Womenspirit Rising: A Feminist Reader in Religion,* eds. Carol Christ and Judith Plaskow (San Francisco: Harper and Row, 1979), p. 3.

13. Mary Daly, *Beyond God the Father: Toward a Philosophy of Women's Liberation* (Boston, MA: Beacon Press, 1973; London: The Women's Press, 1986), p. 19.

14. Christ and Plaskow, *Womanspirit Rising,* p. 3.

15. The move from ideological feminism to neo-paganism is a short one. A survey conducted by Margot Adler for a revised edition of her important study of neo-paganism called *Drawing Down the Moon* asks people to identify the influences which led them to Neo- paganism, and the one cited most frequently was "feminism."

16. In *Full Circle,* a National Film Board of Canada documentary.

17. Hampson, *Swallowing a Fishbone,* p. 15.

18. *Ibid.*

19. *Ibid.,* p. 1.

20. *Ibid.*

21. Hampson, *Theology and Feminism,* p. 145.

22. Starhawk, "Witchcraft and Women's Culture" in Christ and Plaskow, *Womanspirit Rising,* p. 70.

23. Cited in *Either/Or: The Gospel or Neo-Paganism* ed. Carl E. Braaten and Robert W. Jenson (Grand Rapids, Michigan, 1995), p. 3.

24. Rosemary Radford Ruether, "Motherearth and the Megamachine: A Theology of Liberation in a Feminine, Somatic and Ecological Perspective," in Christ and Plaskow, *Womanspirit Rising,* p. 52.

25. Elizabeth Achtemeier, "Exchanging God for 'No Gods': A Discussion of Female Language for God," in Kimel, *Speaking the Christian God,* p. 7.

26. *Ibid.*

27. *Ibid.,* pp. 8–9.

28. Rudy Wiebe, *My Lovely Enemy* (Toronto: McClelland & Stewart, 1983), pp. 140–41.

29. David Scott, "Creation as Christ: A Problematic Theme in Some Feminist Theology" in Kimel, *Speaking the Christian God,* p. 249.

30. *Ibid.,* pp. 245–46.

31. *Ibid.,* p. 9.

32. Janet Soskice, "Can a Feminist Call God Father?" in Kimel, *Speaking the Christian God,* p. 86.

33. *Ibid,* p. 87.

34. *Ibid.*

35. Paul Ricouer, "Fatherhood: from Phantasm to Symbol" in *The Conflict of Interpretations: Essays in Hermeneutics,* ed. D. Ihde (Evanston, IL: Northwestern University Press, 1974), pp. 468 ff.

36. Soskice, p. 89.

37. Ricoeur, "Fatherhood," p. 486, as quoted in Soskice, p. 89.

38. Soskice, p. 90.

39. *Ibid.*

40. *Ibid.*

CHAPTER 7

Homosexuality and the Christian Sex Ethic

Stanley J. Grenz

In October 1996, Christian leaders from across Canada gathered in Toronto for the gala World Shapers '96 conference sponsored by the Evangelical Fellowship of Canada (EFC). While the thousand conferees were putting the final touches on the opening night festivities—heartily singing "Bind Us Together"—members of the Word of Life Church in nearby St. Catharine's broke the unanimity of the event by scattering about pamphlets critical of the EFC. EFC's flagship journal, *Faith Today*, had just published an essay on human sexuality that Word of Life's pastor, Peter Youngren, claimed denied the power of the gospel to deliver homosexuals from their "sinful, God-dishonoring condition."

Barely a year later, a group of concerned citizens (including several conservative Christians) sought to hold an open-air public informational forum in downtown Vancouver to focus on the inappropriateness of using certain literature on homosexuality in the public schools.

The meeting, however, never got off the ground. A cadre of shouting gay and lesbian activists took control of the microphones and intimidated would-be attendees, while law enforcement officers stood idly by.

These two events—instigated by people whom we might dismiss as occupying opposite fringes of the political spectrum—stand as reminders of just how emotionally charged and potentially divisive the issue of homosexuality has become—not only in North American society, but also within the church.

Conservative Christians believe the Bible speaks clearly to this issue, and they note that, throughout its history, the church consistently and unequivocally has opposed homosexual behaviour. But why?

In what follows, I seek to answer this question. My intent is to go beneath the strictures themselves and draw out from the foundational biblical narrative the ethical stance that motivated biblical writers—including Paul and the compiler(s) of the Holiness Code—to declare same-sex intercourse "unnatural" and, thus, unethical.

My assumption is that, despite any influence other sources had on them, these authors were imbued with the narratives of God, acting in human history, that lay at the foundation of the Hebrew and early Christian faith communities.

Consequently, the scriptural injunctions against homosexual practises were embedded in a teleological understanding of the "natural." This understanding derived fundamentally from an outlook towards God's intention for human life as depicted in the biblical narrative. For the biblical writers, then, the "natural" is what is in accordance with God's *telos* (purpose) for human existence. And divine purposes encompass human sexual practice.

In keeping with this assumption, I begin the discussion by placing human sexuality in the context of the biblical narrative. My goal in this first section is to set forth in summary fashion a Christian theological understanding of sexuality and marriage.

The theological understanding of sexuality that emerges from these reflections, in turn, provides the foundation for an ethical appraisal of same-sex intercourse. Then, I next interact with the question of sin as it relates to same-sex intercourse and homosexuality in general. Finally, I round out the discussion with a few comments about homosexuality and sexual expression. In this manner, I develop a basically teleological approach to the contemporary issue, an approach that draws from considerations of God's *telos* for human relationships[1] as given, in part, in the creation narratives.

Human Sexuality in Theological Perspective

An awareness of human sexual distinctions appears almost immediately in the biblical story. Standing at the apex of the first creation narrative is God's fashioning of humankind in the divine image as male and female (Gen 1:27-28).

Sexual differentiation is even more prominent in the second creation story, which focuses on God's creation of the woman to deliver the man from his solitude (Gen 2:18-24).

Throughout the Bible, the creation stories play an ongoing role, even in texts that emerged within different social contexts. Paul, for example, appealed to the Genesis narratives, even though he lived in the more urban, less agrarian culture of the first-century Roman Empire.

Thus, the creation of humankind as male and female is central to the understanding of human sexuality found throughout the entire biblical story. This broader creation-based understanding lies behind the biblical injunctions that depict homosexual intercourse as "unnatural" and, hence, unethical.

The Nature of Human Sexuality

Human beings are sexual creatures. But what is the significance of our sexuality?[2]

One answer, according to the biblical narrative, is procreation. Procreation is a crucial aspect of our creation as male and female, especially after the Fall (e.g., Gen 4:1). Yet, the begetting of children is not the only purpose for our creation as both male and female.

The second creation story suggests that our sexuality is not limited to the physical characteristics and activities associated with male and female reproductive roles. Sexuality encompasses our fundamental existence in the world as embodied people. It includes our way of being in and relating to the world. Above all, however, sexuality represents our incompleteness as embodied creatures. Hence, sexuality lies behind the human quest for completeness. This yearning for wholeness, which we express through our seemingly innate drive to bond with others, forms an important basis for the interpersonal dimension of existence.

This Genesis narrative highlights the interpersonal aspect of human sexuality. The story presents the creation of the woman as God's solution to Adam's solitude. The man enjoyed a relationship with the animals; yet none of them could provide what he truly needed—a partner with whom he could bond. Cognizant of this situation, God created another—the woman—to deliver Adam from his isolation. The man greeted her with the joyous declaration: She is "bone of my bones, and flesh of my flesh" (Gen 2:23). The episode concludes with the narrator's application to the phenomenon of male-female bonding: "For this reason a man will leave his father and mother and be united to his wife, and they will become one flesh" (v. 24). In this manner, the narrator points out that the drive toward bonding finds expression in the coming together of male and female in the unity of people we know as marriage.

The interpersonal dynamic, however, is not limited to the sexual bond. Our creation as male and female also contributes to personal identity development. We discover—or construct—who we are in our embodied maleness or femaleness partly through our interactions with the other sex.

This dimension of our sexuality also is evident in the second creation account. Adam first sensed his own maleness when confronted with the woman. That encounter led him to declare joyfully, "She shall be called 'woman' for she was taken out of man" (Gen 2:23). In a sense, this aspect of the story provides an explanation of the first narrative, which links the *imago dei* to our creation as male and female (Gen 2:27). We discover God's intention for us to be the divine image bearers—and, hence, discover our full humanness—through our interaction with one another as male and female. This can occur within marriage, of course, but it is also operative in all male-female relationships.

The Old Testament narrative views the sexual bond between husband and wife as the foundation for human social relationships—family, tribe and, eventually, nation. Jesus, however, inaugurated one significant alteration to this pattern. Rather than elevating earthly ancestry, he looked to his heavenly parentage, counting as his true family, "whoever does the will of my Father in heaven" (Mt 12:50). In keeping with his own example, Jesus challenged his followers to place their relationship to him above all familial ties (Mt 10:37). And he promised them a new spiritual family to compensate for the loss that discipleship would exact from them (Mk 10:29-30).

According to Jesus, the primary human bond is not marriage and family, as important as these are, but the company of disciples. In this manner, human sexuality—understood as the quest to forsake our solitude through relations with others—finds ultimate fulfillment through participation in the community of believers who enjoy fellowship with God through Christ. And our innate incompleteness, related as it is to our fundamental sexuality, points toward the consummation of God's activity in the community of God's eternal kingdom.

En route to that future day, humans enter into a variety of personal relationships. Most of these are informal and somewhat fluid. Others are permanent and exclusive. Although both are the outworking of the human drive toward bonding and, hence, in this sense are "sexual," they differ widely, including with respect to the type of sexual behaviour proper to each. In this manner, the biblical narrative provides the foundation for a rich understanding of human sexuality that forms a stark contrast to what the Dutch gay theologian, Pim Pronk, bemoans as the modern "static-mechanical" model.

The model Pronk critiques treats human behaviour as divisible into autonomous parts, among which is sexual activity. It draws a sharp distinction between sexual and non-sexual behaviour on the basis of whether or not the sex organs are involved. And it views the link between the sex drive and sexual behaviour somewhat like the connection between "the wound-up alarm clock and its going off."[3]

Pronk concludes that this static-mechanical view suffers from a "one-sided accent on the *private* character of sexual relations" and, as a result, it "fails to do justice to the social dimension" of human sexuality.[4]

Sexuality and Marriage

Historically, the most significant social expression of human sexuality is marriage. Viewed from the perspective of the Bible, marriage entails the coming together of male and female to form an exclusive sexual bond. The biblical writers connect this human relationship with procreation and child-rearing, as well as a focal point for companionship as husband and wife share intimacy and friendship.

Marriage carries another crucial meaning in Scripture: It provides a metaphor of spiritual truth. The bond uniting husband and wife symbolizes certain aspects of the relation between God and God's people.

The Old Testament prophets found in marriage an appropriate vehicle for telling the story of Yahweh's faithfulness in the face of Israel's idolatry.

The New Testament authors drew from this Old Testament imagery (e.g., Rom 9:25; 1 Pet 2:9-10). They spoke of marriage as a picture of the great mystery of salvation—the union of Christ and the Church. Marriage illustrates Christ's self-sacrifice for the Church, as well as submission to Christ (Eph 5:21-33) by people who anticipate the future coming of their Lord (Mt 2:1-13; Rev 19:7; 21:9; 21:2).

In this manner, marriage provides a picture of the exclusive nature of our relationship to God in Christ. Just as marriage is to be an exclusive, inviolate and, hence, holy bond, so also our relationship to God must be exclusive and holy for, as God's covenant people, we can serve no other gods but the one God (Ex 20:3). By extension, the exclusive love shared by husband and wife reflects the holiness of the divine love present within the triune God, which then overflows from God to creation.

The ancient Hebrews clearly viewed marriage as normative. The New Testament, however, opened the way for believers to fulfill a divine vocation as single people, evidenced by John the Baptist, Jesus and Paul. This dimension of the biblical narrative reminds us that, whether married or single, we all enter into a variety of informal relationships and friendships with others. These friendships need not be permanent, they rarely are exclusive (that is, limited to only two people), and they seldom are entered through formal covenant.

Relationships between single people provide the clearest example of a non-exclusive, non-marital friendship bond. Like marriage, friendship carries theological meaning. In contrast to the marital union, the informal friendship bond is less defined and, therefore, more open to the inclusion of others. Further, the dynamic of love involved in friendship generally is not contained within exclusive boundaries. For this reason, friendship reflects the open, non-exclusive, expanding aspect of God's love—the divine love that seeks to include within the circle of fellowship those still outside its boundaries.

Sexuality and the Sex Act

As several contemporary philosophers have pointed out, events are more than physical happenings because every event always occurs within a context that contributes to its meaning. Similarly, the meaning of a human act is dependent not only on the act itself, but also on the context in which it transpires, which includes the actor's intent.[5]

As a human act, sexual intercourse is more than a physical occurrence. It is a highly meaningful metaphor. But the meaning of any act of sexual intercourse is dependent both on the physical act itself and the context in which it occurs. The participants pour meaning into the act by the intent that motivates them and by the relationship they bring to it.

The Christian ethic is based on the belief that God intends the sex act to carry specific meanings. Sexual intercourse is not valuable primarily as a means to some other goal, including such good purposes as pleasure or pregnancy. Rather, the sex act is what Roman Catholic ethicist James Hanigan calls a symbolic or ritual activity. He writes, "Sex, then, finds its proper value as an act which focuses, celebrates, expresses and enhances the meaning of our substantive activities and relationships."[6]

In part, we may view sexual intercourse as the ritual that celebrates committed, loving relationships. Yet, each of us enjoys many such relationships, which we celebrate in various non-genital ways. In fact, sexual intercourse would deeply wound, if not completely destroy, most of these relationships. Consequently, the context in which the sex act occurs is crucial, so much so that in certain contexts the sex act simply is inappropriate. According to the biblical writers, the divinely-intended meanings of the sex act emerge only when the act occurs within one specific context—marriage.

Practised within marriage as the sign of the unconditional, convenantal love of husband and wife, sexual intercourse carries several important meanings. It is a beautiful symbol of the exclusive bond between the marriage partners, through which wife and husband reaffirm their commitment to each other. Further, it is a beautiful celebration of the mutuality of the relationship, as each partner reaffirms his or her desire to give pleasure to the other. And, because of its connection to procreation, the sex act expresses the openness of husband and wife to the new life that may arise from their bond.

Because of the meanings the sex act is intended to carry, the marital bond provides the sole proper context for sexual intercourse. The Old Testament law codified this view (e.g., Ex 20:14), and Jesus and the New Testament apostles reaffirmed it (e.g., Mt 19:3-9; 1 Cor 6:9).

As a result, the traditional Christian sex ethic rightly advocates chastity in the form of abstinence in singleness and fidelity in marriage. This ethic, in turn, provides the foundation for a Christian stance toward homosexuality.

Christian Sex Ethic and Same-Sex Intercourse

Most participants in the contemporary discussion agree that certain homosexual practises—like certain heterosexual practises—are morally wrong. Lists of immoral behaviours commonly include such abuses as prostitution, rape and pederasty. But does this ethical judgment extend to all homosexual acts? More specifically, is same-sex intercourse morally wrong even when practised within the context of a loving gay or lesbian relationship?

In dealing with this question, I will avoid the pattern of some advocates of the traditional position who enumerate the purported harmful physical or psychological effects of involvement in various homosexual behaviours.[7] Nor will I deal with the reciprocal argument of those who claim that homosexual liaisons must be affirmed simply because "they harm no one."[8]

I want to probe the ethics of same-sex intercourse viewed apart from any "side-effects" it may or may not have. My goal here is to determine in what sense the act may be deemed unethical in and of itself. What is it about this practice that makes it morally suspect even when it occurs within the context of a stable homosexual relationship?

Same-Sex Intercourse as a Deficient Act

As previously stated, the significance of any act arises in part from the context in which it occurs. Similarly, the physical act is important as an appropriate carrier of intended meaning: To serve as an authentic ritual, a physical act must have the capacity to symbolize the reality it ritualizes.[9] Viewed from this perspective, same-sex intercourse is deficient as a vehicle for conveying the intended meaning of the sex act. Because it ritually cannot enact the reality it symbolizes, it fails to make that reality present.

According to the biblical understanding, sexual intercourse involves the coming together of two people as sexual beings in one-flesh union. It represents the act of two becoming one at the deepest level of their being (e.g., Gen 2:23-24; Mt 19:4-6).

As a result, the sex act entails more than the experience of sexual climax. (Indeed, sexual climax can occur apart from sexual intercourse.)

More crucial than the ability to attain sexual climax is the capability of the sex act to symbolize the uniting of two sexual people into one. As a ritual act, sexual intercourse must be able to represent physically (and, thus, make present) the two-in-one sexual bond it symbolizes.

This meaning readily is expressed in sexual relations between a man and a woman. Each engages in the sex act through the whole body, of course, but primarily through those body parts (vagina and penis) that most explicitly symbolize their existence as embodied, sexual beings; that most explicitly separate male from female; and that most readily allow male and female to complement each other. In this manner, both their own personal identities and the "otherness" or difference from each other as sexual creatures become the foundation for the expression of the bond they share. As a result, the sex act itself serves as a ritual act, an appropriate symbol of the union of two who are sexually "other" into a sexual bond.

It is not surprising that male-female intercourse provides such a vivid symbol of the sexual bond. As James Hanigan observes, "The unity ritualized and enacted in sexual behaviour is a two-in-one flesh unity, a unity that has its created basis in the physical and biological complementarity of male and female."[10]

The partners in same-sex intercourse also bring to the act the physical features that most deeply represent their existence as sexual beings. But in this act, the specific body part each contributes to the act does not represent what distinguishes them from each other. Nor does it represent the unique contribution each brings to their sexual union because their roles in the act can be interchanged.

Further, in same-sex intercourse, some other body part (finger or artificial penis in lesbian acts, mouth or anus in male homosexual acts) routinely substitutes for the sexual organ that neither partner can provide. But whenever this occurs, one or the other partner presses an aspect of his or her anatomy into the service of the sex act that, because it is not the definitive mark of the person as a sexual being, is not normally viewed as sexual.

In this manner, same-sex intercourse loses the symbolic dimension of two-becoming-one that is present in male-female sex. At best, it only is a simulation of the two-becoming-one ritual that the act of sexual intercourse is designed to be. And a homosexual couple only can imitate the unity of two people joining together as sexual "others," so vividly symbolized in male-female coitus.

Hence, Hanigan is correct in concluding that homosexual acts ultimately are "only pretense or imaginative simulations of the real thing."[11]

Sexual Intercourse within the Wrong Context

If acts derive their meaning from the context in which they occur, then same-sex intercourse also is deficient because it occurs within an improper context. That is, the context in which it is practised—even if it is a stable gay or lesbian relationship—does not confirm the intended meaning of the sex act.

To understand this, we must return to the three meanings of the sex act within the context of marriage. At first glance, it would appear that when practised in the context of a stable, monogamous homosexual relationship, same-sex intercourse could carry at least two of these meanings. The act conceivably could mark the celebration of the lifelong commitment of the two partners to each other, as well as the mutuality of their relationship.

Less possible, obviously, is the third meaning. Because children simply are not procreated in this manner, same-sex intercourse cannot express the openness of the couple to new life arising from their bond. At best, the act serves as an imitation of male-female procreative intercourse.

Are we to conclude, then, that ultimately the only basis on which same-sex intercourse can be discounted is its lack of procreative potential?

No. We drew from the biblical narrative the idea that the sex act is the ritual celebration of the exclusive bond of two people united in a one-flesh union. And we concluded that, when viewed from the biblical perspective, the marriage of male and female is the only appropriate expression of that exclusive sexual bond. Of course, this conclusion rules same-sex sexual bonding out of court, even when it involves a mutual, life-long commitment.

But why privilege heterosexual marriage? Why set up the male-female sexual bond as the standard? Why could we not view same-sex intercourse as the expression of the bond uniting two people of the same sex, analogous to heterosexual intercourse as the ritual sexual act in marriage?

One response arises from another consideration drawn from the physical aspect of the sex act itself. It is instructive to note that, by its very nature, any specific occurrence of male-female sexual intercourse involves—and only can involve—two people, a male and a female. This characteristic forges a close link between the sex act and the reality it ritualizes because the sex act provides a vivid symbol with the begetting of children for, biologically, a child is the union of the contributions of two people—the biological father and the biological mother.

At this point, however, same-sex intercourse fundamentally differs from heterosexual intercourse. There is nothing inherent in this physical act that would limit involvement to two people. This observation leads us to ask: On what ritual basis would any homosexual bond necessarily consist of two and only two? If there is no intrinsic aspect of the ritual act that limits its participants to two, why should anyone privilege "monogamous" homosexual relations?

Further, if nothing intrinsic to the act inherently symbolizes the reality of two-becoming-one, then same-sex intercourse—even when practised within a stable homosexual relationship—simply is unable to ritualize exclusivity. In contrast to heterosexual intercourse, it cannot function as the celebration of an exclusive bond and, therefore, cannot point to the exclusivity of the relationship God desires to have with us. In this way, same-sex intercourse loses the spiritual meaning of the sex act.

The same conclusion arises from a consideration of the nature of the bond being celebrated in the sex act. When viewed from the perspective we outlined earlier, same-sex intercourse entails a confusing of the bond of informal friendship with the male-female sexual bond of marriage.

We already noted that the otherness of the marital relationship is crucial to its symbolic significance. As Max Stackhouse declared, "the marriage bond is a community of love between those who are 'other.' This means not simply 'another' person, but one who is truly 'other.'"[12] Just as homosexual people cannot ritualize a two-become-one unity in the act of intercourse, so also they cannot become become a two-become-one unity in the shared life of unity and difference that typifies the marriage of male and female.[13] Stackhouse reminds us of one reason why this is crucial:

The marriage of a man to a woman...remains the normative physical, social, and moral sign that we are not meant to be isolated individuals or to focus only on relationships with those who are already much like us. We are created for community with the Divine Other and with the human other, and the bonding of sexual otherness is the immediate and obvious evidence of this.[14]

Similarly, psychologist Ruth Tiffany Barnhouse appeals to the Song of Songs in declaring that "sexuality in itself is a symbol of wholeness, of the reconciliation of opposites, of the loving at-one-ment between God and Creation."[15]

These statements lead us back to the central significance of marriage that we noted earlier; namely, its theological symbolism. As the biblical writers themselves suggest, the exclusive bond of husband and wife forms a fitting metaphor of the exclusivity of the divine-human relationship. The sex act, in turn, is the ritual celebration of this exclusive bond. A homosexual relationship is not an appropriate context for the sex act because, in the context of such a relationship, sexual intercourse simply cannot express this intended meaning.

This is evident when we realize that every stable same-sex relation is, in fact, an informal bond between or among friends. As we noted earlier, the friendship bond ought not to find ritualized expression in a sexual act. Several considerations point out why this is so.

First, although like marriage friendship includes unity and difference, the difference exemplified between or among friends is not a sexual difference; same-sex friends do not manifest unity and difference sexually.[16]

Further, friendships can wither and die without necessarily incurring moral fault on the part of any of the friends. Although in marriage both friendship and sexual attraction can and do die, the biblical writers suggest that the severing of the marital relationship itself always involves moral fault, however hard it might be to pinpoint that fault.

Finally, friendship—which generally is neither an exclusive nor a formalized bond—proclaims the inclusive, rather than the exclusive, love of God. The intent of the sex act, however, is to celebrate exclusivity, not inclusivity.

Same-sex intercourse, then, introduces into the friendship bond the language of exclusivity and permanence that properly belongs solely to marriage. Of course, we could back away from the grammar of pair-bonding and conclude that same-sex intercourse intends to say nothing more than "I find you attractive." But mutual attraction never is a sufficient basis for sexual intimacy, regardless of the sexual preference of the people involved. As ethicist Edward Batchelor pointed out, "love does not always justify sexual union." The implication for homosexual attraction follows: "It is every bit as likely that the love of man for man or woman for woman bids them refrain from sexual intercourse as that it urges them to it."[17]

The Christian Ethic and Homosexuality

I have looked at the implications of a Christian theology of sexuality for same-sex intercourse. In this process, I drew from the divine *telos* for human sexual relationships as indicated in the foundational series of Genesis and reiterated in the New Testament to indicate why the sex act properly cannot occur within a homosexual relationship. In this sense, same-sex intercourse is "unnatural."

What does all this have to say about the contemporary phenomenon of homosexuality understood as a stable sexual orientation or preference? Specifically, in what sense, if any, is homosexuality sinful?

En route to an answer, I will look at the contemporary argument favouring a positive outlook toward homosexuality as a sexual "inversion." Only then can I seek to chart an alternative.

The "Naturalness" of Homosexuality

Many proponents of a more open stance view homosexuality as a stable sexual preference, which properly finds expression in acts such as same-sex intercourse. In effect, the apologetic for this position turns the biblical condemnation of homosexual behaviour on its head. In contrast to Paul and others who claim that same-sex acts are "against nature," proponents assert that homosexuality, in fact is "natural."

By "natural," some theorists mean nothing more than homosexuality is a naturally occurring phenomenon among humans. The central foundation for this approach is its purported presence in a variety of societies throughout history.

This approach, however, has been exploded by social constructivists such as David Greenberg,[18] who point out that homosexuality is not a single, identifiable, transcultural human condition. Instead, understandings of same-sex practises vary from culture to culture. These range from the ritualized rites of passage associated with adolescent sexual development found in several tribal societies[19] to the spiritualized pederasty of certain Greek philosophers, who down-played any actual physical content within such relationships.[20]

Other proponents speak of the naturalness of homosexual preference in more individualistic terms. Homosexuality is natural, they assert, in that it is not the product of conscious personal choice. Rather than choosing their sexual orientation, this argument purports, gays and lesbians "discover" their homosexuality as a pre-existing reality. As Christian gay activist and writer Chris Glaser declared, "In my experience, sexual orientation was a given, like race or gender. How I responded in faith to that given was what was spiritually significant to me."[21] Christine Gudorf draws out the erroneous, but commonly asserted, ethical implication:

> The agreement within medical and social science that sexual orientation is not chosen but more commonly discovered absolves homosexual orientation of sinfulness, and calls into question...the unnaturalness of homosexual acts for those with homosexual orientation.[22]

Statements such as these are an important reminder that most people do not consciously set out to develop a specific sexual preference. At the same time, claims about its unchosen nature often harbour an overly simplistic picture of the development of homosexuality.

While the jury still is out on what causes any specific instance, most scientists and psychologists agree that a constellation of factors—biological predispositions, personal experiences and the attitudes and actions of others (including parents)—can contribute to disposing a person toward same-sex preference.

To this list we ought to add the constellation of a social identities and roles that social constructionists like Greenberg declare are involved in the construction of homosexuality. Yet, in this equation, we dare not overlook the likelihood of some element of personal choice. Certain psychologists conclude that homosexuality is a pattern that develops over time and this conclusion opens the possibility of a limited, yet nevertheless active role, of the person himself or herself. In short, as the designation itself suggests, one's sexual orientation also is in some sense his or her sexual "preference," even if once set that preference "can hardly be abolished by an arbitrary act of will," to cite Greenberg's assessment.[23]

More important, however, is the ethical critique of this perspective. Ethicists remind us that to argue from any supposed natural reality to moral rectitude is to commit the "naturalistic fallacy;" that is, to deduce an "ought" from an "is." Ethics, however, is not the condoning of what is natural. Thus, even if homosexuality were indisputably "natural" for certain people, this would not in and of itself justify their engaging in same-sex practises.

Christian ethics takes this critique an additional step: In contrast to those who assert that no one can be held responsible for acting according to his or her true nature, the Christian tradition declares that personal responsibility is not limited to matters in which we have full personal choice.

Why not? This question leads to the concept of sin. Viewed from the biblical perspective, sin means "missing the mark;" that is, failing to live up to God's intention for our lives. Rather than a somewhat localized debilitation, this failure can be felt in all areas of human existence and its presence predates our conscious choices. This, in part, is what the Reformers meant by "depravity."

Because of our depravity, we find at work within us desires, impulses and urges we did not consciously choose but which, instead, feel quite normal. Yet, we dare not entrust ourselves to our natural inclinations for these are not a sure guide to proper conduct. Jesus himself declared that evil deeds proceed from the human heart (Mk 7:21). Consequently, he instructed his disciples to distrust what they may perceive to be their natural inclinations and follow a radically new ethic.

Caution is necessary as much in our sexual conduct as in any aspect of life. The supposed naturalness of a person's same-sex preference does not set aside the biblical call to engage in genital sexual expression exclusively within monogamous heterosexual marriage. To assert otherwise, once again, is to commit the "naturalistic fallacy" of arguing from "what is" to "what ought to be."[24] The same fallacy would be at work if I were to set aside the biblical call to marital fidelity on the basis of the claim that, as a male, I naturally am promiscuous, as contemporary sociobiology suggests.

Rather than excusing us on the basis of the sensed naturalness of our inclinations, the Bible offers divine grace in the midst of the realities of life. This grace brings both forgiveness of our trespasses and power to overcome the workings of our human fallenness in the concrete situations that we face.

This cautionary stance toward the appeal to what is natural must be tempered, however, by one additional consideration. Christian ethics does derive an "ought" from an "is,"[25] and "is" does determine the Christian moral imperative. But this "is" ultimately is neither what once was, nor what now is. Instead, it is a future "is"—a "will be."

Specifically, the "is" that provides the Christian ethical "ought" is the future reality of the new creation. Our calling is to exhibit in our relationships in the here and now God's intentions for human existence, which will be present in their fullness only in the future new community.

While the Christian moral imperative arises out of a future "is," this future does not come as a total contradiction to what is truly natural in the present. As the fullness of God's intention for human relationships, the future community is the completion of what God set forth "in the beginning."

And a crucial aspect of what God has intended for human sexual relationships from the beginning is depicted in the biblical creation narratives. This is why reading those stories in the context of the vision of the new creation provides the foundation for our teleological ethical approach to the question of homosexuality.

The "Sin" of Homosexuality

I have asserted that the felt naturalness of a same-sex sexual preference does not in and of itself provide a sufficient rationale for accepting homosexual behaviour. But the question remains as to whether or not the preference itself is sinful.

Sin, Judgment, Acts and Disposition

The search for an answer leads once again to the biblical understanding of sin. Christian theology maintains that the present world is fallen; that is, creation does not yet correspond to the fullness of God's intention. What can be said about humankind as a whole—and even the universe itself (cf. Rom 8:20-22)—is true of each person as well. Each of us is fallen.

This fallenness extends beyond our specific actions. It encompasses every aspect of our existence, including what might be called our moral disposition (which one day will be conformed to the character of Christ [1 Jn 3:1-3]) and even the body itself in its mortality (which will be transformed at the resurrection [e.g., Rom 8:11, 23]). Is this human fallenness "sin"?

In its widest sense, "sin" refer to every aspect of human life that fails to reflect God's design. Viewed from this perspective, fallenness means that we are sinful in the totality of our existence. At the same time, we generally use the word more narrowly. Thus, we speak about "sins," i.e., specific actions, even transgressions.

The word "sin" immediately conjures up another idea, judgment, that likewise carries two related, yet distinct, meanings. On the one hand, insofar as God one day will transform every dimension of creaturely fallenness, human fallenness comes under divine judgment. On the other hand, the biblical writers consistently reserve the idea of a divine judgment leading to condemnation for sinful acts (e.g., Rom 2:3; 2 Cor 5:10; Rev 20:12).

Putting the two meanings together leads to the conclusion that, as the great physician, God will heal our fallen sinfulness in the new creation and, as our judge, God will condemn our sinful actions. Hence, our fallen disposition is sinful in that it is foundational to our sinning. But it is our sinful acts—which bring God's condemnation upon us—that mark us guilty before God.[26]

Sexual Desire and Lust

God created us as sexual beings. Within us is the drive to leave our isolation and enter into relationships with others and, ultimately with God. We might term this drive "sexual desire" because it arises out of our fundamental embodied existence as sexual creatures.

One aspect of this drive is the "desire for sex"; that is, the urge to form a genital sexual bond with another person.[27] Certain people find at work in their psyche a desire for sex with people of the other sex. For other people, the desire for sex largely, if not exclusively, is targeted toward people of the same sex. At what point does sin enter into the picture? When does what belongs to the goodness of our creaturely existence run counter to God's intention?

It seems that the clearest answer the biblical writers and the Christian tradition offer is "at the point of lust"; that is, at the point when a person harbours the desire for sex with someone who is not his or her spouse (e.g., Mt 5:27-28). Thus, the presence in us of both sexual desire and the desire for sex are the manifestation of the goodness of our creaturely sexuality. These good gifts, however, can come under the power of sin.

With the incursion of sin, the desire for sex gives birth to lust. Lust involves allowing the desire for sex to control us so that the goal of sexual satisfaction has become, in that moment, our god. Lust also entails the harbouring of the desire to engage in inappropriate sexual expressions, including the urge to introduce a genital sexual dimension into relationships in which this dimension would be improper.

What we said earlier suggests that all same-sex relationships are an example of one such improper act. To understand this, we must keep in mind that sexual desire in the sense outlined above does not only lie behind the drive to enter into the bond of marriage, it also gives rise to the desire to enter into friendship bonds—even close, intimate friendships. Such friendships may be formed with people of either sex. The desire to bring genital sexual behaviour into same-sex relationship is problematic ethically because it involves treating a friendship like the marital bond.

But what about the situation of those people for whom homoeroticism has become an ongoing, seemingly stable personal disposition?

A proper response requires that we note where the ethical problem actually lies. The presence of sexual desire or the desire for sex within a person's psyche ethically is not problematic. Instead, the moral difficulty emerges when the person involved harbours—and, thus, creates an ongoing urge—to express the desire for sex in acts that are inappropriate, where the "targets" of these desires are potential or actual friends.

Ultimately, it is lust and its outworking in overt acts—not the gender of those toward whom a person might feel drawn (i.e., a person's disposition)—that incur divine condemnation.

Homosexuality as an Orientation?

One additional question remains to be treated: What about the language of "homosexual orientation" itself? Can we properly talk about "sexual orientation" as separable from sexual acts?

Many evangelical traditionalists find themselves in agreement with proponents of a more open stance at this important point. Both distinguish between a homosexual orientation (or propensity) and homosexual practises.[28] But they do so for quite different reasons.

Gay/lesbian theologians often claim that one's sexual orientation always is good because it is a gift from God. Consequently, the task of the homosexual person is to accept his or her sexual orientation, and this includes acting on the basis of it.

Evangelical traditionalists, in contrast, generally assert that while the Bible condemns homosexual acts, it does not mention the orientation.[29] On this basis, they treat homosexual feelings, attractions, urges, desires and longings as temptations to be mastered, rather than as sins to be confessed. Sin, they add, emerges only when a person acts (whether physically or merely mentally) on these urges. The goal of this approach, of course, is to encourage believers who admit to the ongoing presence of homosexual inclinations, but who are able to resist acting them out.[30]

In a sense, the separation of orientation from behaviour is appropriate. It offers a convenient way of differentiating between what truly requires ethical scrutiny (lust and overt acts) and what does not (the desire for sex as a dimension of human existence). To this end, my argument in the previous section drew from a similar distinction, that of disposition versus conduct. Likewise, the pastoral goal of this separation surely is correct. Feeling guilty about what does not incur guilt simply is not justifiable ethically, and it actually can be counterproductive in the journey of discipleship.

While cautiously affirming its utility, we dare not overlook the dangers that lurk in the use of the contemporary language of sexual orientation. I have noted already that social constructivists object to the idea of homosexuality as a transcultural phenomenon. They point out that the idea of a given, stable same-sex sexual orientation that somehow is natural to a certain percentage of people is more the product of a contemporary social construction than an actual essential reality that sociologically or historically can be documented. By using the language of orientation, we risk transposing a construction of contemporary society into indelible scientific fact.

Further, using this language may encourage a significant group of people to construct, perhaps prematurely, their personal identity (the self) on the basis of these socially-based cognitive tools.

One important potential group is today's adolescents. Research in the human sciences suggests that adolescents often move through a stage in their development in which certain same-sex activities are present. The grammar of sexual orientation may lead certain youths to assume on the basis of such experiences that they constitutionally are homosexual. Ruth Tiffany Barnhouse indicates how such an assumption may work to their detriment:

> Adolescence is a period which requires the utmost of young people in working their way through the enormously difficult transition from childhood to adulthood ... the anxieties surrounding the psychosexual maturation process are severe, and the temptation to opt for less than one is capable of is very great. While it is probably true that one cannot proselytize the invulnerable, there are a great many youngsters whose childhoods have been sufficiently problematic so that homosexuality presented to them as an acceptable alternative would be convincingly attractive.[31]

The "threat," however, is not limited to young people. The widespread use of the language of sexual orientation tempts each of us in a potentially detrimental direction. It may lead us to place our sense of having a sexual orientation, and with it our desire for sex, at the centre of our understanding or ourselves and others.

But as certain radical lesbian theologians have asked rhetorically, "Why should the sex of those we desire to sleep with be the determining characteristic of our identity?"[32] Indeed, just as "one's life does not consist in the abundance of possessions" (Lk 12:15), so also there is more to human existence than the desire for sex.

There is yet a deeper theological issue at stake. The uncritical use of the language of sexual orientation may lead us to blindly accept the therapeutic focus rampant in our society. Traditional psychologists routinely assert that homosexual practises, in the end, are the outworking of a psychological maladjustment or a "disorientation."[33] Such assertions, however, replace the moral discussion with a disease model and turn a debate about ethics into a discussion of cures for a psychological illness. David Greenberg offers this sobering reminder:

> Though the Renaissance sodomite was depicted as a monster whose vice signified a repudiation of God and nature, no one suggested that he suffered from a disease and required therapy ... His repudiation of God and morality was considered volitional; it was his acts, not his physiology or psychology, that made him monstrous.[34]

While Greenberg's choice of the word "monstrous" is unfortunate, his main point is well taken.

The potential problems of "sexual orientation" language ought to give us pause before we too quickly adopt it. Nevertheless, being able to distinguish between homoeroticism and its outworking in thought and overt act—that is, between disposition and conduct—has certain positive benefits in discussing the ethics of homosexuality. Perhaps the best designation, given these considerations, is "sexual preference."

Homosexual People and Sexual Expression

These conclusions raise one final question: What viable options are there for homoerotic people to express their sexuality? And does the stance argued here mean that a same-sex sexual preference "condemns" a person to a life devoid of sexuality?

Sexual Chastity

The position taken in these pages leads to only two ethically feasible options for homosexual people: fidelity within (heterosexual) marriage or abstinent singleness. Invariably, proponents of a more open stance toward homosexuality find this proposal uncharitably narrow. They claim such a narrowing of the options for gays and lesbians simply is unfair.

The fairness critique would carry weight if the call for a life characterized by fidelity in marriage or abstinent singleness were directed solely toward homosexual people. The fact, however, is that the elevation of marriage and abstinent singleness merely is the outworking of an ethic of sexual chastity intended for all people without exception.

Some critics do not find this answer at all compelling. They argue that it is far easier for heterosexual than homosexual people to live out such an ethical proposal. James Nelson, for example, claims that this stance, "demonstrates lack of sensitivity to the gay person's socially-imposed dilemma." Why? Nelson explains: "The heterosexual's abstinence is either freely chosen for a lifetime or it is temporarily until marriage. But the celibacy some Christians would impose on the gay person would be involuntary and unending.[35]

Other critics add that this proposal erroneously assumes that every homosexual person automatically is called to celibacy. Pamela Dickey Young writes, "In making celibacy mandatory for homosexual persons we violate the traditional Protestant emphasis on celibacy as individual calling."[36]

These objections, however, are wide off the mark. The fact that some people may find it easier to live out an ethical ideal does not mitigate against the ideal itself. Each of us could point to dimensions of the Christian ethic that we find ourselves disadvantaged to follow in comparison with other people. But this does not mean that those who uphold the ideal are treating us unjustly.

Further, proponents of a more open stance toward homosexuality often are overly optimistic about the viability of the marriage option for heterosexuals. In contrast to such optimism, many single people attest to the fact that, despite their good intentions and personal willingness, they simply are unable to find a suitable marriage partner.

Likewise, such objections often confuse celibacy and abstinence.[37] Young correctly pointed out that only certain Christians sense a divine call to celibacy, understood as foregoing marriage and genital sexual intimacy for the purpose of special service to God and others.[38] But this is not the same as my proposal that unmarried homosexual people commit themselves to abstinence. Unlike celibacy, abstinence in singleness is not a particular calling for certain people, but an ethical ideal for all who are not married. And unlike celibacy, which is a chosen, permanent (or semi-permanent) response to a sensed call from God, the commitment to abstinence in singleness is a particular, and for many people temporary, outworking of the overarching call to a life of sexual chastity that comes to all. This general call to chastity, while remaining the same call, demands a quite different response from married people than it does from single people.

Finally, the objection that this proposal is unfair rests on a highly questionable emphasis on rights. John McNeill, for example defends homosexual behaviour on the basis that "every human being has a God-given right to sexual love and intimacy."[39]

This claim, however, displays a faulty understanding of what a right entails. Love is a relational reality and sexual love, in particular, requires a partner (a lover). For this reason, no one can claim a personal right to sexual love. Such a right would demand that a lover exist somewhere for every person, but no one is entitled to or can be guaranteed a sexual partner.

Further, such a right would place on someone else the corresponding obligation to enter into a sexual relationship with the person who possesses the right. No one, however, can require that someone else love, let alone become sexually intimate with, him or her.

James Hanigan draws out the implications of these considerations for same-sex relations:

> Since, strictly speaking, there is no positive right to sexual satisfaction, sexual fulfillment and sexual happiness, the human desire for such things and the pursuit of these goods, even the nature human orientation to these goods, cannot itself be a justification for doing just anything to achieve them ...

> Therefore, just because a homosexual relationship may possibly be the only way some people can find, or think they can find, a satisfying degree of humanity in their lives does not make such a relationship morally right by that very fact.[40]

In contrast to contemporary proposals such as McNeill's, the New Testament writers do not build their ethic on an appeal to personal rights. Instead, the early Christian leaders were convinced that discipleship entails a call to follow the example of Jesus, who freely laid aside his personal prerogatives for the sake of a higher good (Phil 2:5-8; 1 Pet 2:18-25). This Jesus calls his disciples to give expression to their fundamental human sexuality in ways that bring glory to the God he himself served. As the New Testament writers concluded, his call requires chastity of all people, a chastity that acknowledges the God-given boundaries of genital sexual expression.[41]

But can we truly expect unmarried people to commit themselves to abstinence?

Jesus himself noted that certain people willingly would set aside the sex act for the sake of God's kingdom (Mt 19:12). The human sciences confirm that sexual activity is not a human necessity, thereby holding open the possibility of abstinence. In the words of Jones and Workman, "There is no basis in behavioral science ... to suggest that abstinence is detrimental to human welfare, or that expression of genital eroticism is necessary for wholeness."[42] Abstinent single Christians stand as living examples of this possibility.

Homosexual People and Sexual Expression

To commit oneself to abstinence outside of marriage does not mean that single homosexual people are "condemned" to lives devoid of sexual expression. On the contrary, people who are not "sexually active" still experience dimensions of affective sexual expression.

The differentiation between sexual desire and the desire for sex suggests how this is so. As the basis for our innate drive toward bonding, sexuality is operative in the lives of all humans. Hence, our sensed need to bond with other humans, to live in community with others, and even to find God all are aspects of human sexual desire. But as most of our day-to-day relationships indicate, sexual desire does not require that we fulfill the desire for sex; that is, that we engage in sexual intercourse. Rather, as I already have argued, the only context in which the desire for sex properly can be expressed is in marriage.

At the same time, we all form non-marital friendship bonds with others. Whenever such bonding occurs, our fundamental sexuality—sexual desire—comes to expression. And as I noted earlier, friendship bonds know no gender boundaries. Hence, our fundamental sexuality readily leads people of the same sex to develop close, even intimate friendships, albeit ones that exclude sexual intimacy in the form of genital relations.

A question commonly asked today is: "Does God really care about whom I sleep with?"

We dare not answer this question in the negative for to do so is to banish God from our sex lives. Rather, Christians seek to understand every aspect of life, including the sexual dimension, within the context of Christian discipleship. Christians seek to place life itself—and, hence, sexual expression—under the lordship of Christ.

Viewed from this perspective, Christians are convinced that God does care about our sexual conduct. And by taking care to live in appropriate sexual chastity, the choice we make as to whom we do—and do not—sleep with becomes a powerful theological statement. This choice speaks loudly about our understanding of ourselves, about our view of the nature of life and, ultimately, about our deepest convictions as to what God is like.

Ultimately, this is the challenge that underlies the discussions about sexual practices so rampant in our society, including the emotionally-charged debate about homosexuality.

Endnotes

1. This focus on teleology is also present among proponents of an open stance. See, for example, John J. McNeill, *The Church and the Homosexual,* 3rd ed. (Boston: Beacon Press, 1988), 130-31.

2. For several contemporary answers to this question, see, for example, the taxonomy and discussion in Peter Coleman, *Gay Christians: A Moral Dilemma* (London: SCM Press, 1989), 191-96, 198-200.

3. Pim Pronk, *Against Nature? Types of Moral Argumentation Regarding Homosexuality* (Grand Rapids, MI: Eerdmans, 1993), 63-64.

4. Pronk, *Against Nature?* 65-66.

5. Maslow notes the implications of this understanding: "It would appear that no single sexual act can per se be called abnormal or perverted. It is only abnormal or perverted individuals who can commit abnormal or perverted acts. That is, the dynamic meaning of the act is far more important than the act itself." Abraham Maslow, "Self-Esteem (Dominance-Feeling) and Sexuality in Women," in *Sexual Behavior and Personality Characteristics,* ed. Manfred F. DeMartino (New York: Citadel Press, 1963), 103.

6. James P. Hanigan, *Homosexuality: The Test Case for Christian Sexual Ethics* (Mahwah, NJ: Paulist, 1988), 77.

7. For a discussion of such harmful effects, see Jeffrey Satinover, *Homosexuality and the Politics of Truth* (Grand Rapids, MI: Baker, 1996), 49-70; Thomas E. Schmidt, *Straight and Narrow? Compassion and Clarity in the Homosexuality Debate* (Downers Grove, IL: InterVarsity, 1995), 100-30.

8. For an example of a slightly more academically credible version of this reasoning, see Michael Keeling, "A Christian Basis for Gay Relationships," in *Towards a Theology of Gay Liberation,* ed. Malcolm Macourt (London: SCM Press, 1977), 104.

9. For a helpful discussion, see Hanigan, 100.

10. Hanigan, 101-2.

11. Hanigan, 102.

12 Max L. Stackhouse, "The Heterosexual Norm," in *Homosexuality and Christian Community,* ed. Choon-Leong Seow (Louisville, KY: Westminster John Knox Press, 1996), 141.

13. Hanigan, 99.

14. Stackhouse, "Heterosexual Norm," 141.

15. Ruth Tiffany Barnhouse, *Homosexuality: A Symbolic Confusion* (New York: Seabury, 1977), 172.

16. Hanigan, *Homosexuality,* 100.

17. Edward Batchelor, Jr., *Homosexuality and Ethics* (New York: Pilgrim, 1980), 76.

18. David F. Greenberg, *The Construction of Homosexuality* (Chicago: University of Chicago Press, 1988).

19. See William H. Davenport, "Sex in Cross-Cultural Perspective," in *Human Sexuality in Four Perspectives,* ed. Frank A. Beach (Baltimore: Johns Hopkins University Press, 1977), 156. See also Milton Diamond and Arno Karlen, *Sexual Decisions* (Boston: Little, Brown and Co., 1980), 228.

20. Michel Foucault, *The History of Sexuality: The Use of Pleasure,* vol. 2 (New York: Pantheon Books: 1985), 245.

21. Chris Glaser, *Uncommon Calling: A Gay Christian's Struggle to Serve the Church* (Louisville, KY: Westminster/John Knox, 1996), 181.

22. Christine E. Gudorf, *Body, Sex, and Pleasure: Reconstructing Christian Sexual Ethics* (Cleveland: Pilgrim, 1994), 16.

23. Greenberg, *Construction of Homosexuality,* 492.

24. For a discussion, see Stanley J. Grenz, *The Moral Quest: Foundation of Christian Ethics* (Downers Grove, IL: InterVarsity, 1997), 46-47, 76-77.

25. For the author's fuller discussion of this idea, see Grenz, *The Moral Quest,* 223-27.

26. For a more extensive discussion from the author's viewpoint, see Stanley J. Grenz, *Theology for the Community of God* (Nashville: Broadman & Holman, 1995), 257-68.

27. For a similar distinction between sexual desire and the desire for sex, see Hanigan, 143.

28. For an evangelical statement, see for example, Ronald M. Enroth and Gerald E. Jamison, *The Gay Church* (Grand Rapids, MI: Eerdmans, 1974), 137.

29. Hence, Alex Davidson, *The Returns of Love: Letters of a Christian Homosexual* (London: Inter-Varsity, 1970), 38, 41.

30. See, for example, William Consiglio, *Homosexual No More* (Wheaton, IL: Victor, 1991), 36.

31. Barnhouse, *Homosexuality,* 152-153.

32. See, for example, Mary E. Hunt, "Lovingly Lesbian: Toward a Feminist Theology of Friendship," in *Sexuality and the Sacred: Sources for Theological Reflection,* ed. James B. Nelson and Sandra P. Longfellow (Louisville, Ky.: Westminster/John Knox, 1994), 170.

33. For this designation, see Consiglio, *Homosexual No More,* 36.

34. Greenberg, *Construction of Homosexuality,* 335.

35. James B. Nelson, *Embodiment* (Minneapolis: Augsburg, 1978), 208.

36. Pamela Dickey Young, "Homosexuality and Ministry: Some Feminist Reflections," in *Theological Reflections on Ministry and Sexual Orientation,* ed. Pamela Dickey Young (Burlington, Ont.: Trinity Press, 1990), 104.

37. For the author's perspective on this distinction, see Grenz, *Sexual Ethics,* 182-85, 196-99.

38. For insight into the positive significance of celibacy, see Jim Cotter, "The Gay Challenge to Traditional Notions of Human Sexuality," in *Towards a Theology of Gay Liberation,* ed. Malcolm Macourt (London: SCM Press, 1977), 67-68.

39. John J. McNeil, "Homosexuality: Challenging the Church to Grow," *Christian Century* 104/8 (11 March 1987): 243. This position was also articulated in McNeill's important work, *The Church and the Homosexual.*

40. Hanigan, 72.

41. A similar understanding of chastity is developed in Donald Georgen, *The Sexual Celibate* (New York: Seabury, 1974), 101-103.

42. Stanton L. Jones and Don E. Workman, "Homosexuality: The Behaviorial Sciences and the Church," *Journal of Psychology and Theology* 17/3 (Fall 1989): 224.

CULTURAL AND
HISTORICAL PERSPECTIVES

Women in the World Christian Movement

Miriam Adeney

A twelve-year old girl was dying. Her dad rushed cross-country to Jesus and begged him to intervene. But when Jesus arrived at the girl's house, he walked into the grief and mourning of the girl's funeral.

Jesus was abrupt. "Clear out! This girl isn't dead. She's sleeping."

Sarcasm rained down on him. What an absurd statement. Jesus ignored it. "Girl, get up," he said. And she did (Luke 8:41–56).

What is a girl? Property? Cheap labour? A sex object? A lineage connector? A social stabilizer? A dangerous pollutant? Or a human being created in the image of God, potentially liberated by Christ's death and resurrection, empowered by the Holy Spirit, and commissioned for active service in God's world? When Jesus met Jairus' daughter, he saw something special. Those around the girl had limited expectations and a dim view of her future. But Jesus saw that this girl had potential. She just needed to be awakened and empowered to get up.

This paper describes women who have learned to see women and men with Jesus' eyes, and to serve them through Christian mission. Limited by time and space, we will focus primarily on North American women. After providing a brief historical framework, we will explore women's motives for doing mission work. Finally, we will consider missiological issues which women have confronted.

History: Where North American Women Began

In 1800, an invalid named Mary Webb founded the Boston Female Society for missionary purposes. Following Mary's example, "cent societies" spread all over New England. In these societies, members challenged each other to save one penny a week for missions. Sally Thomas, a servant girl, gave the first bequest to the American Board of Foreign Missions, her life savings of $345.38. From this humble beginning—the invalid Mary Webb and the servant Sally Thomas—Protestant women "stitched together a missiology of local auxiliaries, sacrificial pennies and ecumenical flexibility that blanketed the continent."[1] By 1910, North American women had founded, were administering, and were supporting over forty mission agencies undergirding over 2500 women missionaries, 6000 indigenous Bible women, 3263 schools, 80 hospitals, 11 colleges and innumerable orphanages and dispensaries.

During these years, in local groups all across the continent, women lavished attention on mission. They read missionary letters, praying over each one, writing back, and sending what they could. When a missionary woman had a concern, these women at home would go to the church administrators and mission administrators and plead the cause that was on their missionary's heart. This bore results. Policies and assignments would be changed on the field. No less significant, the children of the church grew up in mission meetings, absorbing mission concern as naturally as mother's milk.

Yet by the 1930s, denomination after denomination had co-opted the women's societies, absorbing them into general mission committees over the protests of the women. The results were disastrous. Mission became a specialized concern of church committees. It never regained its grass-roots support in the mainline denominations.[2]

There were a few churches, however, where the women would not let go. The Southern Baptists continue to maintain a very strong women's mission auxiliary. To this day, the denomination's major mission funds are raised in the names of two women missionaries. At Christmas, the Lottie Moon offering raises one hundred twenty five million dollars for foreign missions. At Easter, the Annie Armstrong offering raises fifty million dollars for home missions.

Nor did the Canadian Baptists give up their women's mission auxiliary. Today both Canadian and Southern Baptist women are keenly aware of the significance of this heritage. Theses wait to be written here. Unwritten stories lie in the archives of the Canadian Baptist Mission, in the letters of Canadian missionaries to their relatives, and in interviews with their descendants. These are theses that could be published as Canadian history, Canadian feminism,

Canadian international relations, Canadian religious studies, and Canadian multicultural studies, all showing how women in mission have made a difference in the world.

Motives for Mission: Why Women Care

What has propelled North American women into mission? Throughout history, there have been many motives for mission: personal call; obedience to Jesus' command; rescuing the hell-bound; compassion for the hurting; eschatology; God's kingdom; civilization; and the glory of God. Three motives in particular have moved North American women toward mission: first, the experience of the love of God; second, the desire to be useful; and third, empathy with women. In this essay we will focus on the first.

Pentecostal Women

In 1906, Penetecostal theologian Minnie Abrams published *The Baptism of the Holy Ghost and Fire,* in which she developed a "missiology of divine love."

> When a person receives the baptism of the Holy Spirit, Abrams taught, "the fire of God's love will so burn within you that you will desire the salvation of souls. You will accept the Lord's commission to give witness, and realize that he to whom all power is given has imparted some of that power to you, sufficient to do all that he has called you to do."[3]

In particular, speaking in tongues is intended to propel a person to mission as she experiences the love of God. Historian Dana Robert comments: "The prominent healing and compassion ministries of Pentecostals in the 20th century were largely the product of women, an indirect offshoot of the missiology of divine love first espoused by Minnie Abrams."[4]

"Holiness" Women

Not only Pentecostal women have been transformed by God's love. During the "great century" for North American women in mission, "holiness" churchwomen, too, experienced liberation, empowerment, and indeed a compulsion to step into the public arena when they experienced the love of God. In the holiness tradition,

> mission work required the special consecration and sacrificial submission to God's will that could be obtained through an experience of 'perfect love' (a holiness distinctive). Such an experience was important to give women the confidence they needed to travel around

speaking and organizing on behalf of missions and other social causes. . . . Submission to God through acts of consecration not only harnessed women for the cause but provided the means of their own liberation from fear of public speaking, fear of financial management, and fear of traveling alone. Submission to God for the cause of missions empowered women to serve as educators, lay preachers and lay theologians. . . . As women across Methodism experienced holiness, they felt freed from the silence imposed on them by American society, and they began to speak out in church and commit themselves to social service and mission work on behalf of others.[5]

"Mainline" Women

God's love moved women in "mainline" denominations as well. Mary Lyon founded Mt. Holyoke College as a "female seminary" in 1837. Fifty years later, Mt. Holyoke alumnae constituted 20% of the missionary women connected with the American Board of Mission. President Lyon trained women to use their time and manage their small financial resources well so that they would have something to give for mission. Biology was not destiny in her school. But Lyon taught more than a system. She insisted that it was God's love and God's presence with us that give us the courage to act.

"You will find no pleasure like the pleasure of active effort," Lyon exhorted in a graduation address.

Never be hasty to decide that you cannot do because you have not physical or mental strength. Never say you have no faith or hope. Always think of God's strength when you feel your weakness. And remember that you can come nearer to him than to any being in the universe. We have desired to educate you to go among the rich or the poor, to live in the country or the village, in New England, the West, or in a foreign land, and wherever you go remember that God will be with you.[6]

Across the denominations, women have been conscious of weakness, timidity, lack of resources and lack of confidence. In this very weakness, however, they have experienced the dynamizing love of God. This is a major motivation for women in mission even today.

Missiological Issues: What Women Confront

What issues confront women in mission? We will consider five.

Married or Single?

Which is the more effective mission strategy: marriage or singleness? Marriage was required for the first American missionaries, especially for women. Graduating from seminary, a man sometimes discovered that he could not set forth unless he had a wife. If a woman was longing to go to the mission field, she was delighted when a man with a similar vision presented himself.

Many of these marriages worked out well because both the husbands and the wives in this first wave were highly motivated for mission. The focus was on the task, not romance.

The first American women missionaries were among the best educated women of their time. Several of the early wives knew Latin, Greek, and Hebrew, and all had extensive experience in social service and benevolent activities before they went to the field. After her conversion experience, Ann Hasseltine, later Ann Judson, put herself on a course of theological self-study, characteristic of a male student enrolled at Andover Seminary. She read extensively in the works of five leading theologians, especially Jonathan Edwards. She studied Scripture daily, using commentaries and keeping notes on what she did not understand. Whenever a visiting clergyman came along, she would consult with him on obscure points.

In Burma, Ann translated Scripture side by side with her husband, Adoniram. When they had learned enough of the language, they divided up the task. Anne translated Daniel and Jonah and wrote a catechism in Burmese. Then, noticing that no missionary was learning the language of the Thai people who lived in Rangoon, she learned Thai, translated the gospel of Matthew, and wrote a catechism in Thai. She was the first Protestant to translate any of the Bible into that language.

Simultaneously, Ann ran a girls' school. She did regular evangelistic itineration across a large region. She had children. She ran the home. When her husband was imprisoned, she took the children and followed him from prison to prison for two years, keeping him alive physically and politically. Ann had a full life. Unfortunately, like many other early missionary wives, she died young, at the age of 36. Her husband married twice more.

The range of activities in which Ann engaged was not untypical of the first wave of well-educated missionary women. In Iran, Judith Campbell Grant spoke and read six languages. Her Latin was so proficient that she taught herself Syriac through the use of Latin lexicons and grammars. She spoke Turkish and French, read ancient Syriac, wrote in modern Syriac and read her Bible in Greek. She ran a school for girls. She had three children. She died at the age of 25.

Before meeting Judith, the local leaders had not believed that girls could learn. However, Judith so impressed them that they were willing to allow her school to continue after she died. Yet who was available to run it? Back home at Mt. Holyoke College, Principal Mary Lyon presented this opportunity to the student body during evening prayers. "Do any of you feel called to replace Judith?" she asked. Within one hour, forty teachers and students had volunteered.[7] This was the first wave of North American missionary women— married, well-educated pioneers, linguists, evangelists, and teachers. By contrast, when the women's mission agencies exploded in the 1860s, many of these agencies required their members to be single. If a member married on the field, she sometimes had to reimburse the mission agency for her travel expenses.

Public Ministry or Model Homes?

Should women focus on public evangelism, teaching, and service, or should they focus on nurturing model Christian families? Following the early missionaries to Burma came a surge of missionaries to Hawaii. The wives in this group were not strong evangelists or linguists. While they taught in schools, teaching was not a high priority for them. Rather they focused on creating model Christian families. Unfortunately, some went to extremes, not allowing their children to learn the Hawaiian language or even to associate with the people.

Nevertheless, they raised an issue which persists. How should a woman balance ministry in the public arena with ministry in the home? Even single women may feel this crunch. Some contemporary missionaries to Muslims advise Christian women to do ministry from their homes, not venturing further than the neighbourhood. A single woman confesses,

> A team leader in my mission told me recently, 'Joanna, you just need to understand that in Muslim culture women don't have public roles, so you can't have one either if you want to be effective among Muslims.' I was saddened at his ignorance. At the university where I was asked to teach in—, the head of the college of engineering is a woman. Who will reach these women with the gospel if leaders in important mission movements to Muslims have little understanding of them?
>
> During our recent mission conference, I tried to stick to positive, unifying themes, but my retrospective is still dominated by the realization that after years of admiring this mission's bold love for

Muslims, I had joined an organization whose ethos did not encompass me, a single, professional female.[8]

On the other hand, many women feel called to focus on their homes, and to express Christ's love from that base. As a result, there are believers everywhere who have been drawn by the beauty of Christian families.

Multiplying Churches or Ministering Holistically?

Should we focus on church growth, or should we focus on holistic ministry? At least three times in North America's 200 years of mission history, there has been an emphasis on numerical church growth, planting churches and multiplying congregations. After all, missionaries are to make disciples, teaching them to observe all that Christ commanded. Grouping believers into congregations facilitates this. It also aids evaluation, as congregations can be counted.

In the 1840s, Rufus Anderson began a long career as secretary of the American Board of Missions. He fathered the three-self mission theory, which flowered later in the writings of Roland Allen. According to this theory, self-supporting, self-governing and self-propagating congregations are a key measure of mission success. All efforts must be directed toward multiplying these kinds of congregations.

Here Anderson collided with women already on the field. When women encounter needy people, they tend to respond in multifaceted ways. Women were evangelizing, healing, teaching, feeding the hungry, and confronting social abuses when Anderson took up his post. Were they likely to drop all those diverse ministries, or at least subordinate them, in order to focus on planting churches?

Consider healing. Dr. Ida Scudder founded the Vellore Medical Hospital and Training School, one of the outstanding medical schools on the subcontinent. For two generations her family had been missionary doctors in India. Ida had not intended to follow in their footsteps. She went to college in the U.S., and planned a happy life there. But on a visit with her parents in India, her life plans changed.

One night a man knocked on the door. "Excuse me. My wife is having a baby, and something's gone wrong. Is there a doctor who could come?"

Ida's father picked up his medical bag, but the husband objected, "No, not a man doctor. Isn't there a woman doctor?"

There was none, so the young husband went away. Twice more that night husbands came seeking help for wives in childbirth. Twice more they turned away when they discovered there was no woman doctor. In the morning Ida heard that all three women had died. She went back to the U.S., enrolled in medical school, raised funds, and returned with enough finances to start her renowned medical center, which focused on serving and training women. Following Jesus when he reached out to Jairus' daughter, missionaries like Ida have found their vocation in healing.[9]

Community development is another area where women have sparkled. Born in India in 1858, Pandita Ramabai came to faith in Christ as a young widow with a child. Although Indian widows have a hard life, Ramabai's way was smoothed by education and well-placed connections. She hurt for women who were not so fortunate, however. Eventually she started a community for women who had no means of support. It grew large enough to shelter 1900 women and orphans at a time. Today the community continues as the Ramabai Mukti Mission.

Ramabai described this holistic, self-supporting community: "The gardens and the fields, the oil-press and the dairy, the laundry and the bakery, the making of plain, Indian garments, caps, lace, buttons, ropes, brooms and baskets, the spinning of wool and cotton, the weaving of blankets, rugs, saris and other cloths, embroidery and various sorts of fancy work, thread-winding, grain-parching, tinning, culinary utensils, and dying, furnished employment and jobs for hundreds of girls. Within the last few months, a printing press has been added to the establishment."[10]

Ironically, when revivals broke out in this community, the unexpected Pentecostal ethos so offended supporters in the U.S. and India that they withdrew funds. In this lonely abyss, Ramabai took inspiration from mission leaders Hudson Taylor and George Mueller, and for the last 25 years of her life she ran her operation "by faith," rather than by guaranteed support. This faith was nurtured by her Marathi Bible, of which she spent much time making a fresh translation.

As in healing and in community development, women also have pioneered in urban mission. Catherine Booth (1829–1890) was cofounder of the Salvation Army. When Catherine had four children, the eldest aged four (and the prospect of possibly a dozen more) she began to preach. Frequently she addressed two or three thousand people—uneducated, disruptive people of the slums. After the meetings she counseled those who came forward. She struggled to find jobs for these newly reformed prostitutes and pickpockets. For years to come she would correspond with them. Beyond this, whenever possible, Catherine made it her habit throughout her life to visit the families of alcoholics one evening a week.

Catherine continued preaching right through eight children. When she traveled as an evangelist, they often traveled with her. The guest speaker would arrive complete with children, nursery furniture and also a big rug so her offspring would not ruin the carpets in the homes where she stayed. She had one assistant who, more like a sister than a servant, stayed with the Booths all her life, though rarely could they pay her. With one helper for eight sets of diapers without any automatic washer or dryer in rainy England, Catherine and her assistant made all the children's clothes until the children were twelve years old. What kind of mother was she? Her letters to her children pulsate with the passionate individual thought she gave to each child. At the same time, without any word processor, she wrote eight books. Catherine Booth understood that she had been empowered by the love of God to make a difference in God's world. To evangelize, to plant churches—and to minister holistically to needy people in the urban jungle.[11]

Whether urban or rural, women often feel impelled to feed the hungry. Consider Rosario Rivera of Peru. Twenty-five years ago she was a leader in the Shining Path, Peru's fierce Marxist guerrilla movement. Today she runs a breakfast program for 2500 children. Peruvian women volunteers serve out breakfast. While the children eat, the women tell gospel stories. Very poor children start the day with Jesus and with food.[12]

Does such holistic ministry distract from gospel witness and church planting? That is the issue.

Teaching for Domesticity? Or for the Professions?

When teaching girls or women, what is a missionary's goal? Especially in Africa, mission schools often trained girls to act like ladies and run Victorian-style homes. Queen's College in Lagos, Nigeria, was founded for the secondary education of girls. For many years, the curriculum consisted of needlework, domestic science and singing. African parents objected. They wanted academic or professional training. As one remarked, "When an [African] woman is educated, she is expected to *do* something with her education."[13] Schools did not teach income-generating skills which women needed. Some Africans even argued that it was better not to send their girls to school because graduates ended up less competent than their mothers, who were canny market traders.

By contrast, missionary Gertrude Howe trained Chinese women for the professions at a high level. Howe was running a girls' school, and had adopted four Chinese girls, when a Chinese Christian brought his seven-year-old daughter and asked, "Could you prepare her to be a doctor?"

This was a new idea. Prayerfully, Howe observed how Chinese boys were being readied for pre-med studies. She began to teach English to her daughters and her best students. Other missionaries disapproved. "You are raising aspirations that will never be filled. You are making these girls unfit for their role in society," they argued. But Howe persevered, saving money by eating Chinese food and living in a Chinese home. When they were ready, she took her five best pupils to Michigan University, having tutored them in math, chemistry, physics, and Latin so that they could pass the entrance exam. Howe stayed with them in the U.S. for two years, supporting and coaching them. When they returned to China years later, some of these women became very prominent physicians.[14]

"The power of educated womanhood is simply the power of skilled service. We are not in the world to be ministered unto, but to minister. The world is full of need, and every opportunity to help is a duty. Preparation for these duties is education, whatever form it may take, or whatever service it may require."[15] These are the words of Isabella Thoburn, who founded the first women's college in India, located at Lucknow.

Confronting Cultural Abuses versus Affirming a Culture?

"I will have no bound feet in my school," decided Mary Porter en route to China. It was the custom for high class parents to bind their little girls' feet tightly as a mark of beauty and status. Unfortunately, the feet were deformed as they grew. Sometimes bones broke. Such women could not work or even walk much. Yet the hold of custom was strong. While deploring footbinding, most missionaries had decided not to make an issue of it. They focused on spreading the gospel message. Footbinding was simply an unfortunate cultural custom.

But Mary Porter said "I am not going to be a party to this harmful and degrading practice. If a girl wants education, she unbinds her feet. I will have no bound feet in my school." In time, this sentiment spread, and the custom was outlawed at the national level.[16]

Out of empathy with hurting women, Christians often have felt compelled to confront social abuses. In the late nineteenth and early twentieth centuries, the West Coast of North America saw the enslavement of Chinese women. These women were brought to California, for example, to serve in brothels. Baby girls were smuggled in to be raised in the houses of prostitution. Chinese husbands who fell into debt could sell their wives to brothels for $300 to $2,000. Kept as virtual prisoners, the women were used by dozens of men.

Maggie Culbertson, Donaldina Cameron, and volunteers of the

Presbyterian Women's Home Society looked at their communities and saw these Chinese women being enslaved. They decided to do something about it. Between 1875 and 1916, swarms of Presbyterian women periodically descended on a given brothel, intimidating even the guards. They liberated the women and little girls inside, found them places to stay, gave them respite care, trained them for independence, and helped them find jobs. The owners fought back. They hired thugs, and, when that did not work, they hired attorneys. Deputies knocked on the doors of Presbyterian women's houses with warrants for slave girls' arrests. Local politicians opposed the church women. At a time when anti-Chinese sentiment was high, many of Maggie's and Donaldina's fellow church members deplored their focus. "Chinese shouldn't be here in the first place," these parishioners argued. But, having experienced the love of God, Maggie and Donaldina could not stop sharing that love with these needy women.[17]

Abuse calls for loving action, whether the abuse is footbinding or slavery, female circumcision or machismo, unequal pay or harassment. When we confront evils in another culture, however, we tend to exaggerate those evils, while ignoring both the beauties and strengths of that culture and the evils in our own. In any such confrontation, we ought to work with and under local people.

We have explored five issues that confront women in mission. These are not merely academic or female issues, however. Readers of this essay will struggle with similar problems. As members of churches with limited budgets, readers will be faced with the need to decide which projects to support. Their knowledge of missiological theory and strategies will shape their priorities, just as it did for Anne and Catherine, Ramabai and Gertrude, Rosario and Maggie.

Love in the Beginning, Middle, and End

When Jesus met Jairus' daughter, he saw something special. Those around her had a dim view of her future. But Jesus saw that this woman had potential. She just needed to be awakened and empowered.

As Jesus was on the way to Jairus' daughter, he met an older woman who had been suffering from a flow of blood for twelve years. She had spent all her money on doctors—for nothing. Having tried everything, she was burned out, depleted, exhausted, traumatized, used up. Her hope was almost dead. Whereas Jairus had run into Jesus' presence articulate, impassioned, and assertive, this worn-out woman did not have the confidence to speak a word. What was the use? Yet she touched the hem of Jesus' garment. And Jesus spoke to her. Jesus took the initiative. Then, after more than a decade of shame, confusion, stigma and despair, she was healed.

Whether a woman is at the beginning of her creative adult life, like Jairus' daughter, or middle-aged like this bleeding woman, Jesus' love empowers. Even if a woman should be at the end of her life, Jesus' love remains the relevant variable. Faridah was a professor of statistics at a state university in Africa who won a scholarship to do graduate study at the University of British Columbia a few years ago. Although Faridah was raised in a strong Muslim family, a Regent student brought her to Christ. For the next eighteen months—for the rest of her time here—three Regent students from Africa and their families surrounded Faridah and her Muslim husband with Christian love and community. Faridah devoured Scripture. She grew in Christian maturity. Her husband said, "I don't want you going to church," so she didn't. But she came to chapel on Tuesdays at Regent College. Three months before she graduated, she asked to be baptized in a local church. Then she returned home to Africa. Six months later she was dead. Yet, if she were offered a chance to do it over, I don't think she would change her choice. For her, the love of Jesus was life-transforming. The love of Jesus was enough. That has been the testimony of many women, not only in North America but on every continent.

Endnotes

1. Dana Robert, *American Women in Mission: A Social History of their Thought and Practice.* (Machine, Georgia: Mercer University Press, 1996), p. 137.

2. See primary references cited in R. Pierce Beaver, *All Loves Excelling: American Protestant Women in World Mission,* (Grand Rapids, MI: Eerdmans' Publishing Co., 1968); Ruth Tucker and Walter Liefeld, *Daughters of the Church: Women in Ministry from New Testament Times to the Present,* (Grand Rapids, MI: Zondervan Publishing, 1987); and Dana Robert, "Revisioning the Women's Missionary Movement," in ed. Charles Van Engen, et al., *The Good News of the Kingdom.* (Maryknoll, NY: Orbis Books, 1993).

3. Minnie Abrams, *The Baptism of the Holy Ghost and Fire,* 2nd ed. (Kedgaon: Mukti Mission Press, 1906), p.67.

4. Robert , op.cit (1996), p.252.

5. Ibid., pp.140, 144–45, 148.

6. Fidelia Fiske, *Recollections of Mary Lyon, with Selections from her Instructions to the Pupils in Mt. Holyoke Female Seminary.* (Boston: American Tract Society, 1866), pp. 85–65.

7. Robert, op.cit.(1996), pp. 7–10, 17–19, 31, 43–46, 109.

8. Personal communication.

9. Dorothy Clarke Wilson, "The legacy of Ida S. Scudder," in *International Bulletin of Mission Research,* Jan. 1985, p. 26.

10. Quoted in Stephen Neill, *Builders of the Indian Church.* (London: The Livingstone Press, 1934), pp.131–132.

11. Catherine Bramwell-Booth. *Catherine Booth.* (London: Hodder and Stoughton, 1970).

12. John Maust, "Rosario Rivera: Reaching Lima's Children," *Missiology*, July 1987, pp.339–346.

13. Deborah Pellow, *Women in Accra: Options for Autonomy*. (Algonac, Michigan: Reference Publications, Inc., 1977). See also Carol Johnson, "Class and Gender: Yoruba Women in the Colonial Period," in Claire Robertson and Iris Berger, eds. *Women and Class in Africa*. (NY: Holmes and Meier, 1986).

14. Robert, op.cit. (1996), pp.185–86.

15. Quoted in J.M.Thoburn, *Life of Isabella Thoburn*. (Cincinnati: Jennings and Pye, 1903), p. 332.

16. Ethel Daniels Hubbard, *Under Marching Orders: A Story of Mary Porter Gamewell*. (NY: Missionary Education Movement of the U.S. and Canada, 1911).

17. Cathy Luchetti, *Women of the West*. (Ogden, Utah: Antelope Island Press, 1982), pp. 49–55.

CHAPTER 8

"Gender" and the Idea of the Social Construction of Reality

Craig M. Gay

"If the sex of a person is biologically determined," *The Penguin Dictionary of Sociology* (1988) reads, "the gender of a person is culturally and socially constructed. There are thus two sexes (male and female) and two genders (masculine and feminine). The principal theoretical and political issue is whether gender as a socially constructed phenomenon is related to or determined by biology."[1] *The Concise Oxford Dictionary of Sociology* (1994) states: "According to Ann Oakley, who introduced the term to sociology [in 1972], 'Sex' refers to the biological division into male and female; 'gender' to the parallel and socially unequal division into femininity and masculinity. Gender draws attention, therefore, to the socially constructed aspects of differences between women and men."[2] Similarly, in the *Encyclopedia of Psychology* (1994) we read the following: "The use of gender was introduced in behavioral and social sciences to distinguish it from the concept of sex. Gender was distinguished from sex in feminist literature to emphasize that anatomy is not destiny, as sex is biologically defined and gender is culturally constructed."[3] And in *The Encyclopedia of Sociology* (1992) we read: "Gender is the organized pattern of social relations between women and men, not only in face-to-face interaction and within the family but also in the major institutions of society, such as social class, the hierarchies of large-scale organizations, and the occupational structure... The social reproduction of gender in individuals sustains the gendered societal structure; as individuals act out the expectations of their gender status in face-to-face interaction, they are constructing gender and, at the same time, gendered systems of dominance and power."[4]

Of the several things these definitions of "gender" have in common, one of the more intriguing is the notion of "social construction" and the suggestion that a core aspect of personality—i.e., "gender"—is socially constructed. Whereas certain "raw" characteristics of human life are biologically and naturally determined, so the definitions contend, our sense of ourselves as masculine and feminine is socially and culturally constructed. And if something as basic to our individual makeup as "gender" is socially constructed, then it would seem safe to assume that other core aspects of our identities—and perhaps even the notion of "identity" itself—are socially constructed as well.

This is a striking contention. And I would guess that it is more or less at odds with what we take for granted to be true about ourselves. We don't normally think of ourselves as having been "constructed"—at least not by society—but rather as simply "being" in some more fundamental sense, even if the specific quality of our being remains something of a mystery to us.

The contention that "gender"—and, by extension, identity in general—is socially constructed is also more or less at odds with most traditional anthropologies, which tend to place the emphasis upon the "nature of things" in general and upon "human nature" in particular, as well as upon the givenness or createdness of nature. The account of the creation of the first human beings in Genesis 1, for example, states: "And God created man... male and female he created them." Now, although it is possible to read the words "male" and "female" in this and similar texts as referring only to the biological aspects of sex, the suggestion that our experience of maleness and femaleness is socially constructed seems to imply a good deal more plasticity in human nature than this text permits. It also tends to replace God's creative agency with our own, or at least with that of society. We need to take a close look at the notion of social construction in the following essay, and specifically the notion of the social construction of identity.

The notion obviously troubles me. And not because I don't think that it is true in certain respects; I am sure it is. What worries me is the way the notion is being employed in contemporary discourse, and not simply about "gender roles," but about a whole host of social and cultural issues. The social construction of identity seems to me to be one of those half-truths that, because it is presented today as the whole truth, actually obscures the truth of things, making it more and not less difficult to get at many of the problems we face.

The thesis I want to advance with respect to the constructionist position—as I will call the advocacy of the social construction of identity—is modest but pointed. It doesn't have to do with the gender question per se as much as it has to do with the danger of employing the notion of the social construction of identity in the service of gender reconciliation or, indeed, for the purpose of advancing any kind of radical social change. The thesis is as follows: When we contend for radical social change (radical in the sense that it extends to the matter of personal identity) on the basis of the purportedly socially constructed quality of personality (hence underscoring the historical and cultural relativity of identity) we are at risk of placing far, far too much confidence in our own ingenuity and far, far too little (if, indeed, any at all) upon our need to patiently seek out the truth of things. Put differently, by prefacing whatever desires we may have for social change with the proposition that our identities are always and only socially constructed, we assume (albeit perhaps unwittingly) that we are capable of re-constructing ourselves. We imply, furthermore (again, albeit perhaps unwittingly), that we are the sole creators of "meanings" and "values" in the world and that, in effect, we create these "meanings" and "values" ex nihilo. Such a stance, it seems to me, completely cripples the theological task, which assumes to the contrary that the truth of things in general, and the truth of our identities in particular, are not things that we construct, but rather that they are things that must we painstakingly seek and/or painstakingly receive and, indeed, that we must seek and/or receive them from outside of ourselves and our societies.

Sharpening this thesis, we might say that from a theological point of view, adopting a constructionist stance with respect to the question of identity only insures that we will never really discover who we are, and that the reason we will not is precisely because we are not looking outside of ourselves for answers to the question of identity. As Jewish philosopher Martin Buber observed in a collection of essays entitled *The Eclipse of God* (1952): "[I]t has become necessary to proclaim that God is 'dead.' Actually, this proclamation means only that man has become incapable of apprehending a reality absolutely independent of himself and of having a relation with it..."[5] The modern preoccupation with human agency and control, Buber observed, and with knowing solely for the sake of taking control of things—a preoccupation that is not only legitimated but is amplified by the notion of the social construction of identity—has a great deal to do with the widespread impression that God is distant, disinterested, and perhaps even "dead."

Preoccupied with establishing mastery over nature, mastery over our social circumstances, mastery over each other, and even mastery over ourselves, the modern and now postmodern mind has forgotten how to even ask the question of truth. Whatever "truths" are, so the contemporary argument runs, they must somehow be constructed on the basis of human desires. And because the supposition that "truths" must somehow be constructed has animated modern society and culture for quite some time now, it appears to many of our contemporaries that there is no other way to think about human existence. Hence Buber observed: "[T]he unbelieving marrow of the capricious man cannot perceive anything but unbelief and caprice, positing ends and devising means. His world is devoid of sacrifice and grace, encounter and presence, but shot through with ends and means."[6]

Yet if we are ever to achieve gender reconciliation, indeed if we are ever to establish any kind of justice for anyone who is oppressed, it will not be because we have managed to construct it, but only because we have managed to find it and, having found it, only because we have been given the grace to repent of our wayward affections and been allowed to become re-attached to justice, mercy, truthfulness, and to other qualities that God graciously establishes and sustains. In short, it is "the fear of the Lord"—however we may want to express this—and not the exaltation of human creative agency, that is the beginning of wisdom.

The Social Construction of Reality

So that we may fully appreciate the risks associated with employing constructionist rhetoric, I want to fit the notion of the social construction of identity into a somewhat larger conceptual framework—widely accepted these days—called "the social construction of reality." I plan to draw from two principle sources: Peter L. Berger and Thomas Luckmann's seminal work, *The Social Construction of Reality: A Treatise in the Sociology of Knowledge* (New York: Penguin, 1967); and Peter L. Berger's *The Sacred Canopy: Elements of a Sociological Theory of Religion* (Garden City, NY: Anchor, 1969).

Berger and Luckmann's basic proposition is that "reality"—that is, our ordinary, everyday experience of the world—is not naturally and/or instinctively given, but is socially constructed. What passes for "reality" in society, in other words, is something that we determine and construct in society with others. Together with others we decide, more or less deliberately, how our world is to be understood and interpreted, who we are and how we fit into the world, what is important and why, and, conversely, what it is safe to ignore and neglect. This socially-constructed "reality" is held together, furthermore, by way of a whole host of assumptions that we take largely for granted, assumptions which provide a framework for making sense of our natural and social environments. Taken together these assumptions form the stock of knowledge that enables us to know and to tell each other who we are and what in the world is "real."

Synthesizing the insights of a number of social theorists, Berger and Luckmann develop an elegant model to explain how the social construction of reality works and to elucidate the relationship that exists between the societies we live in and the contours of our personalities and identities. This circular model consists of three moments: *externalization, objectivation,* and *internalization,* which may be diagrammed as follows:

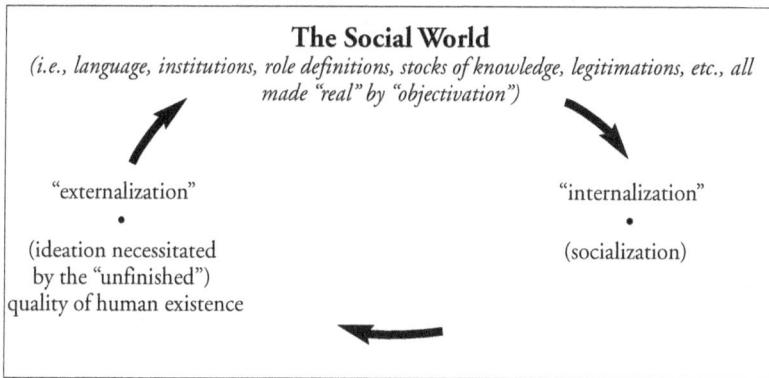

The Social World
(i.e., language, institutions, role definitions, stocks of knowledge, legitimations, etc., all made "real" by "objectivation")

"externalization"   "internalization"

(ideation necessitated   (socialization)
by the "unfinished")
quality of human existence

Identity (i.e., Our Sense of Ourselves)

In short, "externalization" suggests that society is a human product or projection; "objectivation" suggests that once society has been projected it becomes objectively "real" over and against us; and "internalization" submits that our identities are formed out of socially objectivated meanings, institutions, and roles.

Detailing Berger and Luckmann's model, we note that externalization was originally a Hegelian term (*Veräusserung*) denoting our human propensity to project ourselves into the world and to "spit out" ideas. Here Berger and Luckmann refer to Arnold Gehlen's anthropological insight: that, unlike other animals, we human beings are not born with an instinctual "world" that delimits and governs our behaviour. Rather, human beings are, to use Gehlen's phrase, "unfinished animals," and it is because of the "unfinished" quality of

171

our existence that we are, in effect, forced to construct "a world" for ourselves. Because we are social animals, furthermore, we do this together with others in groups. "Society"—the "social world"—is the conglomeration of the meanings, knowledge, and institutions that we have constructed to give order to our existence.

Although there are natural and biological limits to this "world construction" process, Berger and Luckmann insist that they are not nearly as restrictive as we might have supposed. They write:

> It is an ethnological commonplace that the ways of becoming and being human are as numerous as man's cultures. Humanness is socio-culturally variable. In other words, there is no human nature in the sense of a biologically fixed substratum determining the variability of socio-cultural formations. There is only human nature in the sense of anthropological constants (for example, world-openness and plasticity of instinctual structure) that delimit and permit man's socio-cultural formations… While it is possible to say that man has a nature, it is more significant to say that man constructs his own nature, or more simply, that man produces himself.[7]

"What appears at any particular historical moment as 'human nature'," Berger writes elsewhere, "is itself a product of man's world-building activity."[8]

Objectivation refers to the peculiar quality of our social constructions. Following Durkheim's lead, Berger and Luckmann suggest that society is a "thing," i.e., an objective reality every bit as solid and real as rocks, trees, and other "things" we bump into and occasionally trip over. The international border separating Canada and the USA is as good an example of an objectivated social reality as any. The border is a purely social construction (needless to say, the 49th parallel does not exist in nature), as are the two "nation-states" that maintain and patrol it, but the fact that it is socially-constructed does not diminish its "reality" as far as I am concerned when I drive from Vancouver to Seattle. I am forced—by people armed with lethal weapons—to respect the conventions of border-crossing when I cross through the Peace Arch. And the same is true—though perhaps less dramatically—of a host of other social constructions that make up our society, including the legitimations that sustain them.

Internalization, which is more commonly termed "socialization," is the process by which the objective institutions, roles, and legitimations of the social world become core elements of our own identities. The learning of language is without doubt the most important element in this process of internalization; for a language *is* a world; it provides us with a "ready-made" universe of values, purposes, and meanings.

According to Berger and Luckmann, then, the three processes of externalization, objectivation, and internalization occur simultaneously and in an ongoingly circular fashion in any given society. Taken together they interpret the shape of society and the range of identities possible within it at any given time.

Ideally, our identities will perfectly reflect the objective structures of our society and we will feel perfectly "at home" playing our roles within society's institutions and perfectly comfortable with the meanings and legitimations that interpret them. Yet, as Berger and Luckmann note, such perfect symmetry rarely, if ever, actually exists. The process of socialization is never completely successful, and human beings continue to externalize new ideas and novel institutional arrangements that tend to unsettle whatever *status quo* may hitherto have been established. When these new ideas and/or novel institutional arrangements manage to attach themselves to powerful enough social interests, furthermore, there will be pressure toward social change.

Discussion

There is something more-or-less obviously true about the contention that knowledge and ideas, indeed, that all cultural meaning, is socially and historically locatable. The staggering variety of human institutions, both historically and cross-culturally, does appear to warrant Berger and Luckmann's suggestion that the only anthropological constant, i.e., the only consistent aspect of what we might call "human nature," is to continually produce and reproduce knowledge, institutions, and roles that enable us, more or less fleetingly, to tell ourselves who we are and what the world means. In this connection, I have found Berger and Luckmann's model quite useful in theological self-examination. It is always a good idea to ask ourselves to what extent have we allowed "the traditions of men," which was Jesus' term for socially constructed meaning, to eclipse the Word of God in our churches.

We also note in passing that the proposition of the social construction of reality lies at the heart of what is called "postmodernism." Postmodernism's celebrated incredulity with respect to metanarratives stems directly from the assumption that "reality" is socially constructed.

And it is not at all difficult to see why cultural revolutionaries, revisionists, and iconoclasts of various stripes would find the constructionist position attractive, for it serves to relativize opposition to social change, and particularly opposition made in the name of "natural" and/or "moral" order.

Indeed, if the existing status quo, including its conceptions of right and wrong and its understanding of human purposes and "human nature," is at bottom merely a social construct, then nothing prevents us from deconstructing it and then reconstructing it as we see fit. The natural place to begin this deconstructive and reconstructive process, furthermore, will be in language, i.e., in first-order legitimations of the social world.

It is also fairly easy to see why those who adopt a constructionist stance, and who would deconstruct the existing status quo for the sake of reconstructing something new, are assertive and occasionally even combative *vis-à-vis* "the powers that be." For if it is assumed that the existing social situation was originally constructed by those in positions of power, and that it continues to be legitimated in the interests of the powerful, then the only way to change matters will be to marshal countervailing social forces, and by whatever means are necessary. The old cynical adage has it that "might makes right," and while few today would be so bold (or so clumsy) as to defend such an openly Machiavellian sentiment, the constructionist view must, it seems to me, tend in this direction. To put this a bit more delicately, principled persuasion on the basis of the truth of things or, for that matter, on the basis of the will of God is not a particularly obvious strategy from the constructionist point of view. Indeed, I think you will find that the notion of the social construction of reality and the word "truth" only very rarely, if ever, occur in the same sentence; that is, unless the word "truth" has been neutralized by means of inverted commas.

But, of course, this raises a difficult question with respect to the constructionist position: on what basis can social reconstruction ever be legitimated? It cannot really be proposed in the name of justice or equity or goodness, etc., for the constructionist already knows that all such notions are historically and culturally relative. Serious postmodern theorists recognize this problem and so typically refrain from using the imperative voice, suggesting instead that the way forward is, in effect, for each of us to simply do what is right in our own eyes. But many others, including those most concerned about gender questions, do continue to contend for the rightness of their proposals in spite of the fact that the theoretical stance they have adopted empties the word "right" of all but rhetorical force. This inconsistency should not simply be brushed aside, for it suggests that something is fundamentally amiss in the constructionist argument.

And so in spite of what we just said earlier, it must also be said that there is something more or less obviously *untrue* about the constructionist position, for surely not every idea is culturally and/or historically relative, or at least not in the way that the word "relativity" is commonly intended as a synonym for "novel." Rather a strong case can be made that all culturally-conditioned values are only recognizable as such because they reflect, however dimly, those *true* values that are built into the truth of being. As C. S. Lewis argued so eloquently in *The Abolition of Man*:

> This thing that I have called for convenience the *Tao*, and which others may call Natural Law or Traditional Morality or the First Principles of Practical Reason or the First Platitudes, is not one among a series of possible systems of value. It is the sole source of all value judgments. If it is rejected, all value is rejected. If any value is retained, it is retained. The effort to refute it and raise a new system of value in its place is self-contradictory. There never has been, and never will be, a radically new judgment of value in the history of the world. What purport to be new systems or (as they now call them) 'ideologies', all consist of fragments from the *Tao* itself, arbitrarily wrenched from their context in the whole and then swollen to madness in their isolation, yet still owing to the *Tao* and to it alone such validity as they possess. If my duty to parents is a superstition, then so is my duty to posterity. If Justice is a superstition, then so is my duty to my country or my race. If the pursuit of scientific knowledge is a real value, then so is conjugal fidelity. The rebellion of new ideologies against the *Tao* is a rebellion of the branches against the tree: if the rebels could succeed they would find that they had destroyed themselves. The human mind has no more power of inventing a new value than of imagining a new primary colour, or, indeed, of creating a new sun and a new sky for it to move in.[9]

Either there *are* values and they are unchanging, Lewis reasons, or there *are not* (which, of course, is not to say that these values may not have been forgotten, or that they may not be ignored). The constructionist position assumes that the latter is the case, that is, that "values" are simply things that people construct to make sense of themselves and their circumstances. Such a position is coherent and is either true or false. Those who employ constructionist arguments, however, seem often to want to have it both ways. They want to claim that the "values" they oppose are simply socially constructed, but that the values they affirm are just and right. Now, here again, if this is done in such a way as to juxtapose "the traditions of men" over and against something like the Word of God, then this is perfectly legitimate. Yet the radical theory upon which the constructionist argument is based is such as to make it all but impossible to appeal to the Word of God. Indeed, the "constructionist" position is—at least implicitly—atheistic, and in the most serious sense of this term; for it is premised upon the assumption that all social meanings—including religious ideas—are ultimately only human projections. To see why this is the case, it may help to take a moment to locate the constructionist position in the history of ideas.

As Berger and Luckmann indicate at the outset of their treatise, the notion of the social construction of reality emerged out of the context of nineteenth-century German historical scholarship, and specifically in response to the radical historical/cultural relativity that such scholarship had apparently unearthed. They observe:

> Historicism, especially as expressed in the work of Wilhelm Dilthey, immediately preceded the sociology of knowledge. The dominant theme here was an overwhelming sense of the relativity of all perspectives on human events, that is, of the inevitable historicity of human thought. The historicist insistence that no historical situation could be understood except in its own terms could readily be translated into an emphasis on the social situation of thought. Certain historicist concepts, such as "situational determination" *(Standortsgebundenheit)* and "seat in life" *(Sitz im Leben)* could be directly translated as referring to the "social location" of thought.[10]

The late nineteenth-century historicist assertion of the radical historical-cultural relativity of all knowledge was, in its own turn, premised upon the rejection of the possibility of revealed religion in the name of enlightened science. The plausibility of the historicist account of history and culture, in other words, presupposed the repudiation of traditional religious accounts of both, and particularly that of traditional Christianity. To put this in contemporary terms, it was incredulity with respect to the traditional Christian "metanarrative" that precipitated the emergence of the notion of the social construction of reality, a notion that has, by now, led to postmodern incredulity with respect to all metanarratives.

Berger and Luckmann also note that the proposition that "reality" is socially constructed owes a great deal to Marx's celebrated assertion that our consciousness is determined by our social circumstances. "The production of ideas, of conceptions, of consciousness," Marx had written ca. 1844:

> is at first directly interwoven with the material activity and the material intercourse of men, the language of real life. Conceiving, thinking, the mental intercourse of men appear... as the direct *efflux* of their material behaviour. The same applies to mental production as expressed in the

language of the politics, laws, morality, religion, metaphysics of a people. Men are the producers of their conceptions, ideas, etc.—real, active men, as they are conditioned by a definite development of their productive forces and of the intercourse corresponding to these.... Consciousness can never be anything else than conscious existence, and the existence of men in their actual life-process.[11]

Marx's emphasis here upon "material intercourse" and "productive forces," incidentally, helps to explain why constructionists of various stripes almost always insist that the matter of one's identity must be linked, ultimately, to one's relative position within the marketplace.

Lastly, Berger and Luckmann note that the notion of the social construction of reality has borrowed a thorough-going "*anti*-idealism" from Nietzsche, that is, a refusal to believe that the ongoing social construction of reality has any larger meaning or serves any larger purpose. "Truths," Nietzsche had insisted, are simply "illusions about which one has forgotten that this is what they are."[12] And so the "constructionist" position tends to assume—contra the historicism of Hegel and Marx—that the social construction of "reality" is always and only driven by the struggle for survival and power against the backdrop of an absolutely indifferent universe (*multi*verse, really). In this connection, the nihilism that tends to permeate the constructionist position today is evident in the following passage taken from Berger's *The Sacred Canopy*:

[T]he marginal situations of human existence [i.e., death and suffering] reveal the innate precariousness of all social worlds. Every socially defined reality remains threatened by lurking "irrealities." Every socially constructed nomos must face the constant possibility of its collapse into *anomy*. Seen in the perspective of society, every nomos is an area of meaning carved out of a vast mass of meaninglessness, a small clearing of lucidity in a formless, dark, always ominous jungle. Seen in the perspective of the individual, every nomos represents the bright "dayside" of life, tenuously held onto against the sinister shadows of the "night." In both perspectives, every nomos is an edifice erected in the face of the potent and alien forces of chaos. This chaos must be kept at bay at all cost.[13]

And so it appears that two closely-linked affirmations form the doctrinal core of the onto-theology (or *anti*-theology) upon which the constructionist position is based: a) that our projection of "meanings" and "values" always and only occurs against a backdrop of chaos and meaninglessness; and b) that the social construction of "reality" is therefore always and only motivated by the struggle for survival and the will-to-power. Apart from these terrible assumptions, the insight that ideas and institutions are inevitably socially and historically locatable doesn't really extend any further than common sense, which is perhaps what explains why constructionist rhetoric is often attractive to many people, including many Christians, who ought to know better.

Conclusion

What, then, are we to make of all this? In the first instance, the fact that we are socially and culturally situated in a social "world" is undeniable. Yet our "situatedness" will not prevent us from seeking to understand the *truth* of things unless we have somehow become convinced that there is no truth to find. And this is precisely the problem with employing constructionist rhetoric, for the force of the constructionist argument *hinges* upon our having already despaired over the possibility of ever knowing the truth of things. If it didn't, constructionists would spend far less of their time and effort on historical and cultural analysis, and those analyses they did undertake would be quite clearly placed in the service of normative reasoning, which alone is able to appeal to conscience and to produce conviction.

Of course, it is usually at this point in the discussion that constructionists adduce empirical evidence to "prove" that such things as sexual morality, family structure, gender relations, conceptions of freedom, conceptions of "god," and so forth, are historically and culturally relative. But this is only a rhetorical ploy and nothing more. For the assertion that there is no truth cannot be either empirically proven or disproven. The fact that there are any number of religions, for example, each with its own peculiar view of "god" or "the gods," does not mean that the true nature of God cannot be known, but only that confusion has existed and perhaps still exists with respect to the question. The fact that any number of cultures have come up with any number of institutions governing the relations between men and women, does not mean that the relations between men and women are infinitely plastic, but only that such relations have, for whatever reason, been subject to confusion and change. Similarly, the fact that various cultures have produced a variety of conflicting understandings of such things as "human nature" or "justice" or "freedom" does not mean that human nature, justice, and freedom do not exist apart from our construction of them, but, again, only that confusion has existed and still exists with respect to these matters. None of this "evidence" has any bearing whatsoever on the question of whether there might not be a *right* way to conceive of God, or a *right* way to conceive of the relations between men and women, or a *right* way to conceive of justice and freedom. Christians, of all people, should not be misled by those who would represent social-scientific "facts" in an attempt to convince us that "truth" is always and only socially constructed.

Of course, there is a place for the kind of sociology of knowledge analysis that Berger and Luckmann and others have developed, but it must be completely shorn of its nihilistic presuppositions to be of any genuinely constructive use. The scriptural repudiation of idolatry, for example, is quite similar to the analysis we have outlined above, entailing externalization, objectivation, and internalization. "Why do the nations say, 'Where is their God?'," the Psalmist writes, for example in Psalm 115 (verses 2–8):

> Our God is in heaven;
>> he does whatever pleases him.
> But their idols are silver and gold,
>> made by the hands of men. [Note: externalization; objectivation]
> They have mouths, but cannot speak,
>> eyes, but they cannot see;
> they have ears, but cannot hear,
>> noses, but they cannot smell;
> they have hands, but cannot feel,
>> feet, but they cannot walk;
>> nor can they utter a sound with their throats.
> Those who make them will be like them,
>> and so will all who trust in them. [Note: internalization]

But, of course, the point of this prophetic denunciation is not to empower us to construct newer and better idols, nor is it meant to laud and encourage human ingenuity and cleverness. Rather the point is to encourage us to turn from the worship of idols—or, in our case, ideologies—to the living God. When it comes to the matter of gender reconciliation, this is exactly what we must we must encourage each other to do.

Endnotes

1. Nicholas Abercombie, Stephen Hill & Bryan S. Turner (eds.), *The Penguin Dictionary of Sociology*, 2nd ed (New York: Penguin, 1988), 103.

2. Gordon Marshall (ed.), *The Concise Dictionary of Sociology* (Oxford: Oxford University Press, 1994), 197.

3. Raymond J. Corsini (ed.), *Encyclopedia of Psychology*, Vol. 2, 2nd ed (New York: John Wiley & Sons, 1994), 53.

4. Edgar F. Borgatta & Marie L. Borgatta (eds.), *Encyclopedia of Sociology*, Vol. 2 (New York: Macmillan, 1992), 748.

5. Martin Buber, *The Eclipse of God: Studies in the Relation Between Religion and Philosophy* (New York: Harper & Row, 1952), 14.

6. Martin Buber, *I and Thou*, translated by Walter Kaufmann (New York: Charles Scribner's Sons, 1970 [1937]): 110.

7. Peter Berger.and Thomas Luckmann, *The Social Construction of Reality: a Treatise in the Sociology of Knowledge* (Garden City, N.Y.: Doubleday & Co., 1966), 67.

8. Peter Berger, *The Sacred Canopy*, (New York: Doubleday, 1969), 7.

9. C. S. Lewis, *The Abolition of Man* (Glasgow: Collins, 1978 [1943]), 29–30.

10. Berger & Luckmann, *The Social Construction of Reality*, 19.

11. Karl Marx, *The German Ideology in The Portable Karl Marx*, ed. Eugene Kamenka (New York: Viking Penguin, 1983), 169.

12. "On Truth and Lie in an Extra-Moral Sense," in *The Portable Nietzsche*, translated and edited by Walter Kaufmann [New York: Penguin, 1976], 47

13. Berger, *The Sacred Canopy*, 23–24.

Women and the Church:
A North American Perspective

Barbara Horkoff Mutch

One of my earliest memories of women and the church is of my mother teaching Sunday School in our little church in Burnaby, British Columbia. The women of St. Matthew's United Church played an important role in teaching, organizing and serving the fledgling congregation. The women of my mother's generation contributed their intelligence, industry, and countless volunteer hours to the church.

Ten years later, following a family move to the Canadian prairies, my mother and I briefly attended a church led by an ordained woman, Brenda Fergusson. Although we never knew the minister personally, I still remember her name and one of her sermons. By my early teens, I had seen women in lay leadership and women in pastoral leadership, and been nurtured by the ministry of each.

In my later teens and early twenties, I was exposed to an interpretation of Scripture that emphasized "creation order" and the headship of men. While studying at a conservative Christian school, I encountered limits to what women could do in the church, at least the church in North America. Upon graduation, I began to direct children's ministry at a Baptist Union church. Over time, the congregation began to ask me to take on additional responsibilities. Ministry to children grew into a ministry to the whole family.

My understanding of what women could contribute to the church broadened.

Then my church requested that I consider ordination. I had been blessed by the ministry of an ordained woman, yet had been taught that ordination of women was not appropriate. However, I believed in congregational authority. I believed even more strongly that the Holy Spirit gives gifts to the whole people of God. My church community believed that ordination was an appropriate response to what they saw as the gifts of the Spirit in my life. All my study, then and now, has led me to believe that equally godly, equally scholarly men and women will continue to interpret Scripture differently on the subject of women and the church.

I was ordained in 1988 and continued to serve that congregation until I had completed fifteen years of pastoral ministry. I was blessed with unfailing support from my congregation, colleagues and family. I worked hard to learn what it means to be a minister. Now I work with a new generation of men and women. Some are heading toward lay leadership, like my mother. Others are training for pastoral leadership, like the minister in Benito, Manitoba. It is a privilege to help these men and women discover and use their Spirit-given gifts. I love the church and believe that it is God's chosen way to meet the world. From this perspective, I would like to make five observations about women and the church in North America.

Public Work and Volunteer Work

There is a significant difference between the church my mother served as a Sunday School teacher in the 1960s and the church of the third millennium. The transitions symbolized by the movement of women into public work have affected the number of volunteer hours women can give to the church. By the mid-1970s, over half the women younger than fifty-five in North America had joined the paid labour force. In the next fifteen years, employment rates rose dramatically. At the end of this millennium, most women younger than fifty have public work. For some parts of the North American population, particularly African-American, these statistics are nothing new. As early as 1880, 50 percent of black women were in the paid labour force compared with 15 percent of white women.[1] Most of these women worked in domestic situations, primarily in the homes of white women.

Most of the women involved in public work remain in monotonous, low-wage, sometimes hazardous jobs. More women are working to pay bills than are working for luxuries. Despite the addition of employment outside the home, most women continue to take the major responsibility for their family, working a second shift when they get home. While men often do more housework and parenting than did their fathers, it is not yet equal between women and men. "We share it 50-50" was the response of 43 percent of the men and only 19 percent of the women in a recent survey. There appears to be distinctly different understandings of parental and household tasks. Both genders still describe it as helping women with the housework. Even when women work full-time, most still define wife and mother as their primary roles. Their husbands usually agree. While men are at work, they think about family less than women do. When they are at home, they do less of the housework. It is perhaps not surprising that working men are more satisfied with their marriage and family life than are working women.[2]

Women have always worked, but the work now, largely, takes place in the public sphere as well as within the home. This raises all kinds of issues of working and loving. It illuminates the difficulties of "conceiving in professional and familial ways at the same time."[3] Experimentation characterizes work and family life, and that shifting spills over into people's church lives.

One of the challenges facing the church in North America is learning how to support women in their struggle to resolve the conflict inherent in loving and working. The lives of women and men are very different from the 1960s, yet church expectations of women have not adapted well to the changes in their lives. The church must affirm both the public and the home-based work that women and men do as their service to God in the world. The church is called to extend expectations of volunteer time equally to women and men, and to actively support both women and men in their struggle to live faithfully to their various commitments.

Diversity of Women's Experience

The introduction of a new title of choice for many women represents a second area of societal transition that has implications for the church. In 1970, the letters "r" and "is" caused a commotion by their absence. The letters were the missing parts of the titles "Mrs." and "Miss." Instead of these titles, some women began using "Ms." Women, like men, now had the option of a title that did not designate marital status. The social codes that made obvious a woman's legal relationship to a man were cast away. It was a very unsettling time for many persons. Also unsettling was a married woman calling herself by the same name she had before she was married. Although men had used the same construct for years, some religious leaders condemned the use of Ms. as an attack on the family.[4]

The now common singular title of Ms. represents a rich diversity of women's experience. Women in our churches and in our world include the never-married and the single parent, the divorcing and the divorced, the widowed and the married and the lesbian. Within those categories are both celibate and sexually active women, women who parent and those who do not.

Pastoral care should not be reserved for those whose wounds have our approval. We must extend compassion and care to all. Our churches must become sanctuaries of inclusion, healing and care. Affirmation of personhood should be a high priority of the church. Because not all men and women are married, the sensitive church creates structures that are independent of marital status. Because not all men and women have children, leaders of worship should think carefully about the ways in which we celebrate Mother's Day and Father's Day in our congregations. Because single persons are sexual beings, we must recognize that celibacy does not negate sexuality. And because for as many as 26 million women in North America, female experience includes the reality of depression, we must determine to be sensitive to the essential loneliness at the core of every human being. We must allow that sensitivity to characterize the church's response to the diversity of human experience.

Sense of Self Rooted Within Relationships

The formation of women's sense of self is rooted within the matrix of relationships. For much of this century, theorists have seen human development as a process of separation.[5] Required developmental tasks are identified as the child separating from the mother, the adolescent from the family, and the adult from teachers and mentors. The goal for human development found in the theories of leading developmental theorists Erik Erikson and Daniel Levinson is to "become one's own man."[6] Neither learning how to draw near to others nor contributing to the growth of others is a priority in these theories. Individual achievement is valued over community. Independence is valued over relationship, and autonomy over connectedness.

It is not surprising that developmentalists have had trouble fitting women into this model of individuation. In a 1976 study, in which the playtime activities of 10- and 11-year-old children were observed, it was found that boys play competitive games more often than girls do, and that boys' games last longer.[7] During the study, boys were frequently seen quarrelling, but not once was a game ended because of a quarrel. In addition, boys never interrupted a game for more than seven minutes. It seemed that the boys enjoyed the legal debates and the elaboration of rules as much as they did the game itself.

In contrast, when a dispute erupted during girls' games, the girls often ended the game. They were tolerant in their attitudes toward rules and more willing to make exceptions. In the games that girls often chose, such as hopscotch and jump-rope, one person's success did not require another's failure. Disputes emerged with less frequency, but when they did, girls were likely to end the game. They chose to subordinate the continuation of the game to the continuation of the relationships.

For many years, the way boys developed was considered the norm for human development. However, approximately twenty-five years ago, a new batch of developmentalists began to look at things in a different light. They suggested that the primary experience of self for females is neither competitive nor rule-oriented but relational.[8] Women organize and develop the self in important relationships. Intimacy develops alongside identity. The female comes to know herself in important relationships with others. All growth occurs within emotional connection, rather than separation from it. Healthy, dynamic relationships are the motivating force for growth.

The familiar Old Testament words spoken by Ruth to her mother-in-law illustrate the deep truth that identity and intimacy are connected for women. It is in their most meaningful relationships that women discover who they are.

> Do not press me to leave you or to turn back from following you!
> Where you go, I will go; where you lodge, I will lodge;
> your people shall be my people, and your God my God.
> Where you die, I will die—there will I be buried.
> May the Lord do thus and so to me, and more as well,
> if even death parts me from you. (Ruth 1:16-17)

Relational needs are primary for women. Women need friendships, not as a luxury, but for reasons of discovering God-given potential. Women need friendships, not as a frill, but to continue to discover identity. Women need healthy, dynamic friendships with both women and men because these relationships bring growth. A relational way of understanding women's formation and growth is foundational to the development of effective ministries for women.

Churches that are responding well to the relational needs of women are doing so in at least three ways. First, churches are boldly offering opportunities for women to connect with other women within the family of faith. Bible studies, prayer groups, book groups and mission task groups for women offer a place of belonging and learning. In a society that often labels single-gender fellowships as regressive, these churches understand what Jesus modelled in his vulnerability with twelve others of his own gender.

Second, churches are steadfastly providing women places to be served as well as to serve. Traditionally, women in the church have not experienced a shortage of opportunities to serve. They have loved their neighbours well, sometimes much more than they have loved themselves. The Samaritan in Jesus' parable serves as a powerful image for women. He cared for the wounded person while also continuing his own journey. The Samaritan relied on the host of the inn, showing us that many must share the provision of care.[9]

Third, churches that are responding well to the relational needs of women are graciously reminding women of their creation in the image of God, and that their primary relationship is found with him. It is in their deepest relationships that women learn who they most truly are. Churches that provide effective ministries for women clearly lead women toward Christ at every stage of their development.

It appears that adolescent women are having a particularly hard time with their sense of self. The results of recent reports, such as *A Capella: A Report on the Realities, Concerns, Expectations and Barriers Experienced by Adolescent Women in Canada* and *Reviving Ophelia*[10] note how difficult it is for young women to forge independent identities in today's world. The high incidence of cigarette smoking, sexual activity at young ages, and an increased awareness of violence among adolescent females gives testimony to the difficult passage that adolescence presents for some girls.

To use Nelle Morton's phrase, we need to hear women of all ages into speech.[11] Congregations can help women learn to name their experiences of God and to claim those experiences as holy. Church families can help women learn to tell their spiritual stories. Many women struggle to believe their experience with God is valuable. When such women are genuinely heard by a representative of God, they can gain the capacity to open up to the powerful presence of the Spirit of God.

Need for Mutual Respect

In recent years, we have witnessed the unprecedented emergence on the national stage of issues surrounding gender encounters. The reality and prevalence of sexual abuse, sexual harassment, date rape and the battering of women have exploded into our consciousness. As individuals and as the church, we can deny their awful presence no longer. Wounded, soul-damaged women are in our society and in our churches, and their brokenness has come at the hands of gender encounters of a devastating kind.

The difficult truth is that, for many women in North America, gender encounters have been damaging. The truth is that we continue to be a racist, classist, sexist people in spite of the gospel announcement of parity in Christ. We have heard Galatians 3:28 expounded, yet too often in the last two thousand years, the church of Jesus Christ has failed to practise what it has preached. Our churches have shortchanged many girls and women. They have discouraged them from developing their own voices. They have prevented them from exercising their gifts in their houses of faith. They have have silenced or oppressed them with interpretations of Scripture.

This brokenness affects women on every level. They find it difficult to trust themselves or others. They are wary of the institutional church and male authority structures. Unable to concentrate or to maintain employment, women who have suffered in gender encounters have many things in common, most particularly, damaged souls.

Empirical studies have shown that both women and men have highly paternal conceptions of God.[12] Persons tend intuitively to think of God in male/father imagery. When violence, injustice or an abuse of power are introduced into that understanding or experience of maleness, confusion arises about the nature of God. When this confusion is compounded by those who would use the name of God to justify their behaviour, or by a church that disbelieves or silences its victims, religious confusion deepens. The inability to pray intensifies.

I believe that the problem involves the abuse of power. Much of the wrong that takes place between men and women concerns the violation of power perpetrated by a person who has more power over someone who is vulnerable. The violation often takes a sexual form, but it involves much more than sex. It involves a breach of trust, a breaking of boundaries, and a profound violation of the survivor's sense of self. Abuse of power causes difficulty with prayer. It causes women to doubt their sense of worth and their place in the family of God. Abuse of power also damages the souls and cripples the spirits of some of half of God's children.

The nature of our relationships as men and women needs to change. We need to replace devastation with healing. We need to learn to be together in ways that nurture esteem and not shame. We need to relate in ways that sustain mutuality, not power used for domination. As the church and in the church, we must get serious about how we relate to one another as men and women.

We need to become increasingly intentional about praying for and working toward healing encounters in the church. We must commit ourselves to the creation of new relationships that represent socially what is true theologically. The Apostle Paul establishes an absence of hierarchy between Jews and

Gentiles in the church of the new creation. The work of the risen Christ similarly affects the relationship between men and women. Jews and Gentiles, men and women, share a common spiritual status. The theological relationship is reciprocal, not hierarchical.

Moreover, what is true in status is now true at the level of function. The Spirit has given gifts to all without any restrictions. Jews and Gentiles, men and women, are included in the New Creation. Jews and Gentiles, men and women have been gifted by the Spirit. The privileges of equal status ought to be accompanied by the experience of equal status.

We are called to functionalize this theological truth in relationships and behaviours. It is clear that Paul fully expected this new status to result in observable differences within the believing community. Gentiles were not to be treated by Jews as they had been in the past. Women are not to be treated by men as they have been in the past. As a result of the work of Christ, something radical and revolutionary is intended to happen to the old ways of relating. The theological status obtained in Christ is meant to affect our experience in the community of faith. Once excluded, Gentiles now claim full status and freedom to function within the new creation. It is time for this to be fully true for women, as well. We must commit ourselves to the creation of new relationships in which there is justice and inclusion for all.

We also must become increasingly sensitive to the language we use. The way we speak shapes our reality. Language can be used as a tool of domination or as a means to bring freedom and life. This is illustrated through the contrasting ways of referring to the initial scaling of Mount Everest: "the conquest of Everest" in the West or "the befriending of Everest" in the East. Conquest or befriending, domination or restoration: the difference is both deep and deeply imbedded within the ways that we think and speak.

"Before the world was created, the Word already existed.... From the very beginning, the Word was with God.... The Word was the source of life, and this life brought life to humankind" (Jn 1:1,2,4). We must learn to speak this Word as fully as possible, for only in so doing can Word, words, women and men weave together a tapestry of freedom, transformation and justice.

We must learn to ask ourselves the questions, Does the language with which we speak of God and the experience of faith speak the truth? Does it demonstrate the radical, new relationship that God has established with the world and the church through the work and life of Jesus Christ? Does the language we use foster mutuality and justice, rather than rendering some of God's creation invisible and powerless? Will the language that we use enable us to be more attentive to the ways that God works in our world? If the language with which we speak of God is salted only with male imagery, where does that leave the female experience? If life in the community of faith is more comfortable for men than for women, how does that speak of the reign of God? We must commit ourselves to awareness of the ways in which we use language and learn to speak of the Word with all the fullness that is present in the Godhead.

We must learn to live with respect for one another. Without respect, we cannot relate with courage and wholeness. Without respect for God, for ourselves and for others, we cannot create a community of love and faith. Disrespect has devastating effects on a person's ability to be found in faith. Our experiences of life in community affect our spirituality. Our wounding occurs through our experiences in community. It is only through community that we become healed.

A profound lesson about that which lies at the heart of gender encounters of a healing kind can be found in an ancient Arthurian story. King Arthur, in his youth, was caught poaching in the kingdom of a neighbouring king. He might well have been killed immediately, for that was the punishment for trangressing the laws of property and ownership. But the neighbouring king was touched by Arthur's youth and winsome character. He offered Arthur freedom if he could find the answer to a very difficult question within one year. The question was: What does woman really want? This question would stagger the wisest of men and seemed insurmountable for the youth. But it was better than hanging, so Arthur returned home and began questioning everyone he could find. Harlot and nun, princess and queen, wise man and court fool–all were questioned but none could give a convincing answer. Each advised, however, that the old witch in the forest would know, although she would charge an exorbitant fee.

The last day of the year arrived. Arthur was driven to consult the old hag. She agreed to provide an answer which would satisfy the accusing king, but required for her price marriage to Gawain, the noblest knight of the Round Table and Arthur's lifelong and closest friend. Arthur looked at the old witch in horror. She was ugly, had only one tooth, emitted a stench that would sicken a goat, made obscene noises and was humpbacked. Never was there a more loathsome sight! Arthur vowed not to ask, but Gawain insisted that he pay this price for his friend.

The wedding was announced and the hag spoke her infernal wisdom. What does woman really want? The answer: She wants sovereignty over her own life.[13] Everyone knew instantly that great wisdom had been spoken, and Arthur would live.

The wedding still had to be endured. All the court was there, with none more torn between relief and distress than Arthur himself. The witch exhibited her worst manners, wolfing the food from her plate without using any utensils, and making hideous noises and smells. Through it all, Gawain was courteous, gentle and respectful.

Finally, Gawain and the witch retired to prepare for their wedding night. To Gawain's utter astonishment, his bride appeared to him as the loveliest maiden he had ever seen! When Gawain asked what had happened, she replied that because Gawain had been courteous to her, she would show him her hideous self half the time, and her gracious side the other half. Which of the two did he choose for the day and which for the night? This was a cruel question and Gawain did rapid calculation. Did he want a lovely maiden to show during the day where all his friends could see, and a hideous hag at night in the privacy of their chamber? Or did he want a hideous hag during the day and a lovely maiden in the intimate moments of their life? Noble man that he was, Gawain replied that he would let her choose for herself. At this, the maiden announced that she would be a fair damsel to him both day and night, because he had given her respect and sovereignty over her own life.

Respect brings healing. We model redemption through the respectful ways in which we relate with one another.

Increase of Women in Theological Education

One of the most observable differences in the North American church arena is the increased presence of women in theological education. The last twenty years has witnessed a dramatic rise in the number of women students. Historically the domain of men, some theological schools currently see women comprise more than half of the student body, and a number of denominations ordain more women than men.[14] The presence of women, feminist theology and new religious practices have significantly changed the nature of theological education. New voices and faces in Christian history have been uncovered. New areas of research, new resources and new models have been identified, as well. Ways of speaking have changed.[15]

Although many aspects of theological education and church life have changed in recent years, there is still progress to be made. Recent research within the Canadian Baptist Federation indicates that some of the experiences of women within the North American church are still painful.[16] In some churches, women are denied the exercise of spiritual gifts because of gender. Some are dismissed as "feminist" for advocating the use of inclusive language for people. Others feel misunderstood or marginalized for the contribution they would like to make.

At the same time, women in both lay and pastoral leadership report positive affirmation from those to whom they minister. They affirm that lives are touched and spiritual gifts identified. Leading communion, teaching adults, directing a camp program and serving on an ordination examining council are all expressions of ministry which bring these women joy.

As reported in a recent Canadian graduate thesis,[17] Canadian women concluded that to be a woman in ministry in the current Canadian evangelical church requires a commitment of conviction which will be carried out within the context of challenge. The confrontation may vary in intensity and origin, but it will occur. The public nature of ministry brings with it a certain "fish bowl" dimension. Questions such as "How can your husband be the head of the home when you preach?" and "Why is he looking after the child?" prove to be a challenge. Ministry for women in the North American church, while at times incredibly fulfilling, is also often lonely and stressful. But women do endure. There are glimmers of hope. The African-American tradition has long known that women are strong. The church needs strong people.

Once there was a Sunday School classroom in which children were preparing to act out the day's Bible story. The roles were awarded without regard to sex since the characters in the story were all men and the class was evenly divided between boys and girls. When the role of Jesus was announced, a girl was asked to play the part. Immediately a boy called out, "You can't be Jesus—you're a girl!"

Before the teachers could intervene, the girl shot back, "A girl can be Jesus, a girl can be Jesus!" She wasn't exactly crying, but her voice was full of emotion, and it fell on one of those class moments when everything else seemed momentarily silent.

It has been suggested that this is the question over which the church in North America is most polarized. Can a woman represent God to the church? Can a woman put on a pastoral robe and minister in servant leadership to a congregation? Is it true that women and men are equally saved, equally gifted and equally called? Many believe that women are, and that it is a matter of gospel importance.

The North American church faces a number of significant challenges. Societal transitions illustrated by the tension between public and volunteer work and the wide diversity of human experience require sensitivity and creativity in the church's response. The role of relationships, both in the formation of women's sense of self and between men and women, impact the experience of the whole community of faith. The increased presence of women in theological education and pastoral leadership affects the dynamics of the church in additional ways.

Many women come to the community of faith ready to contribute. Like my mother, they bring their intelligence, industry, Spirit-gifts and much of their precious volunteer time. Like Brenda Fergusson in a little country church, they also bring their theological training and their call to pastoral vocation and service. Both have the capacity to enrich the church as the church discerns how to welcome their ministry with grace.

Endnotes

1. Joanna Bowen Gillespie, "Gender and Generations in Congregations," *Episcopal Women*, Catherine Prelinger, ed. New York: Oxford University, 1993. See also Joanna Bowen Gillespie, *Women Speak: of God, Congregations and Change* Valley Forge, PA: Trinity Press International, 1995).

2. Ibid.

3. Bonnie J. Miller-McLemore, "Women Who Work and Love: Caught Between Cultures," *Women in Travail and Transition*, Maxine Glaz and Jeanne Stevenson Moessner, eds. (Minneapolis: Fortress Press, 1991) p. 65.

4. Priscilla L. Denham, "Life-styles: A Culture in Transition," *Women in Travail*, Glaz and Moessner, eds., p. 162.

5. Jean Baker Miller, "The Development of Women's Sense of Self," *Women's Growth in Connection*, Judith V. Jordan, Alexandra G. Kaplan, Jean Baker Miller, Irene P. Stiver, and Janet L. Surrey (New York: Guilford Press, 1991) p. 11.

6. See Daniel J. Levinson, *The Seasons of a Man's Life* (New York: Knopf, 1978); and Erik Erikson, *Identity and the Life Cycle* (New York: International Universities Press, 1959).

7. Janet Lever, "Sex Differences in the Games Children Play," *Social Problems* 23 (1976), p. 480.

8. Carol Gilligan, *In a Different Voice* (Cambridge, MA: Harvard University Press, 1982) p. 17.

9. Jeanne Stevenson Moessner, "A New Pastoral Paradigm and Practice," *Women in Travail*, Glaz and Moessner, eds., p. 203.

10. Mary Bray Pipher, *Reviving Ophelia: Saving the Selves of Adolescent Girls* (New York: G. P. Putnam, 1994) and *A Cappella: A Report on the Realities, Concerns, Expectations and Barriers Experienced by Adolescent Women in Canada* (Ottawa: Canadian Teachers' Federation, 1990).

11. Nelle Morton, *The Journey is Home* (Boston: Beacon Press, 1985) p. 13.

12. William Justice and Warren Lambert. "A Comparitive Study of the Language People Use to Describe the Personality of God and Their Earthly Parents." *Journal of Pastoral Care* 40:2 (June 1986) pp. 166-173.

13. Connie Zweig, ed. *To Be a Woman* (Los Angeles: Jeremy P. Tarcher, Inc., 1990), pp. 268-270.

14. Rebecca Chopp, *Saving Work: Feminist Practices of Theological Education* (Louisville, KY: Westminster/John Knox Press, 1995).

15. Ibid.

16. Barbara Mutch, Women in the Church Workshop, Research done at The Canadian Baptist Gathering in Calgary, July 1998.

17. Cheryl Busse, "Evangelical Women in the 1990s: Examining Internal Dynamics." Graduate Thesis, Briercrest Biblical Seminary, 1998.

CHAPTER 9

The Uses of History in Evangelical Gender Debates

John G. Stackhouse, Jr.

When it comes to theological and ethical controversy, evangelicals reflexively look to the Bible. And so we should. Thus in the debates over gender that have arisen among evangelicals, especially in the last few decades, most evangelical attention has been devoted to Bible study.

Yet evangelicals have referred to other resources as well. Logical reasoning, of course, has been invoked—if not always used to the satisfaction of one's critics. Personal experience often has come into play, whether happy stories or sad about, say, women performing pastoral functions on the mission field, or testimonies of women to a call of God to ministries that their tradition did not open to them.[1]

We evangelicals are not renowned, however, for our historical conscious-ness. Yet history in fact shows up at several levels in the evangelical debate over gender. Evangelicals naturally tend to begin with biblical history. Sometimes the history of the church is mentioned. Frequently, facets of cultural history show up in the argument. And occasionally, evangelicals look to the contemporary history of evangelicalism itself for guidance.

The point of the following essay is to set out, as fairly as possible, the various ways history has been used in these debates so as to provide some perspective for those who encounter this or that evangelical argument regarding gender. In this discussion, I will simplify things by referring usually to just two main types of approach to gender issues: the one called variously "patriarchal," "hierarchical," "traditional," or "complementarian," and the other customarily called "egalitarian" or "feminist." The last section of this discussion will make clear that evangelicals have in fact defended more than just one or the other of these views along the way. Still, use of these types can be helpful as they represent the main positions articulated in the controversial literature on this subject.

Biblical History

"In the beginning" what relationship existed between the sexes? As other essays in this series show, reference to the creation narratives has yielded, to put it mildly, more than one conclusion. In this primordial history, Adam and Eve are created together, male and female, in the image of God. Yet Adam is created first, and this priority of creation indicates precedence in a hierarchy—according to some (including, it seems, the Apostle Paul: so 1 Cor 11:7–10; but cf. vv. 11–12). On the other hand, Eve is created out of Adam's rib, a symbol of their mutual partnership—as some have seen it. Traditionalists respond that in Eden, Adam names everything and everyone else in the story (except God, of course), including Eve. This privilege of naming (as superiors name inferiors) might show his legitimate position of "headship," whatever that means—or it might not. And so the debate has gone.

What no one disputes, however, is that the rest of the Old Testament—starting at least as early as Genesis 3—shows patriarchy as the universal form of gender relations in the home, tribe and cult.[2] What is in dispute, of course, is what lesson modern Christians should draw from this pattern. Are we to see this pattern as normative for all of God's people all the time? Or are we to see instead this pattern as rooted in the Fall and flowering quickly to become the norm of human relations, but a pattern to be repudiated in the New Covenant—as, say, polygamy, slavery, and other unhappy human relationships that were common among the patriarchs are nonetheless to be redeemed in Christ?

Indeed, the inauguration of the church at Pentecost invokes Old Testament prophecy that includes two startling references to gender from the prophecy of Joel:

> "This is what was spoken through the prophet Joel: 'In the last days it will be, God declares, that I will pour out my Spirit upon all flesh, and your sons *and your daughters* shall prophesy, and your young men shall

see visions, and your old men shall dream dreams. Even upon my slaves, both men *and women*, in those days I will pour out my Spirit; and they shall prophesy'" (Acts 2:16–18; italics added).

In regard to biblical history, then, we encounter the thorny hermeneutical question of just how Christians are to make appropriate use of God's gift of the Old Testament. We can agree on what is recorded in the Old Testament as having actually happened regarding gender—but what is the significance of each instance for us today under the New Covenant?

A parallel question emerges as we consider the New Testament. Jesus called twelve apostles, and in both the New Testament and subsequent Christian tradition "the Twelve" have special status among Jesus' band of disciples. It is clear that all twelve were male. It is also clear that Jesus himself was male. Proponents of some traditional positions typically make much of this pattern of maleness—especially those in more catholic communions whose understanding of the nature priesthood includes personally representing Christ and his chief apostles. Since Christ and the Twelve were male, it thus follows that priests must be male.

Yet, egalitarians counter, Christ and the Twelve were also Jews, and no one insists on an exclusively Jewish priesthood for Christians. Furthermore, egalitarians remark, what is most interesting about the makeup of Jesus' band of followers is not the typical prominence of men but the startling dignity afforded women, particularly Jesus' close friends Mary and Martha and Jesus' special disciple Mary Magdalene—who was first to see the risen Lord and thus the first to bear the Easter message. Indeed, egalitarians continue, the category "disciple" is not exclusively the province of the Twelve. Tabitha is called a "disciple" (Acts 9:36), and Jesus' references to "disciple" are often made in quite generic terms, as in "If anyone wants to be my disciple...."

Complementarians, for their part, are not bowled over by most of these observations. After all, it remains that Jesus and the Twelve *were* male. Moreover, it is clear that the churches depicted in the New Testament were led by men, and that this was what Paul saw as normal "in all the churches" (1 Cor 14:33, 34).

Still, egalitarians point out, the early church apparently did also have some female leaders: Junia, called an "apostle" by Paul himself (Rom 16:7); Lydia, patroness of the church at Philippi (Acts 16:14, 15); Prisca/Priscilla (whom some, among them Martin Luther, have guessed to be the author of the Epistle to the Hebrews, perhaps because of the teaching role she exercises in Scripture); and more. Some egalitarians wonder, then, about just how normative patriarchy is to be. They recall that most of the prophets of the Old Testament were male—but not all. And all of the judges were male—except Deborah, arguably the most noble of the lot! The mere fact of a preponderance of males in a role may or may not speak to God's preferences, let alone his eternal will, in the matter.

In sum, the Bible contains not only precepts regarding gender, but also stories of gender relations in several, very different, contexts. A thorough treatment of gender and the Bible must account for all of these glimpses of the roles of women and men in home, society, and cult.

Church History

"Traditionalists" get their name in this debate in part because they seek to uphold the pattern of gender relations that has predominated in Christian history. Male leadership is what the church has always taught, traditionalists affirm, and it is what the church has always practised. The burden of proof from history, traditionalists plausibly claim, therefore falls upon those who would justify innovation after twenty centuries.

Feminists sometimes have responded by pointing out that patriarchy has eroded in a number of churches, particularly in the modern West. It is thus simply not true, they observe, that the church everywhere and always has taught complementarian roles: nowadays many churches teach otherwise, and many of those are orthodox, even evangelical, churches.

Indeed, feminists go on, in times of revival and missionary zeal, many Christians—evangelicals sometimes prominent among them—have enlisted women in all aspects of the Christian cause, including "frontline" evangelism, church planting, pastoral leadership, and so on. The regrettable pattern in fact has been that the church reverts to the patriarchy that has been typical of society at large precisely as renewal fires cool and missionary zeal wanes.[3]

A peculiar historical argument against female church leadership has been advanced by some evangelicals—notably Walter Martin, author of the widely-used textbook on alternative religious movements, *The Kingdom of the Cults*. They argue that the history of deviant religious groups shows what terrible things can happen when a woman is given religious authority. "It is one of the strange historical peculiarities of the saga of cultism that at least six cults were either started by women or were influenced in a major way by the allegedly weaker sex," among these being Christian Science, Theosophy, the Jehovah's Witnesses, and Unity.[4]

Egalitarians, for their part, wryly observe that all of the "cults" that were not led by women were led by—who else?—men. And that would be most cults, of course. Some egalitarians also question whether there is a kind of vicious circle here in which groups that feature female leadership have been branded "cultic" partly because of that very trait: so Montanism in the early church, and denominations such as the Salvation Army and Pentecostals in our own era.[5]

Cultural History

I once participated in a congregational discussion over whether or not this particular church would take the step of calling a woman as senior pastor—she would become only the sixth woman to exercise that ministry in the history of the denomination. The congregation was well educated and serious about Christian discipleship, so I was deeply impressed as I heard arguments on both sides that rested on assumptions drawn from people's experiences in one culture or another.

Some argued from their experience of that denomination's own culture, in which they had never witnessed a woman in ecclesiastical leadership. Such people therefore declared, "I can't imagine a woman preaching!" Others in the church argued from their experience in the secular workplace, in which women had now come to exercise authority in the most senior positions— including the presidency of the nearby University of Chicago. From their experience, they affirmed, they couldn't imagine a woman *not* being allowed to lead.

Another form of argument from cultural history seeks to respond to the latter feminist move of reasoning from the success of women in secular leadership roles to the legitimacy of women playing the same roles as men in ecclesiastical or domestic spheres. Mary Kassian, for example, has argued at length that so-called biblical feminism is merely a capitulation to secular feminism. First there was Betty Friedan and Gloria Steinem, so this line runs, and latterly come along the kowtowing Christian egalitarians.[6]

What traditionalists such as Kassian don't acknowledge in this regard, so feminists counter, is the previous history of Christian women on the front lines of the feminist movement, whether for women's suffrage, property rights, and so on, stemming from the nineteenth century. One could plausibly argue that secular feminism is in fact a latter-day product of a movement that originally was strongly influenced by evangelical Christianity.[7]

Furthermore, egalitarians argue, cultural interpreters such as Kassian, James Dobson, and others have read the "vector of influence" pointing the wrong way. The church's patriarchy should itself be seen as a capitulation—or, at best, an accommodation—to the predominance of patriarchy in human cultures. This accommodation, parallel with the accommodation of slavery, should be done away with once the cultural moment emerges in which such unhappy hierarchies can be questioned.

It seems to me, in sum, that changing historical circumstances have always been occasions for new Christian thought, whether the formulation of new creeds, the exploration of new evangelistic techniques, or the consideration of gender in home, church and society. Sometimes, furthermore, historical circumstances have also provided impetus for Christian thought, for better or worse. But historical interpreters must exercise care in tracing a causal relationship in any given case, and particularly beware of the fallacy of *post hoc ergo propter hoc* (X occurred before Y, therefore X caused Y).

Contemporary Evangelical History

Elsewhere I have argued that evangelicals in fact have not divided neatly into "for" and "against" parties on these issues. In fact, they have also sponsored women to exercise pastoral leadership on the foreign mission field, even as the very same evangelicals would not let such women serve in such ministries at home (what I call the "missionary exception"). Such an exception has similarly been extended by some evangelicals to women in so-called parachurch groups (in what I call the "parachurch parenthesis"). Female staff workers for InterVarsity Christian Fellowship, or Bible school teachers, or curriculum writers for small-group Bible studies, or inspirational speakers—all of these have flourished among evangelicals who would never allow a woman to preach from a pulpit, much less appoint her as pastor. And a third variety has emerged in which women (perhaps most notably Elisabeth Elliot) carry on preaching and teaching roles but "under the authority" of the proper males— in her case, her husband, her church elders, and the elders of whatever church she visits to serve.

These exceptions to the "all-or-nothing" typology have been dangerous to the views of traditionalists, of course. As young people benefit from the pastoral work of Bible teaching, prayer, worship leading, and counseling rendered by women throughout their childhood and then early adulthood, it becomes hard for some of them to draw the line at this or that form of pastoral ministry. The undoubted success of women in these various roles—including, to repeat, actual pastoral leadership on the mission field, as well as pastoral ministries of various sorts at home—has caused many evangelicals to wonder whether we understand the Bible's teaching on gender aright.[8]

Conclusion: History and Theological Method

Evangelicals—indeed, all Christians—who seek God's guidance on the question of gender do well to take full account of history in these several respects. Most arguments to date have instead drawn largely upon Scripture and reason, while neglecting to an important degree the actual tradition and experience of Christians through the ages. We need a comprehensive view of the historical data in order to construct a theology of gender that makes sense of what has happened, as well as making sense of the biblical teachings *per se*.

Such a healthy regard for history, furthermore, ought to cultivate in us the theological virtue of humility. We should regard with due modesty the advantages and disadvantages of our particular viewpoint, the strengths, limitations and distortions inherent in our outlook at this historical juncture. As we see others in the past apparently captivated by this or that tradition, this or that contemporary current, and this or that unquestioned prejudice, we do well to admit that we ourselves are embedded in a particular set of overlapping cultures (this church, this denomination, this neighbourhood, this country, this ethnic group, and so on). Perhaps what seems merely "obvious" and "evident" to us at present will not look so compelling from another point of view, including our own point of view a few years down the road.

Finally, such chastening in the light of the complicated historical record might prompt us to realize that the theological question we should ask as finite and fallen human beings is not "What's the clear, final answer?" Instead, all we can ask, and all we should ask of the Holy Spirit and of each other is this: "What is the best paradigm we can find, the best way to make sense of all the data—intellectually and practically—with both humility and conviction, and with both openness to hear other opinions and courage to press our own?"

For it remains that none of us—on this matter, or on any other—have transcended history.

Endnotes

1. For an introduction to these matters, see my "Women in Public Ministry in Twentieth-Century Canadian and American Evangelicalism: Five Models," in *Studies in Religion/Sciences Religieuses* 17 (Fall 1988): 471–85.

2. By "cult," here and in most of the remainder of this paper, I mean that part of culture that is focused upon worship. I do *not* usually mean to refer to "offshoot religions," usually referred to nowadays in social scientific literature as New Religious Movements. At least once in what follows, however, I do mean these groups, and I trust context will guide the reader clearly in each case as to which definition is meant.

3. Ruth A. Tucker and Walter Liefeld, *Daughters of the Church: Women and Ministry from New Testament Times to the Present* (Grand Rapids, MI: Academie Books [Zondervan], 1987).

4. Walter R. Martin, *The Kingdom of the Cults.* rev. ed. (Minneapolis, MN: Bethany Fellowship, 1974 [1965]), 223.

5. See Howard A. Snyder, *Signs of the Spirit: How God Reshapes the Church* (Grand Rapids, MI: Academie Books [Zondervan], 1989), 15–28.

6. Mary A. Kassian, *The Feminist Gospel: The Movement to Unite Feminism with the Church* (Wheaton, IL: Crossway, 1992).

7. A pioneering study on this question is Nancy A. Hardesty, *Women Called to Witness: Evangelical Feminism in the Nineteenth Century* (Nashville, TN: Abingdon, 1984).

8. Again, see my article on "Women in Public Ministry."

Scripture Index

General Index

www.ingramcontent.com/pod-product-compliance
Lightning Source LLC
Chambersburg PA
CBHW031252090426

42742CB00007B/426